HAMMOND

PORTABLE

Atlas

OF THE WORLD

Contents

Interpreting Maps

Geographic Comparisons

Maps of the World

Index

Entire Contents
© Copyright MCMXCIV by Hammond Incorporated
All rights reserved. No part of this book may be reproduced or utilized in any form or by any means, electronic or mechanical, including photocopying, recording or by any information storage and retrieval system, without permission in writing from the Publisher. Printed in The United States of America.

ISBN 1-56865-079-5

Map Projections

Simply stated, the map-maker's challenge is to project the earth's curved surface onto a flat plane.

To achieve this elusive goal, cartographers have developed map projections — equations which govern this conversion of geographic data.

This section explores some of the most widely used projections. It also introduces a new projection, the Hammond Optimal Conformal.

GENERAL PRINCIPLES AND TERMS

The earth rotates around its axis once a day. Its end points are the North and South poles; the line circling the earth midway between the poles is the equator. The arc from the equator to either pole is divided into 90 degrees of latitude. The equator represents 0° latitude. Circles of equal latitude, called parallels, are traditionally shown at every fifth or tenth degree.

The equator is divided into 360 degrees. Lines circling the globe from pole to pole through the degree points on the equator are called meridians, or great circles. All meridians are equal in length, but by international agreement the meridian passing through the Greenwich Observatory near London has been chosen as the prime meridian or 0° longitude. The distance in degrees from the prime meridian to any point east or west is its longitude.

While meridians are all equal in length, parallels become shorter as they approach the poles. Whereas one degree of latitude represents approximately 69 miles (112 km.) anywhere on the globe, a degree of longitude varies from 69 miles (112 km.) at the equator to zero at the poles. Each degree of latitude and longitude is divided into 60 minutes. One minute of latitude equals one nautical mile (1.15 land miles or 1.85 km.).

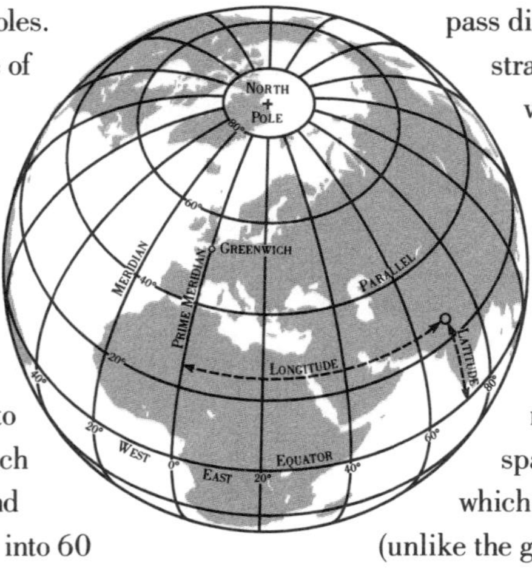

HOW TO FLATTEN A SPHERE: THE ART OF CONTROLLING DISTORTION

There is only one way to represent a sphere with absolute precision: on a globe. All attempts to project our planet's surface onto a plane unevenly stretch or tear the sphere as it flattens, inevitably distorting shapes, distances, area (sizes appear larger or smaller than actual size), angles or direction.

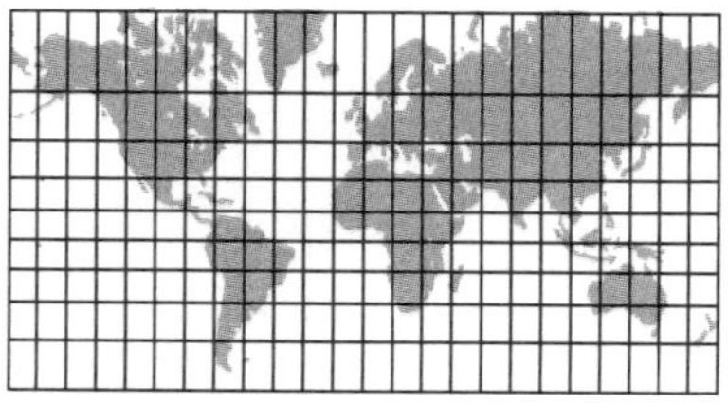

Since representing a sphere on a flat plane always creates distortion, only the parallels or the meridians (or some other set of lines) can maintain the same length as on a globe of corresponding scale. All other lines must be either too long or too short. Accordingly, the scale on a flat map cannot be true everywhere; there will always be different scales in different parts of a map. On world maps or very large areas, variations in scale may be extreme. Most maps seek to preserve either true area relationships (equal area projections) or true angles and shapes (conformal projections); some attempt to achieve overall balance.

PROJECTIONS: SELECTED EXAMPLES

Mercator (Fig. 1): This projection is especially useful because all compass directions appear as straight lines, making it a valuable navigational tool. Moreover, every small region conforms to its shape on a globe — hence the name conformal. But because its meridians are evenly-spaced vertical lines which never converge (unlike the globe), the horizontal parallels must be drawn farther and farther apart at higher latitudes to maintain a correct relationship.

Only the equator is true to scale, and the size of areas in the higher latitudes is dramatically distorted.

Robinson (Fig. 2): To create the thematic maps in Global Relationships and the two-page world map in the Maps of the World section, the Robinson projection was used. It combines elements of both conformal and equal area projections to show the whole earth with relatively true shapes and reasonably equal areas.

Conic (Fig. 3): This projection has been used frequently for air navigation charts and to create most of the national and regional maps in this atlas. (See text in margin at left).

HAMMOND'S OPTIMAL CONFORMAL. As its name implies, this new conformal projection (Fig. 4) presents the optimal view of an area by reducing shifts in scale over an entire region to the minimum degree possible. While conformal maps generally preserve all small shapes, large shapes can become very distorted because of varying scales, causing considerable inaccuracy in distance measurements. The concept underlying the Optimal Conformal is that for any region on the globe, there is an ideal projection for which scale variation can be made as small as possible. Consequently, unlike other projections, the Optimal Conformal does not use one standard formula to construct a map. Each map is a unique projection — the optimal projection for that particular area.

After a cartographer defines the subject area, a sophisticated computer program evaluates the size and shape of the region, projecting the most distortion-free map possible. All of the continent maps in this atlas, except Antarctica, have been drawn using the Optimal projection.

FIGURE 1 Mercator Projection

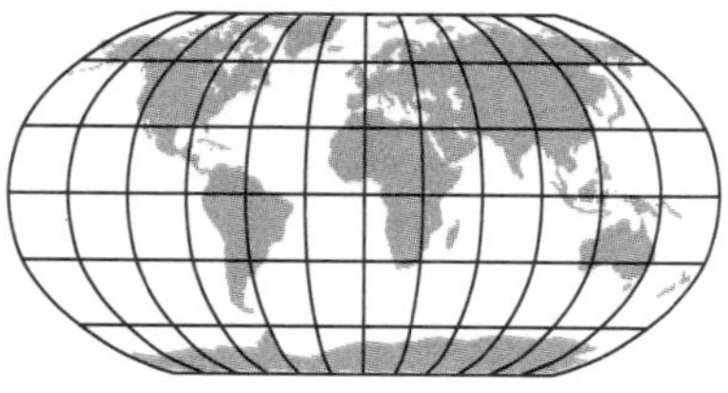

FIGURE 2 Robinson Projection

FIGURE 3 — Conic Projection

The original idea of a conic projection is to cap the globe with a cone, and then project onto the cone from the planet's center the lines of latitude and longitude (the parallels and meridians). To produce a working map, the cone is simply cut open and laid flat. The conic projection used here is a modification of this idea. A cone can be made tangent to any standard parallel you choose. One popular version of a conic projection, the Lambert Conformal Conic, uses two standard parallels near the top and bottom of the map to further reduce the errors of scale.

STANDARD PARALLEL

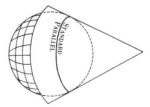

FIGURE 4 — Hammond's Optimal Conformal Projection

Like all conformal maps, the Optimal projection preserves angles exactly and minimizes distortion in shapes. This projection is more successful than any previous projection at spreading curvature across the entire map, producing the most distortion-free map possible.

Using This Atlas

T his new atlas is created from a unique digital database, and its computer-generated maps represent a new phase in map-making technology.

How to Locate Information Quickly

Our Maps of the World section is organized by continent. If you're looking for a major region of the world, consult the Contents on page two.

How Computer-Generated Maps Are Made

To build a digital database capable of generating this world atlas, the latitude and longitude of every significant town, river, coastline, natural and political border, transportation network and peak elevation was researched and digitized. Hundreds of millions of data points describing every important geographic feature are organized into thousands of different map feature codes.

There are no maps in this unique system. Rather, it consists entirely of coded points, lines and polygons. To create a map, cartographers simply determine what specific information they wish to show, based upon considerations of scale, size, density and importance of different features.

New technology developed by mathematical physicist Mitchell Feigenbaum uses fractal geometry to describe and re-configure coastlines, borders and mountain ranges to fit a variety of map scales and projections. Dr. Feigenbaum has also created a computerized type placement program which allows thousands of map labels to be placed accurately in minutes. After these steps have been completed, the computer then draws the final map.

Each section of this atlas has been designed to be both easy and enjoyable to use. Familiarizing yourself with its organization will help you to benefit fully from its use.

World Flags and Reference Guide

This colorful section portrays each nation of the world, its flag, important geographical data, such as size, population and capital, and its location in the Maps of the World section.

World Reference Guide

This concise guide lists the countries of the world alphabetically. If you're looking for the largest scale map of any country, you'll find a page and alpha-numeric reference at a glance, as well as information about each country, including its flag.

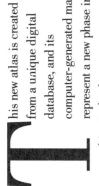

Australia
Page/Location: 70
Area: 2,966,136 sq
7,682,300 s
Population: 17,2
Capital: Canb
Largest

Master Index

When you're looking for a specific place or physical feature, your quickest route is the Master Index. This 6,000-entry alphabetical index lists both the page number and alpha-numeric reference for major places and features in Maps of the World.

Merlimont, Fran...
Mersch, Luxembou...
Mers-les-Bains, France
69/F4 Mertert, Luxembourg
69/F4 Mertesdorf, Germany
69/G6 Mertzwiller, France
68/B5 Méru, France
68/B2 Merville, France
69/F2 Merzenich, Germany
69/F5 Merzig, Germany
'4   Messancy, Belg...

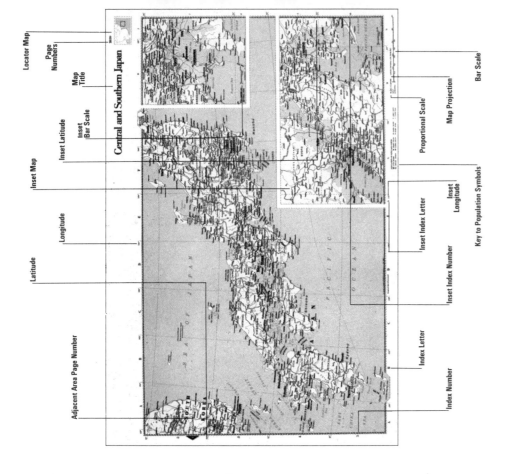

Central and Southern Japan

Map reference labels: Locator Map · Page Numbers · Map Title · Inset Latitude · Inset Bar Scale · Inset Map · Longitude · Latitude · Adjacent Area Page Number · Index Letter · Index Number · Inset Index Letter · Inset Index Number · Inset Longitude · Key to Population Symbols · Proportional Scale · Map Projection · Bar Scale

Symbols Used on Maps of the World

Boundaries & Lines	Area Types	Point Symbols
First Order (National) Boundary	City and Urban Area Limits	Rome — First Order (National) Capital
First Order Water Boundary	Demilitarized Zone	Belfast — Second Order (Internal) Capital
First Order Disputed Boundary	National Park/Preserve/Scenic Area	Hall — Third Order (Internal) Capital
Second Order (Internal) Boundary	National Forest/Forest Reserve	Neighborhood
Second Order Water Boundary	National Wilderness/Grassland	Pass
Second Order Disputed Boundary	National Recreation Area/Monument	Ruins
Third Order (Internal) Boundary	National Seashore/Lakeshore	Falls
Undefined Boundary	National Wildlife/Wilderness Area	Rapids
International Date Line	Native Reservation/Reserve	Dam
Shoreline, River	Military/Government Reservation	Point Elevation
Intermittent River	Lake, Reservoir	Park
Canal/Aqueduct	Intermittent Lake	Wildlife Area
Continental Divide	Dry Lake	Point of Interest
Highways/Roads	Salt Pan	Well
Railroads	Desert/Sand Area	International Airport
Ferries	Swamp	Other Airport
Tunnels (Road, Railroad)	Lava Flow	Air Base
Ancient Walls	Glacier	Naval Base

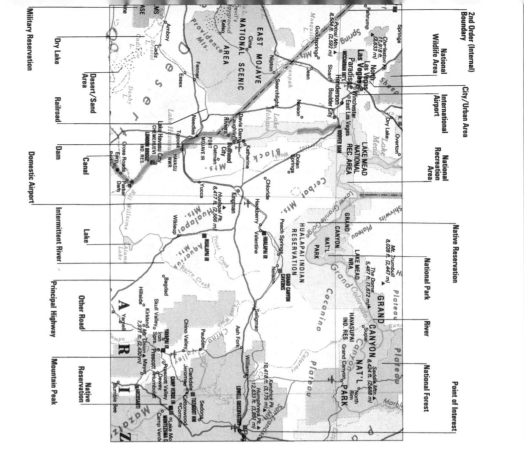

Map Legend

- 2nd Order (Internal) Boundary
- National Wildlife Area
- International Airport
- National Recreation Area
- Native Reservation
- National Park
- River
- National Forest
- Point of Interest
- Military Reservation
- Dry Lake
- Railroad
- Domestic Airport
- Desert/Sand Area
- Canal
- Dam
- Intermittent River
- Lake
- Other Road
- Mountain Peak
- City/Urban Area
- Principal Highway
- Native Reservation

PRINCIPAL MAP ABBREVIATIONS

Abor. Rsv.	Aboriginal Reserve	Ind. Res.	Indian Reservation	NWR	National Wildlife Reserve
Admin.	Administration	Int'l.	International	Obl.	Oblast
AFB	Air Force Base	IR	Indian Reservation	Occ.	Occupied
Amm. Dep.	Ammunition Depot	Isth.	Isthmus	Okr.	Okrug
Arch.	Archipelago	Jct.	Junction	Par.	Parish
Arpt.	Airport	L.	Lake	Passg.	Passage
Aut.	Autonomous	Lag.	Lagoon	Pen.	Peninsula
B.	Bay	Lakesh.	Lakeshore	Pk.	Peak
Bfld.	Battlefield	Mem.	Memorial	Plat.	Plateau
Bk.	Brook	Mil.	Military	PN	Park National
Bor.	Borough	Miss.	Missile	Pref.	Prefecture
Br.	Branch	Mon.	Monument	Prom.	Promontory
C.	Cape	Mt.	Mount	Prov.	Province
Can.	Canal	Mtn.	Mountain	Prsv.	Preserve
Cap.	Capital	Mts.	Mountains	Pt.	Point
C.G.	Coast Guard	Nat.	Natural	R.	River
Chan.	Channel	Nat'l.	National	RA	Recreation Area
Co.	County	Nav.	Naval	Rec.	Recreation(al)
Cr.	Creek	NB	Naval	Ref.	Refuge
Ctr.	Center	NBP	National Battlefield Park	Reg.	Region
Depr.	Depression	NBS	National Battlefield Site	Rep.	Republic
Dept.	Department	NHP	National Historical Park	Res.	Reservation, Reservoir, National
Des.	Desert	NHPP	National Park and Preserve	Rwy.	Railway
Dist.	District	NHS	National Historic Site		Riverway
DMZ	Demilitarized Zone	NL	National Lakeshore	Sa.	Sierra
Dpcy.	Dependency	NM	National Monument	Sd.	Sound
Eng.	Engineering	NMEMP	National Memorial Park	Seash.	Seashore
Est.	Estuary	NMILP	National Military Park	So.	Southern
Fd.	Fiord, Ford	No.	Northern	SP	State Park
Fed.	Federal	NP	National Park	Spr., Sprs.	Spring, Springs
Fk.	Fork	NPP	National Park and Preserve	Sta.	Station
Fld.	Field	NPRSV	National Preserve	Ste.	State
For.	Forest	NRA	National Recreation Area	Stm.	Stream
Ft.	Fort	NRSV	National Reserve	Str.	Strait
G.	Gulf	NS	National Seashore	Terr.	Territory
Gov.	Governor			Tun.	Tunnel
Govt.	Government			Twp.	Township
Gd.	Grand			Val.	Valley
Gt.	Great			Vill.	Village
Har.	Harbor			Vol.	Volcano
Hd.	Head			Wild.	Wildlife, Wilderness
Hist.	Historic(al)			Wtr.	Water
Hts.	Heights				
I., Is.	Island(s)				

WORLD STATISTICS

This atlas lists the dimensions of the earth's principal mountains, islands, rivers and lakes, along with other useful geographic information.

MAPS OF THE WORLD

These detailed regional maps are arranged by continent, and introduced by a political map of that continent. The continent maps, which utilize Hammond's new Optimal Conformal projection, are distinguished by individual colors for each country to highlight political divisions.

On the regional maps, different colors and textures highlight distinctive features such as parks, forests, deserts and urban areas. These maps also provide considerable information concerning geographic features and political divisions.

Hammond also uses accepted conventional names for certain major foreign places. Usually, space permits the inclusion of the local form in parentheses. To make the maps more readily understandable to English-speaking readers, many foreign physical features are translated into more recognizable English forms.

MASTER INDEX

This is an A-Z listing of names found on the political maps. It also has its own abbreviation list which, along with other Index keys, appears on page 110.

MAP SCALES

A map's scale is the relationship of any length on the map to an identical length on the earth's surface. A scale of 1:3,000,000 means that one inch on the map represents 3,000,000 inches (47 miles, 76 km.) on the earth's surface. Thus, a 1:1,000,000 scale is larger than 1:3,000,000, just as 1/1 is larger than 1/3.

The most densely populated areas are shown at a scale of 1:1,170,000, while selected metropolitan areas are covered at either 1:587,000 or 1:1,170,000. Other populous areas are presented at 1:3,500,000 and 1:7,000,000, allowing you to accurately compare areas and distances of similar regions. Remaining regions are scaled at 1:10,500,000. The continent maps, as well as the United States, Canada, Russia, Pacific and World have smaller scales.

Boundary Policies

This atlas observes the boundary policies of the U.S. Department of State. Boundary disputes are customarily handled with a special symbol treatment, but de facto boundaries are favored if they seem to have any degree of permanence, in the belief that boundaries should reflect current geographic and political realities. The portrayal of independent nations in the atlas follows their recognition by the United Nations and/or the United States government.

A Word About Names

Our source for all foreign names and physical names in the United States is the decision lists of the U.S. Board of Geographic Names, which contain hundreds of thousands of place names. If a place is not listed, the name form appearing on official foreign maps or in official gazetteers of the country concerned. For rendering domestic city, town and village names, this atlas follows the forms and spelling of the U.S. Postal Service.

World Flags and Reference Guide

Afghanistan
Page/Location: 53/H2
Area: 250,775 sq. mi.
649,507 sq. km.
Population: 16,450,000
Capital: Kabul
Largest City: Kabul
Highest Point: Noshaq
Monetary Unit: afghani

Albania
Page/Location: 39/F2
Area: 11,100 sq. mi.
28,749 sq. km.
Population: 3,335,000
Capital: Tiranë
Largest City: Tiranë
Highest Point: Korab
Monetary Unit: lek

Algeria
Page/Location: 76/F2
Area: 919,591 sq. mi.
2,381,740 sq. km.
Population: 26,022,000
Capital: Algiers
Largest City: Algiers
Highest Point: Tahat
Monetary Unit: Algerian dinar

Andorra
Page/Location: 35/F1
Area: 188 sq. mi.
487 sq. km.
Population: 53,000
Capital: Andorra la Vella
Largest City: Andorra la Vella
Highest Point: Coma Pedrosa
Monetary Unit: Fr. franc, Sp. peseta

Angola
Page/Location: 82/C3
Area: 481,351 sq. mi.
1,246,700 sq. km.
Population: 8,668,000
Capital: Luanda
Largest City: Luanda
Highest Point: Morro de Môco
Monetary Unit: kwanza

Antigua and Barbuda
Page/Location: 104/F3
Area: 171 sq. mi.
443 sq. km.
Population: 64,000
Capital: St. John's
Largest City: St. John's
Highest Point: Boggy Peak
Monetary Unit: East Caribbean dollar

Argentina
Page/Location: 109/C4
Area: 1,072,070 sq. mi.
2,776,661 sq. km.
Population: 32,664,000
Capital: Buenos Aires
Largest City: Buenos Aires
Highest Point: Cerro Aconcagua
Monetary Unit: Argentine peso

Armenia
Page/Location: 45/H5
Area: 11,506 sq. mi.
29,800 sq. km.
Population: 3,283,000
Capital: Yerevan
Largest City: Yerevan
Highest Point: Alagez
Monetary Unit: Armenian ruble

Australia
Page/Location: 70
Area: 2,966,136 sq. mi.
7,682,300 sq. km.
Population: 17,288,000
Capital: Canberra
Largest City: Sydney
Highest Point: Mt. Kosciusko
Monetary Unit: Australian dollar

Austria
Page/Location: 33/L3
Area: 32,375 sq. mi.
83,851 sq. km.
Population: 7,666,000
Capital: Vienna
Largest City: Vienna
Highest Point: Grossglockner
Monetary Unit: schilling

Azerbaijan
Page/Location: 45/H4
Area: 33,436 sq. mi.
86,600 sq. km.
Population: 7,029,000
Capital: Baku
Largest City: Baku
Highest Point: Bazardyuzyu
Monetary Unit: manat

Bahamas
Page/Location: 104/B2
Area: 5,382 sq. mi.
13,939 sq. km.
Population: 252,000
Capital: Nassau
Largest City: Nassau
Highest Point: 207 ft. (63 m)
Monetary Unit: Bahamian dollar

Bahrain
Page/Location: 52/F3
Area: 240 sq. mi.
622 sq. km.
Population: 537,000
Capital: Manama
Largest City: Manama
Highest Point: Jabal Dukhān
Monetary Unit: Bahraini dinar

Bangladesh
Page/Location: 60/E3
Area: 55,126 sq. mi.
142,776 sq. km.
Population: 116,601,000
Capital: Dhaka
Largest City: Dhaka
Highest Point: Keokradong
Monetary Unit: taka

Barbados
Page/Location: 104/G4
Area: 166 sq. mi.
430 sq. km.
Population: 255,000
Capital: Bridgetown
Largest City: Bridgetown
Highest Point: Mt. Hillaby
Monetary Unit: Barbadian dollar

Bhutan
Page/Location: 62/E2
Area: 18,147 sq. mi.
47,000 sq. km.
Population: 1,598,000
Capital: Thimphu
Largest City: Thimphu
Highest Point: Kula Kangri
Monetary Unit: ngultrum

Belarus
Page/Location: 18/F3
Area: 80,154 sq. mi.
207,600 sq. km.
Population: 10,200,000
Capital: Minsk
Largest City: Minsk
Highest Point: Dzerzhinskaya
Monetary Unit: Belarusian ruble

Belgium
Page/Location: 30/C2
Area: 11,781 sq. mi.
30,513 sq. km.
Population: 9,922,000
Capital: Brussels
Largest City: Brussels
Highest Point: Botrange
Monetary Unit: Belgian franc

Belize
Page/Location: 102/D2
Area: 8,867 sq. mi.
22,966 sq. km.
Population: 228,000
Capital: Belmopan
Largest City: Belize City
Highest Point: Victoria Peak
Monetary Unit: Belize dollar

Benin
Page/Location: 79/F4
Area: 43,483 sq. mi.
112,620 sq. km.
Population: 4,832,000
Capital: Porto-Novo
Largest City: Cotonou
Highest Point: Nassoukou
Monetary Unit: CFA franc

Brazil
Page/Location: 105/D3
Area: 3,284,426 sq. mi.
8,506,663 sq. km.
Population: 155,356,000
Capital: Brasília
Largest City: São Paulo
Highest Point: Pico da Neblina
Monetary Unit: cruzeiro real

Brunei
Page/Location: 66/D2
Area: 2,226 sq. mi.
5,765 sq. km.
Population: 398,000
Capital: Bandar Seri Begawan
Largest City: Bandar Seri Begawan
Highest Point: Bukit Pagon
Monetary Unit: Brunei dollar

Bolivia
Page/Location: 106/F7
Area: 424,163 sq. mi.
1,098,582 sq. km.
Population: 7,157,000
Capital: La Paz; Sucre
Largest City: La Paz
Highest Point: Nevado Ancohuma
Monetary Unit: Bolivian peso

Bosnia and Herzegovina
Page/Location: 40/C3
Area: 19,940 sq. mi.
51,645 sq. km.
Population: 4,124,256
Capital: Sarajevo
Largest City: Sarajevo
Highest Point: Maglić
Monetary Unit: —

Botswana
Page/Location: 52/D5
Area: 224,764 sq. mi.
582,139 sq. km.
Population: 1,258,000
Capital: Gaborone
Largest City: Gaborone
Highest Point: Tsodilo Hills
Monetary Unit: pula

Burma
Page/Location: 63/G3
Area: 261,789 sq. mi.
678,034 sq. km.
Population: 42,112,000
Capital: Rangoon
Largest City: Rangoon
Highest Point: Hkakabo Razi
Monetary Unit: kyat

Burundi
Page/Location: 82/E1
Area: 10,747 sq. mi.
27,835 sq. km.
Population: 5,831,000
Capital: Bujumbura
Largest City: Bujumbura
Highest Point: 8,760 ft. (2,670 m)
Monetary Unit: Burundi franc

Bulgaria
Page/Location: 41/G4
Area: 42,823 sq. mi.
110,912 sq. km.
Population: 8,911,000
Capital: Sofia
Largest City: Sofia
Highest Point: Musala
Monetary Unit: lev

Burkina Faso
Page/Location: 79/E3
Area: 105,869 sq. mi.
274,200 sq. km.
Population: 9,360,000
Capital: Ouagadougou
Largest City: Ouagadougou
Highest Point: 2,405 ft. (733 m)
Monetary Unit: CFA franc

Brunei

Cambodia
Page/Location: 65/D3
Area: 69,898 sq. mi.
181,036 sq. km.
Population: 7,146,000
Capital: Phnom Penh
Largest City: Phnom Penh
Highest Point: Phnum Aoral
Monetary Unit: riel

Cameroon
Page/Location: 76/H7
Area: 183,568 sq. mi.
475,441 sq. km.
Population: 11,390,000
Capital: Yaoundé
Largest City: Douala
Highest Point: Mt. Cameroon
Monetary Unit: CFA franc

Canada
Page/Location: 86
Area: 3,851,787 sq. mi.
9,976,139 sq. km.
Population: 27,296,859
Capital: Ottawa
Largest City: Toronto
Highest Point: Mt. Logan
Monetary Unit: Canadian dollar

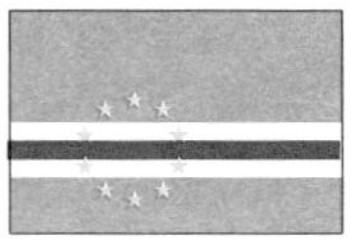

Cape Verde
Page/Location: 74/K9
Area: 1,557 sq. mi.
4,033 sq. km.
Population: 387,000
Capital: Praia
Largest City: Praia
Highest Point: 9,282 ft. (2,829 m)
Monetary Unit: Cape Verde escudo

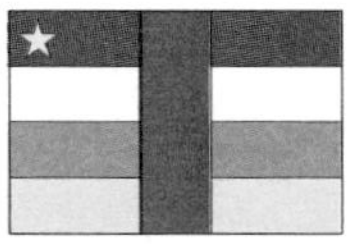

Central African Republic
Page/Location: 77/J6
Area: 242,000 sq. mi.
626,780 sq. km.
Population: 2,952,000
Capital: Bangui
Largest City: Bangui
Highest Point: Mt. Kayagangiri
Monetary Unit: CFA franc

Chad
Page/Location: 77/J4
Area: 495,752 sq. mi.
1,283,998 sq. km.
Population: 5,122,000
Capital: N'Djamena
Largest City: N'Djamena
Highest Point: Emi Koussi
Monetary Unit: CFA franc

Chile
Page/Location: 109/B3
Area: 292,257 sq. mi.
756,946 sq. km.
Population: 13,287,000
Capital: Santiago
Largest City: Santiago
Highest Point: Nevado Ojos del Salado
Monetary Unit: Chilean peso

China
Page/Location: 48/J6
Area: 3,691,000 sq. mi.
9,559,690 sq. km.
Population: 1,151,487,000
Capital: Beijing
Largest City: Shanghai
Highest Point: Mt. Everest
Monetary Unit: yuan

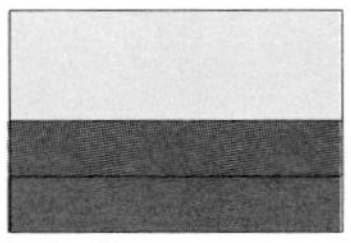

Colombia
Page/Location: 106/D3
Area: 439,513 sq. mi.
1,138,339 sq. km.
Population: 33,778,000
Capital: Bogotá
Largest City: Bogotá
Highest Point: Pico Cristóbal Colón
Monetary Unit: Colombian peso

Comoros
Page/Location: 74/G6
Area: 719 sq. mi.
1,862 sq. km.
Population: 477,000
Capital: Moroni
Largest City: Moroni
Highest Point: Karthala
Monetary Unit: Comorian franc

Congo
Page/Location: 74/D5
Area: 132,046 sq. mi.
342,000 sq. km.
Population: 2,309,000
Capital: Brazzaville
Largest City: Brazzaville
Highest Point: Lékéti Mts.
Monetary Unit: CFA franc

Costa Rica
Page/Location: 103/F4
Area: 19,575 sq. mi.
50,700 sq. km.
Population: 3,111,000
Capital: San José
Largest City: San José
Highest Point: Cerro Chirripó Grande
Monetary Unit: Costa Rican colón

Croatia
Page/Location: 40/C3
Area: 22,050 sq. mi.
57,110 sq. km.
Population: 4,601,469
Capital: Zagreb
Largest City: Zagreb
Highest Point: Veliki Troglav
Monetary Unit: Croatian dinar

Cuba
Page/Location: 103/F1
Area: 44,206 sq. mi.
114,494 sq. km.
Population: 10,732,000
Capital: Havana
Largest City: Havana
Highest Point: Pico Turquino
Monetary Unit: Cuban peso

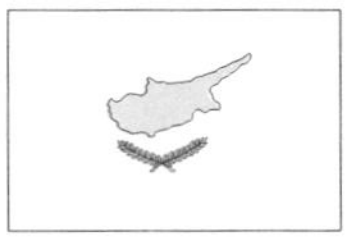

Cyprus
Page/Location: 49/C2
Area: 3,473 sq. mi.
8,995 sq. km.
Population: 709,000
Capital: Nicosia
Largest City: Nicosia
Highest Point: Olympus
Monetary Unit: Cypriot pound

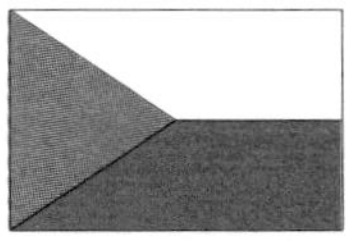

Czech Republic
Page/Location: 27/H4
Area: 30,449 sq. mi.
78,863 sq. km.
Population: 10,291,927
Capital: Prague
Largest City: Prague
Highest Point: Sněžka
Monetary Unit: Czech koruna

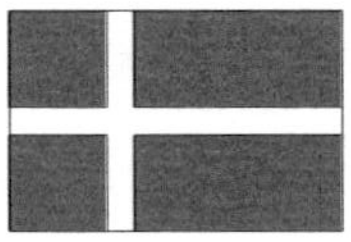

Denmark
Page/Location: 20/C5
Area: 16,629 sq. mi.
43,069 sq. km.
Population: 5,133,000
Capital: Copenhagen
Largest City: Copenhagen
Highest Point: Yding Skovhøj
Monetary Unit: Danish krone

Djibouti
Page/Location: 77/P5
Area: 8,880 sq. mi.
23,000 sq. km.
Population: 346,000
Capital: Djibouti
Largest City: Djibouti
Highest Point: Moussa Ali
Monetary Unit: Djibouti franc

Dominica
Page/Location: 104/F4
Area: 290 sq. mi.
751 sq. km.
Population: 86,000
Capital: Roseau
Largest City: Roseau
Highest Point: Morne Diablotin
Monetary Unit: Dominican dollar

Dominican Republic
Page/Location: 104/D3
Area: 18,704 sq. mi.
48,443 sq. km.
Population: 7,385,000
Capital: Santo Domingo
Largest City: Santo Domingo
Highest Point: Pico Duarte
Monetary Unit: Dominican peso

Ecuador
Page/Location: 106/C4
Area: 109,483 sq. mi.
283,561 sq. km.
Population: 10,752,000
Capital: Quito
Largest City: Guayaquil
Highest Point: Chimborazo
Monetary Unit: sucre

Egypt
Page/Location: 77/L2
Area: 386,659 sq. mi.
1,001,447 sq. km.
Population: 54,452,000
Capital: Cairo
Largest City: Cairo
Highest Point: Mt. Catherine
Monetary Unit: Egyptian pound

El Salvador
Page/Location: 102/D3
Area: 8,260 sq. mi.
21,393 sq. km.
Population: 5,419,000
Capital: San Salvador
Largest City: San Salvador
Highest Point: Santa Ana
Monetary Unit: Salvadoran colón

Equatorial Guinea
Page/Location: 76/G7
Area: 10,831 sq. mi.
28,052 sq. km.
Population: 379,000
Capital: Malabo
Largest City: Malabo
Highest Point: Pico de Santa Isabel
Monetary Unit: CFA franc

Eritrea
Page/Location: 77/N4
Area: 36,170 sq. mi.
93,679 sq. km.
Population: 3,500,000
Capital: Āsmera
Largest City: Āsmera
Highest Point: Soira
Monetary Unit: birr

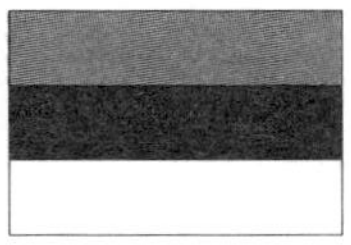

Estonia
Page/Location: 42/E4
Area: 17,413 sq. mi.
45,100 sq. km.
Population: 1,573,000
Capital: Tallinn
Largest City: Tallinn
Highest Point: Munamägi
Monetary Unit: kroon

Ethiopia
Page/Location: 77/N6
Area: 435,606 sq. mi.
1,128,220 sq. km.
Population: 51,617,000
Capital: Addis Ababa
Largest City: Addis Ababa
Highest Point: Ras Dashen Terara
Monetary Unit: birr

Fiji
Page/Location: 68/G6
Area: 7,055 sq. mi.
18,272 sq. km.
Population: 744,000
Capital: Suva
Largest City: Suva
Highest Point: Tomaniivi
Monetary Unit: Fijian dollar

Finland
Page/Location: 20/H2
Area: 130,128 sq. mi.
337,032 sq. km.
Population: 4,991,000
Capital: Helsinki
Largest City: Helsinki
Highest Point: Kahperusvaara
Monetary Unit: markka

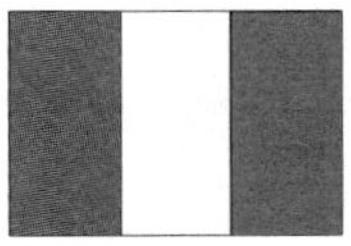

France
Page/Location: 32/D3
Area: 210,038 sq. mi.
543,998 sq. km.
Population: 58,073,553
Capital: Paris
Largest City: Paris
Highest Point: Mont Blanc
Monetary Unit: French franc

Gabon
Page/Location: 76/H7
Area: 103,346 sq. mi.
267,666 sq. km.
Population: 1,080,000
Capital: Libreville
Largest City: Libreville
Highest Point: Mt. Iboundji
Monetary Unit: CFA franc

Gambia
Page/Location: 78/B3
Area: 4,127 sq. mi.
10,689 sq. km.
Population: 875,000
Capital: Banjul
Largest City: Banjul
Highest Point: 98 ft. (30 m)
Monetary Unit: dalasi

Georgia
Page/Location: 45/G4
Area: 26,911 sq. mi.
69,700 sq. km.
Population: 5,449,000
Capital: Tbilisi
Largest City: Tbilisi
Highest Point: Kazbek
Monetary Unit: lari

Germany
Page/Location: 26/E3
Area: 137,753 sq. mi.
356,780 sq. km.
Population: 79,548,000
Capital: Berlin
Largest City: Berlin
Highest Point: Zugspitze
Monetary Unit: Deutsche mark

Ghana
Page/Location: 79/E4
Area: 92,099 sq. mi.
238,536 sq. km.
Population: 15,617,000
Capital: Accra
Largest City: Accra
Highest Point: Afadjoto
Monetary Unit: cedi

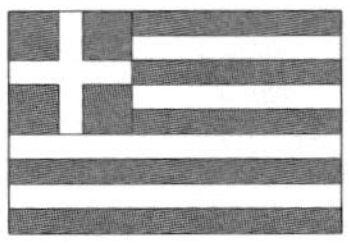

Greece
Page/Location: 39/G3
Area: 50,944 sq. mi.
131,945 sq. km.
Population: 10,043,000
Capital: Athens
Largest City: Athens
Highest Point: Mt. Olympus
Monetary Unit: drachma

Grenada
Page/Location: 104/F5
Area: 133 sq. mi.
344 sq. km.
Population: 84,000
Capital: St. George's
Largest City: St. George's
Highest Point: Mt. St. Catherine
Monetary Unit: East Caribbean dollar

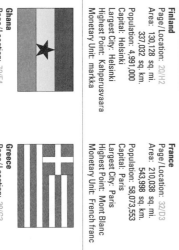

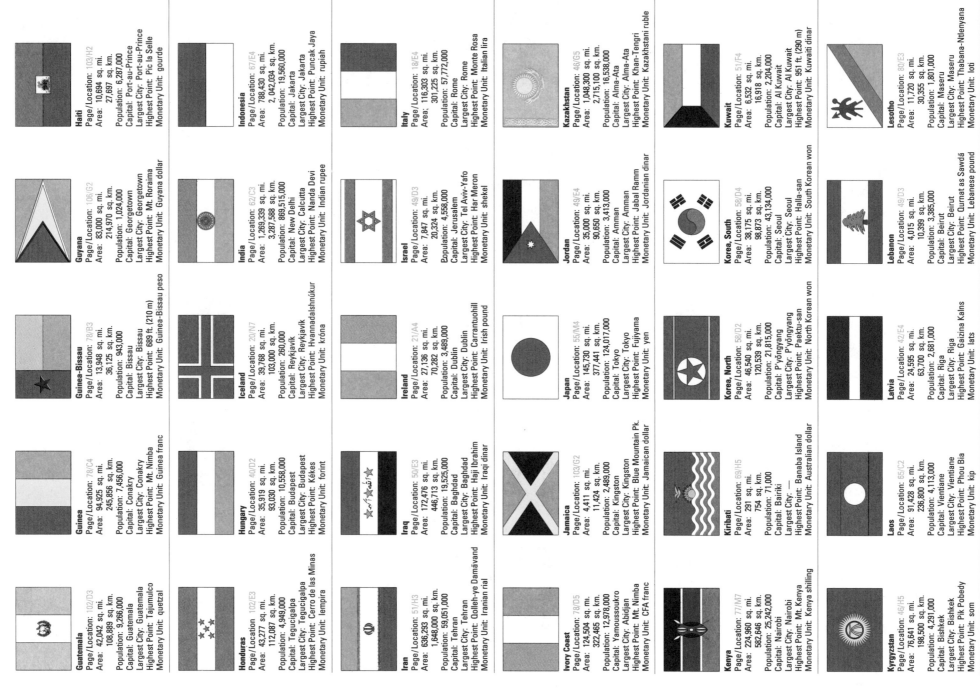

Guatemala
Page/Location: 102/D3
Area: 42,042 sq. mi.
108,889 sq. km.
Population: 9,266,000
Capital: Guatemala
Largest City: Guatemala
Highest Point: Tajumulco
Monetary Unit: quetzal

Guinea
Page/Location: 78/C4
Area: 94,925 sq. mi.
245,856 sq. km.
Population: 7,456,000
Capital: Conakry
Largest City: Conakry
Highest Point: Mt. Nimba
Monetary Unit: Guinea franc

Guinea-Bissau
Page/Location: 78/B3
Area: 13,948 sq. mi.
36,125 sq. km.
Population: 943,000
Capital: Bissau
Largest City: Bissau
Highest Point: 689 ft. (210 m)
Monetary Unit: Guinea-Bissau peso

Guyana
Page/Location: 106/G2
Area: 83,000 sq. mi.
214,970 sq. km.
Population: 1,024,000
Capital: Georgetown
Largest City: Georgetown
Highest Point: Mt. Roraima
Monetary Unit: Guyana dollar

Haiti
Page/Location: 103/H2
Area: 10,694 sq. mi.
27,697 sq. km.
Population: 6,287,000
Capital: Port-au-Prince
Largest City: Port-au-Prince
Highest Point: Pic la Selle
Monetary Unit: gourde

Honduras
Page/Location: 102/E3
Area: 43,277 sq. mi.
112,087 sq. km.
Population: 4,949,000
Capital: Tegucigalpa
Largest City: Tegucigalpa
Highest Point: Cerro de las Minas
Monetary Unit: lempira

Hungary
Page/Location: 40/D2
Area: 35,919 sq. mi.
93,030 sq. km.
Population: 10,558,000
Capital: Budapest
Largest City: Budapest
Highest Point: Kékes
Monetary Unit: forint

Iceland
Page/Location: 20/N7
Area: 39,768 sq. mi.
103,000 sq. km.
Population: 260,000
Capital: Reykjavik
Largest City: Reykjavik
Highest Point: Hvannadalshnúkur
Monetary Unit: króna

India
Page/Location: 62/C3
Area: 1,269,339 sq. mi.
3,287,588 sq. km.
Population: 869,515,000
Capital: New Delhi
Largest City: Calcutta
Highest Point: Nanda Devi
Monetary Unit: Indian rupee

Indonesia
Page/Location: 67/E4
Area: 788,430 sq. mi.
2,042,034 sq. km.
Population: 19,560,000
Capital: Jakarta
Largest City: Jakarta
Highest Point: Puncak Jaya
Monetary Unit: rupiah

Iran
Page/Location: 51/H3
Area: 636,293 sq. mi.
1,648,000 sq. km.
Population: 59,051,000
Capital: Tehran
Largest City: Tehran
Highest Point: Qolleh-ye Damávand
Monetary Unit: Iranian rial

Iraq
Page/Location: 50/E3
Area: 172,476 sq. mi.
446,713 sq. km.
Population: 19,525,000
Capital: Baghdad
Largest City: Baghdad
Highest Point: Haji Ibrahim
Monetary Unit: Iraqi dinar

Ireland
Page/Location: 21/A4
Area: 27,136 sq. mi.
70,282 sq. km.
Population: 3,489,000
Capital: Dublin
Largest City: Dublin
Highest Point: Carrantuohill
Monetary Unit: Irish pound

Israel
Page/Location: 49/D3
Area: 7,847 sq. mi.
20,324 sq. km.
Population: 4,558,000
Capital: Jerusalem
Largest City: Tel Aviv-Yafo
Highest Point: Har Meron
Monetary Unit: shekel

Italy
Page/Location: 18/E4
Area: 116,303 sq. mi.
301,225 sq. km.
Population: 57,772,000
Capital: Rome
Largest City: Rome
Highest Point: Monte Rosa
Monetary Unit: Italian lira

Ivory Coast
Page/Location: 78/D5
Area: 124,504 sq. mi.
322,465 sq. km.
Population: 12,978,000
Capital: Yamoussoukro
Largest City: Abidjan
Highest Point: Mt. Nimba
Monetary Unit: CFA franc

Jamaica
Page/Location: 103/G2
Area: 4,411 sq. mi.
11,424 sq. km.
Population: 2,489,000
Capital: Kingston
Largest City: Kingston
Highest Point: Blue Mountain Pk.
Monetary Unit: Jamaican dollar

Japan
Page/Location: 55/M4
Area: 145,730 sq. mi.
377,441 sq. km.
Population: 124,017,000
Capital: Tokyo
Largest City: Tokyo
Highest Point: Fujiyama
Monetary Unit: yen

Jordan
Page/Location: 49/E4
Area: 35,000 sq. mi.
90,650 sq. km.
Population: 3,413,000
Capital: Amman
Largest City: Amman
Highest Point: Jabal Ramm
Monetary Unit: Jordanian dinar

Kazakhstan
Page/Location: 46/G5
Area: 1,048,300 sq. mi.
2,715,100 sq. km.
Population: 16,538,000
Capital: Alma-Ata
Largest City: Alma-Ata
Highest Point: Khan-Tengri
Monetary Unit: Kazakhstani ruble

Kenya
Page/Location: 77/M7
Area: 224,960 sq. mi.
582,646 sq. km.
Population: 25,242,000
Capital: Nairobi
Largest City: Nairobi
Highest Point: Mt. Kenya
Monetary Unit: Kenya shilling

Kiribati
Page/Location: 69/H5
Area: 291 sq. mi.
754 sq. km.
Population: 71,000
Capital: Bairiki
Largest City: —
Highest Point: Banaba Island
Monetary Unit: Australian dollar

Korea, North
Page/Location: 58/D2
Area: 46,540 sq. mi.
120,539 sq. km.
Population: 21,815,000
Capital: P'yŏngyang
Largest City: P'yŏngyang
Highest Point: Paektu-san
Monetary Unit: North Korean won

Korea, South
Page/Location: 58/D4
Area: 38,175 sq. mi.
98,873 sq. km.
Population: 43,134,000
Capital: Seoul
Largest City: Seoul
Highest Point: Halla-san
Monetary Unit: South Korean won

Kuwait
Page/Location: 51/F4
Area: 6,532 sq. mi.
16,918 sq. km.
Population: 2,204,000
Capital: Al Kuwait
Largest City: Al Kuwait
Highest Point: 951 ft. (290 m)
Monetary Unit: Kuwaiti dinar

Kyrgyzstan
Page/Location: 46/H5
Area: 76,641 sq. mi.
198,500 sq. km.
Population: 4,291,000
Capital: Bishkek
Largest City: Bishkek
Highest Point: Pik Pobedy
Monetary Unit: som

Laos
Page/Location: 65/C2
Area: 91,428 sq. mi.
236,800 sq. km.
Population: 4,113,000
Capital: Vientiane
Largest City: Vientiane
Highest Point: Phou Bia
Monetary Unit: kip

Latvia
Page/Location: 42/E4
Area: 24,595 sq. mi.
63,700 sq. km.
Population: 2,681,000
Capital: Riga
Largest City: Riga
Highest Point: Gaizina Kalns
Monetary Unit: lats

Lebanon
Page/Location: 49/D3
Area: 4,015 sq. mi.
10,399 sq. km.
Population: 3,385,000
Capital: Beirut
Largest City: Beirut
Highest Point: Qurnat as Sawdá
Monetary Unit: Lebanese pound

Lesotho
Page/Location: 80/E3
Area: 11,720 sq. mi.
30,355 sq. km.
Population: 1,801,000
Capital: Maseru
Largest City: Maseru
Highest Point: Thabana-Ntlenyana
Monetary Unit: loti

Liberia
Page/Location: 78/C4
Area: 43,000 sq. mi.
111,370 sq. km.
Population: 2,730,000
Capital: Monrovia
Largest City: Monrovia
Highest Point: Mt. Wuteve
Monetary Unit: Liberian dollar

Libya
Page/Location: 77/J2
Area: 679,358 sq. mi.
1,759,537 sq. km.
Population: 4,353,000
Capital: Tripoli
Largest City: Tripoli
Highest Point: Bette
Monetary Unit: Libyan dinar

Liechtenstein
Page/Location: 37/F3
Area: 61 sq. mi.
158 sq. km.
Population: 28,000
Capital: Vaduz
Largest City: Vaduz
Highest Point: Grauspitz
Monetary Unit: Swiss franc

 **Madagascar**
Page/Location: 81/H8
Area: 226,657 sq. mi.
587,041 sq. km.
Population: 12,185,000
Capital: Antananarivo
Largest City: Antananarivo
Highest Point: Maromokotro
Monetary Unit: Malagasy franc

 Malawi
Page/Location: 82/F3
Area: 45,747 sq. mi.
118,485 sq. km.
Population: 9,438,000
Capital: Lilongwe
Largest City: Blantyre
Highest Point: Mulanje Mts.
Monetary Unit: Malawi kwacha

 Maldives
Page/Location: 48/G9
Area: 115 sq. mi.
298 sq. km.
Population: 226,000
Capital: Male
Largest City: Male
Highest Point: 20 ft. (6 m)
Monetary Unit: rufiyaa

 Lithuania
Page/Location: 42/D5
Area: 25,174 sq. mi.
65,200 sq. km.
Population: 3,690,000
Capital: Vilnius
Largest City: Vilnius
Highest Point: Nevaišiŭ
Monetary Unit: litas

Malaysia
Page/Location: 67/C2
Area: 128,308 sq. mi.
332,318 sq. km.
Population: 17,982,000
Capital: Kuala Lumpur
Largest City: Kuala Lumpur
Highest Point: Gunung Kinabalu
Monetary Unit: ringgit

Mali
Page/Location: 76/E4
Area: 464,873 sq. mi.
1,204,021 sq. km.
Population: 8,339,000
Capital: Bamako
Largest City: Bamako
Highest Point: Hombori Tondo
Monetary Unit: CFA franc

Luxembourg
Page/Location: 31/F4
Area: 999 sq. mi.
2,587 sq. km.
Population: 388,000
Capital: Luxembourg
Largest City: Luxembourg
Highest Point: Ardennes Plateau
Monetary Unit: Luxembourg franc

 **Marshall Islands**
Page/Location: 68/G3
Area: 70 sq. mi.
181 sq. km.
Population: 48,000
Capital: Majuro
Largest City: —
Highest Point: —
Monetary Unit: U.S. dollar

 Mauritania
Page/Location: 76/C4
Area: 419,229 sq. mi.
1,085,803 sq. km.
Population: 1,996,000
Capital: Nouakchott
Largest City: Nouakchott
Highest Point: Kediet Ijill
Monetary Unit: ouguiya

 Mauritius
Page/Location: 81/S15
Area: 790 sq. mi.
2,046 sq. km.
Population: 1,081,000
Capital: Port Louis
Largest City: Port Louis
Highest Point: 2,713 ft. (827 m)
Monetary Unit: Mauritian rupee

Malta
Page/Location: 38/D5
Area: 122 sq. mi.
316 sq. km.
Population: 356,000
Capital: Valletta
Largest City: Sliema
Highest Point: 830 ft. (253 m)
Monetary Unit: Maltese lira

Macedonia
Page/Location: 39/G2
Area: 9,889 sq. mi.
25,612 sq. km.
Population: 1,909,136
Capital: Skopje
Largest City: Skopje
Highest Point: Korab
Monetary Unit: denar

Monaco
Page/Location: 33/G5
Area: 368 acres
149 hectares
Population: 30,000
Capital: Monaco
Largest City: Monaco
Highest Point: —
Monetary Unit: French franc

Mongolia
Page/Location: 54/D2
Area: 606,163 sq. mi.
1,569,962 sq. km.
Population: 2,247,000
Capital: Ulaanbaatar
Largest City: Ulaanbaatar
Highest Point: Tavan Bogd Uul
Monetary Unit: tughrik

Morocco
Page/Location: 76/C1
Area: 172,414 sq. mi.
446,550 sq. km.
Population: 26,182,000
Capital: Rabat
Largest City: Casablanca
Highest Point: Jebel Toubkal
Monetary Unit: Moroccan dirham

Mexico
Page/Location: 84/G7
Area: 761,601 sq. mi.
1,972,546 sq. km.
Population: 90,007,000
Capital: Mexico City
Largest City: Mexico City
Highest Point: Citlaltépetl
Monetary Unit: Mexican peso

Maldives flag area

Mozambique
Page/Location: 82/G4
Area: 303,769 sq. mi.
786,762 sq. km.
Population: 15,113,000
Capital: Maputo
Largest City: Maputo
Highest Point: Monte Binga
Monetary Unit: metical

Micronesia
Page/Location: 68/D4
Area: 271 sq. mi.
702 sq. km.
Population: 108,000
Capital: Kolonia
Largest City: —
Highest Point: —
Monetary Unit: U.S. dollar

Moldova
Page/Location: 41/J2
Area: 13,012 sq. mi.
33,700 sq. km.
Population: 4,341,000
Capital: Chişinău
Largest City: Chişinău
Highest Point: —
Monetary Unit: leu

 Nepal
Page/Location: 62/D2
Area: 54,663 sq. mi.
141,577 sq. km.
Population: 19,612,000
Capital: Kathmandu
Largest City: Kathmandu
Highest Point: Mt. Everest
Monetary Unit: Nepalese rupee

 New Zealand
Page/Location: 71/Q10
Area: 103,736 sq. mi.
268,676 sq. km.
Population: 3,309,000
Capital: Wellington
Largest City: Auckland
Highest Point: Mt. Cook
Monetary Unit: New Zealand dollar

 Niger
Page/Location: 76/G4
Area: 489,189 sq. mi.
1,267,000 sq. km.
Population: 8,154,000
Capital: Niamey
Largest City: Niamey
Highest Point: Bagzane
Monetary Unit: CFA franc

Netherlands
Page/Location: 28/B5
Area: 15,892 sq. mi.
41,160 sq. km.
Population: 15,022,000
Capital: The Hague, Amsterdam
Largest City: Amsterdam
Highest Point: Vaalserberg
Monetary Unit: Netherlands guilder

Nicaragua
Page/Location: 103/E3
Area: 45,698 sq. mi.
118,358 sq. km.
Population: 3,752,000
Capital: Managua
Largest City: Managua
Highest Point: Pico Mogotón
Monetary Unit: córdoba

 **Namibia**
Page/Location: 82/C5
Area: 317,827 sq. mi.
823,172 sq. km.
Population: 1,521,000
Capital: Windhoek
Largest City: Windhoek
Highest Point: Brandberg
Monetary Unit: rand

Nauru
Page/Location: 68/D4
Area: 7.7 sq. mi.
20 sq. km.
Population: 9,000
Capital: Yaren (district)
Largest City: —
Highest Point: 230 ft. (70 m)
Monetary Unit: Australian dollar

 Nigeria
Page/Location: 76/G6
Area: 357,000 sq. mi.
924,630 sq. km.
Population: 122,471,000
Capital: Abuja
Largest City: Lagos
Highest Point: Dimlang
Monetary Unit: naira

 Norway
Page/Location: 20/C3
Area: 125,053 sq. mi.
323,887 sq. km.
Population: 4,273,000
Capital: Oslo
Largest City: Oslo
Highest Point: Glittertinden
Monetary Unit: Norwegian krone

 **Oman**
Page/Location: 53/G4
Area: 120,000 sq. mi.
310,800 sq. km.
Population: 1,534,000
Capital: Muscat
Largest City: Muscat
Highest Point: Jabal ash Shām
Monetary Unit: Omani rial

 Pakistan
Page/Location: 53/H3
Area: 310,403 sq. mi.
803,944 sq. km.
Population: 117,490,000
Capital: Islamabad
Largest City: Karachi
Highest Point: K2 (Godwin Austen)
Monetary Unit: Pakistani rupee

Panama
Page/Location: 103/F4
Area: 29,761 sq. mi.
77,082 sq. km.
Population: 2,476,000
Capital: Panamá
Largest City: Panamá
Highest Point: Barú
Monetary Unit: balboa

Papua New Guinea
Page/Location: 68/D5
Area: 183,540 sq. mi.
475,369 sq. km.
Population: 3,913,000
Capital: Port Moresby
Largest City: Port Moresby
Highest Point: Mt. Wilhelm
Monetary Unit: kina

Paraguay
Page/Location: 105/D5
Area: 157,047 sq. mi.
406,752 sq. km.
Population: 4,799,000
Capital: Asunción
Largest City: Asunción
Highest Point: Sierra de Amambay
Monetary Unit: guaraní

World Flags and Reference Guide

Peru
Page/Location: 106/C5
Area: 496,222 sq. mi.
1,285,215 sq. km.
Population: 22,362,000
Capital: Lima
Largest City: Lima
Highest Point: Nevado Huascarán
Monetary Unit: nuevo sol

Philippines
Page/Location: 48/M8
Area: 115,707 sq. mi.
299,681 sq. km.
Population: 65,759,000
Capital: Manila
Largest City: Manila
Highest Point: Mt. Apo
Monetary Unit: Philippine peso

Poland
Page/Location: 27/K2
Area: 120,725 sq. mi.
312,678 sq. km.
Population: 37,800,000
Capital: Warsaw
Largest City: Warsaw
Highest Point: Rysy
Monetary Unit: zloty

Portugal
Page/Location: 34/A3
Area: 35,549 sq. mi.
92,072 sq. km.
Population: 10,388,000
Capital: Lisbon
Largest City: Lisbon
Highest Point: Serra da Estrela
Monetary Unit: Portuguese escudo

Qatar
Page/Location: 52/F3
Area: 4,247 sq. mi.
11,000 sq. km.
Population: 518,000
Capital: Doha
Largest City: Doha
Highest Point: Dukhán Heights
Monetary Unit: Qatari riyal

Romania
Page/Location: 41/F3
Area: 91,699 sq. mi.
237,500 sq. km.
Population: 23,397,000
Capital: Bucharest
Largest City: Bucharest
Highest Point: Moldoveanul
Monetary Unit: leu

Russia
Page/Location: 46/H3
Area: 6,592,812 sq. mi.
17,075,400 sq. km.
Population: 147,386,000
Capital: Moscow
Largest City: Moscow
Highest Point: El'brus
Monetary Unit: Russian ruble

Rwanda
Page/Location: 82/E1
Area: 10,169 sq. mi.
26,337 sq. km.
Population: 7,903,000
Capital: Kigali
Largest City: Kigali
Highest Point: Karisimbi
Monetary Unit: Rwanda franc

São Tomé and Príncipe
Page/Location: 76/G7
Area: 372 sq. mi.
963 sq. km.
Population: 128,000
Capital: São Tomé
Largest City: São Tomé
Highest Point: Pico de São Tomé
Monetary Unit: dobra

Saudi Arabia
Page/Location: 104/F3
Area: 829,995 sq. mi.
2,149,687 sq. km.
Population: 17,870,000
Capital: Riyadh
Largest City: Riyadh
Highest Point: Jabal Sawdā'
Monetary Unit: Saudi riyal

Saint Vincent and the Grenadines
Page/Location: 104/F4
Area: 150 sq. mi.
388 sq. km.
Population: 114,000
Capital: Kingstown
Largest City: Kingstown
Highest Point: Soufrière
Monetary Unit: East Caribbean dollar

San Marino
Page/Location: 33/K5
Area: 23.4 sq. mi.
60.6 sq. km.
Population: 23,000
Capital: San Marino
Largest City: San Marino
Highest Point: Monte Titano
Monetary Unit: Italian lira

Sierra Leone
Page/Location: 78/B4
Area: 27,925 sq. mi.
72,325 sq. km.
Population: 4,275,000
Capital: Freetown
Largest City: Freetown
Highest Point: Loma Mansa
Monetary Unit: leone

Singapore
Page/Location: 66/B3
Area: 226 sq. mi.
585 sq. km.
Population: 2,756,000
Capital: Singapore
Largest City: Singapore
Highest Point: Bukit Timah
Monetary Unit: Singapore dollar

Slovakia
Page/Location: 27/K4
Area: 18,924 sq. mi.
49,013 sq. km.
Population: 4,991,168
Capital: Bratislava
Largest City: Bratislava
Highest Point: Gerlachovský Štit
Monetary Unit: Slovak koruna

Seychelles
Page/Location: 74/H5
Area: 145 sq. mi.
375 sq. km.
Population: 69,000
Capital: Victoria
Largest City: Victoria
Highest Point: Morne Seychellois
Monetary Unit: Seychellois rupee

Saint Kitts and Nevis
Page/Location: 104/F3
Area: 104 sq. mi.
269 sq. km.
Population: 40,000
Capital: Basseterre
Largest City: Basseterre
Highest Point: Mt. Misery
Monetary Unit: East Caribbean dollar

Saint Kitts and Nevis

Saint Lucia
Page/Location: 104/F4
Area: 238 sq. mi.
616 sq. km.
Population: 153,000
Capital: Castries
Largest City: Castries
Highest Point: Mt. Gimie
Monetary Unit: East Caribbean dollar

Solomon Islands
Page/Location: 68/E6
Area: 11,500 sq. mi.
29,785 sq. km.
Population: 347,000
Capital: Honiara
Largest City: Honiara
Highest Point: Mt. Makarakomburu
Monetary Unit: Solomon Islands dollar

Somalia
Page/Location: 77/D6
Area: 246,200 sq. mi.
637,658 sq. km.
Population: 6,709,000
Capital: Mogadishu
Largest City: Mogadishu
Highest Point: Shimber Berris
Monetary Unit: Somali shilling

Senegal
Page/Location: 78/B3
Area: 75,954 sq. mi.
196,720 sq. km.
Population: 7,953,000
Capital: Dakar
Largest City: Dakar
Highest Point: Fouta Djallon
Monetary Unit: CFA franc

South Africa
Page/Location: 80/C3
Area: 455,318 sq. mi.
1,179,274 sq. km.
Population: 40,601,000
Capital: Cape Town; Pretoria
Largest City: Johannesburg
Highest Point: Injasuti
Monetary Unit: rand

Slovenia
Page/Location: 40/B3
Area: 7,898 sq. mi.
20,456 sq. km.
Population: 1,891,864
Capital: Ljubljana
Largest City: Ljubljana
Highest Point: Triglav
Monetary Unit: tolar

Sudan
Page/Location: 77/L5
Area: 967,494 sq. mi.
2,505,809 sq. km.
Population: 27,220,000
Capital: Khartoum
Largest City: Omdurman
Highest Point: Jabal Marrah
Monetary Unit: Sudanese pound

Suriname
Page/Location: 107/G3
Area: 55,144 sq. mi.
142,823 sq. km.
Population: 402,000
Capital: Paramaribo
Largest City: Paramaribo
Highest Point: Juliana Top
Monetary Unit: Suriname guilder

Swaziland
Page/Location: 81/E2
Area: 6,705 sq. mi.
17,366 sq. km.
Population: 859,000
Capital: Mbabane
Largest City: Mbabane
Highest Point: Emlembe
Monetary Unit: lilangeni

Sri Lanka
Page/Location: 62/D6
Area: 25,332 sq. mi.
65,610 sq. km.
Population: 17,424,000
Capital: Colombo
Largest City: Colombo
Highest Point: Pidurutalagala
Monetary Unit: Sri Lanka rupee

Sweden
Page/Location: 20/E3
Area: 173,665 sq. mi.
449,792 sq. km.
Population: 8,564,000
Capital: Stockholm
Largest City: Stockholm
Highest Point: Kebnekaise
Monetary Unit: krona

Spain
Page/Location: 34/C2
Area: 194,881 sq. mi.
504,742 sq. km.
Population: 39,385,000
Capital: Madrid
Largest City: Madrid
Highest Point: Pico de Teide
Monetary Unit: peseta

Switzerland
Page/Location: 36/D4
Area: 15,943 sq. mi.
41,292 sq. km.
Population: 6,784,000
Capital: Bern
Largest City: Zürich
Highest Point: Dufourspitze
Monetary Unit: Swiss franc

Syria
Page/Location: 50/D3
Area: 71,498 sq. mi.
185,180 sq. km.
Population: 12,966,000
Capital: Damascus
Largest City: Damascus
Highest Point: Jabal ash Shaykh
Monetary Unit: Syrian pound

Taiwan
Page/Location: 61/J3
Area: 13,971 sq. mi.
36,185 sq. km.
Population: 16,609,961
Capital: Taipei
Largest City: Taipei
Highest Point: Yü Shan
Monetary Unit: new Taiwan dollar

Tajikistan
Page/Location: 46/H6
Area: 55,251 sq. mi.
143,100 sq. km.
Population: 5,112,000
Capital: Dushanbe
Largest City: Dushanbe
Highest Point: Communism Peak
Monetary Unit: Tajik ruble

Tanzania
Page/Location: 82/F2
Area: 363,708 sq. mi.
942,003 sq. km.
Population: 26,869,000
Capital: Dar es Salaam
Largest City: Dar es Salaam
Highest Point: Kilimanjaro
Monetary Unit: Tanzanian shilling

Thailand
Page/Location: 65/C3
Area: 198,455 sq. mi.
513,998 sq. km.
Population: 56,814,000
Capital: Bangkok
Largest City: Bangkok
Highest Point: Doi Inthanon
Monetary Unit: baht

Togo
Page/Location: 79/F4
Area: 21,622 sq. mi.
56,000 sq. km.
Population: 3,811,000
Capital: Lomé
Largest City: Lomé
Highest Point: Mt. Agou
Monetary Unit: CFA franc

Tonga
Page/Location: 69/H7
Area: 270 sq. mi.
699 sq. km.
Population: 102,000
Capital: Nuku'alofa
Largest City: Nuku'alofa
Highest Point: Kao Island
Monetary Unit: pa'anga

Trinidad and Tobago
Page/Location: 104/F5
Area: 1,980 sq. mi.
5,128 sq. km.
Population: 1,285,000
Capital: Port-of-Spain
Largest City: Port-of-Spain
Highest Point: El Cerro del Aripo
Monetary Unit: Trin. & Tobago dollar

Tunisia
Page/Location: 76/G1
Area: 63,378 sq. mi.
164,149 sq. km.
Population: 8,276,000
Capital: Tunis
Largest City: Tunis
Highest Point: Jabal ash Sha'nabi
Monetary Unit: Tunisian dinar

Turkey
Page/Location: 50/C2
Area: 300,946 sq. mi.
779,450 sq. km.
Population: 58,581,000
Capital: Ankara
Largest City: Istanbul
Highest Point: Mt. Ararat
Monetary Unit: Turkish lira

Turkmenistan
Page/Location: 46/F6
Area: 188,455 sq. mi.
488,100 sq. km.
Population: 3,534,000
Capital: Ashkhabad
Largest City: Ashkhabad
Highest Point: Rize
Monetary Unit: manat

Tuvalu
Page/Location: 68/G5
Area: 9.78 sq. mi.
25.33 sq. km.
Population: 9,000
Capital: Fongafale
Largest City: —
Highest Point: 16 ft (5 m)
Monetary Unit: Australian dollar

Uganda
Page/Location: 77/M7
Area: 91,076 sq. mi.
235,887 sq. km.
Population: 18,690,000
Capital: Kampala
Largest City: Kampala
Highest Point: Margherita Peak
Monetary Unit: Ugandan shilling

Ukraine
Page/Location: 44/D2
Area: 233,089 sq. mi.
603,700 sq. km.
Population: 51,704,000
Capital: Kiev
Largest City: Kiev
Highest Point: Goverla
Monetary Unit: grivna

United Arab Emirates
Page/Location: 52/F4
Area: 32,278 sq. mi.
83,600 sq. km.
Population: 2,390,000
Capital: Abu Dhabi
Largest City: Dubayy
Highest Point: Hajar Mts.
Monetary Unit: Emirian dirham

United Kingdom
Page/Location: 21
Area: 94,399 sq. mi.
244,493 sq. km.
Population: 57,515,000
Capital: London
Largest City: London
Highest Point: Ben Nevis
Monetary Unit: pound sterling

United States
Page/Location: 88
Area: 3,623,420 sq. mi.
9,384,658 sq. km.
Population: 252,502,000
Capital: Washington
Largest City: New York
Highest Point: Mt. McKinley
Monetary Unit: U.S. dollar

Uruguay
Page/Location: 109/E3
Area: 72,172 sq. mi.
186,925 sq. km.
Population: 3,121,000
Capital: Montevideo
Largest City: Montevideo
Highest Point: Cerro Catedral
Monetary Unit: Uruguayan peso

Uzbekistan
Page/Location: 46/G5
Area: 173,591 sq. mi.
449,600 sq. km.
Population: 19,906,000
Capital: Tashkent
Largest City: Tashkent
Highest Point: Khodzha-Pir'yakh
Monetary Unit: Uzbek ruble

Vanuatu
Page/Location: 68/F6
Area: 5,700 sq. mi.
14,763 sq. km.
Population: 170,000
Capital: Vila
Largest City: Vila
Highest Point: Tabwemasana
Monetary Unit: vatu

Vatican City
Page/Location: 38/C2
Area: 108.7 acres
44. hectares
Population: 1,000
Capital: —
Largest City: —
Highest Point: —
Monetary Unit: Italian lira

Venezuela
Page/Location: 106/E2
Area: 352,143 sq. mi.
912,050 sq. km.
Population: 20,189,000
Capital: Caracas
Largest City: Caracas
Highest Point: Pico Bolivar
Monetary Unit: bolivar

Vietnam
Page/Location: 65/D2
Area: 128,405 sq. mi.
332,569 sq. km.
Population: 67,568,000
Capital: Hanoi
Largest City: Ho Chi Minh City
Highest Point: Fan Si Pan
Monetary Unit: dong

Western Samoa
Page/Location: 69/H6
Area: 1,133 sq. mi.
2,934 sq. km.
Population: 190,000
Capital: Apia
Largest City: Apia
Highest Point: Mt. Silisili
Monetary Unit: tala

Yemen
Page/Location: 52/E5
Area: 188,321 sq. mi.
487,752 sq. km.
Population: 10,063,000
Capital: Sanaa
Largest City: Sanaa
Highest Point: Nabi Shu'ayb
Monetary Unit: Yemeni rial

Yugoslavia
Page/Location: 40/E3
Area: 38,989 sq. mi.
100,982 sq. km.
Population: 11,371,275
Capital: Belgrade
Largest City: Belgrade
Highest Point: Daravica
Monetary Unit: Yugoslav new dinar

Zaire
Page/Location: 74/E5
Area: 905,063 sq. mi.
2,344,113 sq. km.
Population: 37,832,000
Capital: Kinshasa
Largest City: Kinshasa
Highest Point: Margherita Peak
Monetary Unit: zaire

Zambia
Page/Location: 82/E3
Area: 290,586 sq. mi.
752,618 sq. km.
Population: 8,446,000
Capital: Lusaka
Largest City: Lusaka
Highest Point: Sunzu
Monetary Unit: Zambian kwacha

Zimbabwe
Page/Location: 82/E4
Area: 150,803 sq. mi.
390,580 sq. km.
Population: 10,720,000
Capital: Harare
Largest City: Harare
Highest Point: Inyangani
Monetary Unit: Zimbabwe dollar

World Statistics

ELEMENTS OF THE SOLAR SYSTEM

	Mean Distance from Sun: in Miles	in Kilometers	Period of Revolution around Sun	Period of Rotation on Axis	Equatorial Diameter in Miles	in Kilometers	Surface Gravity (Earth = 1)	Mass (Earth = 1)	Mean Density (Water = 1)	Number of Satellites
Mercury	35,990,000	57,900,000	87.97 days	59 days	3,032	4,880	0.38	0.055	5.5	0
Venus	67,240,000	108,200,000	224.70 days	243 days†	7,523	12,106	0.90	0.815	5.25	0
Earth	93,000,000	149,700,000	365.26 days	23h 56m	7,926	12,755	1.00	1.00	5.5	1
Mars	141,730,000	228,100,000	687.00 days	24h 37m	4,220	6,790	0.38	0.107	4.0	2
Jupiter	483,880,000	778,700,000	11.86 years	9h 50m	88,750	142,800	2.87	317.9	1.3	16
Saturn	887,130,000	1,427,700,000	29.46 years	10h 39m	74,580	120,020	1.32	95.2	0.7	23
Uranus	1,783,700,000	2,870,500,000	84.01 years	17h 24m†	31,600	50,900	0.93	14.6	1.3	15
Neptune	2,795,500,000	4,498,800,000	164.79 years	17h 50m	30,200	48,600	1.23	17.2	1.8	8
Pluto	3,667,900,000	5,902,800,000	247.70 years	6.39 days(?)	1,500	2,400	0.03(?)	0.01(?)	0.7(?)	1

† Retrograde motion

DIMENSIONS OF THE EARTH

	Area in: Sq. Miles	Sq. Kilometers
Superficial area	196,939,000	510,073,000
Land surface	57,506,000	148,941,000
Water surface	139,433,000	361,132,000

	Distance in: Miles	Kilometers
Equatorial circumference	24,902	40,075
Polar circumference	24,860	40,007
Equatorial diameter	7,926.4	12,756.4
Polar diameter	7,899.8	12,713.6
Equatorial radius	3,963.2	6,378.2
Polar radius	3,949.9	6,356.8

Volume of the Earth	2.6×10^{11} cubic miles	10.84×10^{11} cubic kilometers
Mass or weight	6.6×10^{21} short tons	6.0×10^{21} metric tons
Maximum distance from Sun	94,600,000 miles	152,000,000 kilometers
Minimum distance from Sun	91,300,000 miles	147,000,000 kilometers

OCEANS AND MAJOR SEAS

	Area in: Sq. Miles	Sq. Kms.	Greatest Depth in: Feet	Meters
Pacific Ocean	64,186,000	166,241,700	36,198	11,033
Atlantic Ocean	31,862,000	82,522,600	28,374	8,648
Indian Ocean	28,350,000	73,426,500	25,344	7,725
Arctic Ocean	5,427,000	14,056,000	17,880	5,450
Caribbean Sea	970,000	2,512,300	24,720	7,535
Mediterranean Sea	969,000	2,509,700	16,896	5,150
South China Sea	895,000	2,318,000	15,000	4,600
Bering Sea	875,000	2,266,250	15,800	4,800
Gulf of Mexico	600,000	1,554,000	12,300	3,750
Sea of Okhotsk	590,000	1,528,100	11,070	3,370
East China Sea	482,000	1,248,400	9,500	2,900
Yellow Sea	480,000	1,243,200	350	107
Sea of Japan	389,000	1,007,500	12,280	3,740
Hudson Bay	317,500	822,300	846	258
North Sea	222,000	575,000	2,200	670
Black Sea	185,000	479,150	7,365	2,245
Red Sea	169,000	437,700	7,200	2,195
Baltic Sea	163,000	422,170	1,506	459

THE CONTINENTS

	Area in: Sq. Miles	Sq. Kms.	Percent of World's Land
Asia	17,128,500	44,362,815	29.5
Africa	11,707,000	30,321,130	20.2
North America	9,363,000	24,250,170	16.2
South America	6,875,000	17,806,250	11.8
Antarctica	5,500,000	14,245,000	9.5
Europe	4,057,000	10,507,630	7.0
Australia	2,966,136	7,682,300	5.1

MAJOR SHIP CANALS

	Length in: Miles	Kms.	Minimum Depth in: Feet	Meters
Volga-Baltic, Russia	225	362	–	–
Baltic-White Sea, Russia	140	225	16	5
Suez, Egypt	100.76	162	42	13
Albert, Belgium	80	129	16.5	5
Moscow-Volga, Russia	80	129	18	6
Volga-Don, Russia	62	100	–	–
Göta, Sweden	54	87	10	3
Kiel (Nord-Ostsee), Germany	53.2	86	38	12
Panama Canal, Panama	50.72	82	41.6	13
Houston Ship, U.S.A.	50	81	36	11

LARGEST ISLANDS

	Area in: Sq. Miles	Sq. Kms.
Greenland	840,000	2,175,600
New Guinea	305,000	789,950
Borneo	290,000	751,100
Madagascar	226,400	586,376
Baffin, Canada	195,928	507,454
Sumatra, Indonesia	164,000	424,760
Honshu, Japan	88,000	227,920
Great Britain	84,400	218,896
Victoria, Canada	83,896	217,290
Ellesmere, Canada	75,767	196,236
Celebes, Indonesia	72,986	189,034
South I., New Zealand	58,393	151,238
Java, Indonesia	48,842	126,501
North I., New Zealand	44,187	114,444
Newfoundland, Canada	42,031	108,860
Cuba	40,533	104,981
Luzon, Philippines	40,420	104,688
Iceland	39,768	103,000
Mindanao, Philippines	36,537	94,631
Ireland	31,743	82,214
Sakhalin, Russia	29,500	76,405
Hispaniola, Haiti & Dom. Rep.	29,399	76,143

	Area in: Sq. Miles	Sq. Kms.
Hokkaido, Japan	28,983	75,066
Banks, Canada	27,038	70,028
Ceylon, Sri Lanka	25,332	65,610
Tasmania, Australia	24,600	63,710
Svalbard, Norway	23,957	62,049
Devon, Canada	21,331	55,247
Novaya Zemlya (north isl.), Russia	18,600	48,200
Marajó, Brazil	17,991	46,597
Tierra del Fuego, Chile & Argentina	17,900	46,360
Alexander, Antarctica	16,700	43,250
Axel Heiberg, Canada	16,671	43,178
Melville, Canada	16,274	42,150
Southhampton, Canada	15,913	41,215
New Britain, Papua New Guinea	14,100	36,519
Taiwan, China	13,836	35,835
Kyushu, Japan	13,770	35,664
Hainan, China	13,127	33,999
Prince of Wales, Canada	12,872	33,338
Spitsbergen, Norway	12,355	31,999
Vancouver, Canada	12,079	31,285
Timor, Indonesia	11,527	29,855
Sicily, Italy	9,926	25,708

	Area in: Sq. Miles	Sq. Kms.
Somerset, Canada	9,570	24,786
Sardinia, Italy	9,301	24,090
Shikoku, Japan	6,860	17,767
New Caledonia, France	6,530	16,913
Nordaustlandet, Norway	6,409	16,599
Samar, Philippines	5,050	13,080
Negros, Philippines	4,906	12,707
Palawan, Philippines	4,550	11,785
Panay, Philippines	4,446	11,515
Jamaica	4,232	10,961
Hawaii, United States	4,038	10,458
Viti Levu, Fiji	4,010	10,386
Cape Breton, Canada	3,981	10,311
Mindoro, Philippines	3,759	9,736
Kodiak, Alaska, U.S.A.	3,670	9,505
Cyprus	3,572	9,251
Puerto Rico, U.S.A.	3,435	8,897
Corsica, France	3,352	8,682
New Ireland, Papua New Guinea	3,340	8,651
Crete, Greece	3,218	8,335
Anticosti, Canada	3,066	7,941
Wrangel, Russia	2,819	7,301

Name	Height in: Feet	Meters
Everest, Nepal-China	29,028	8,848
K2 (Godwin Austen), Pakistan-China	28,250	8,611
Makalu, Nepal-China	27,789	8,470
Dhaulagiri, Nepal	26,810	8,172
Nanga Parbat, Pakistan	26,660	8,126
Annapurna, Nepal	26,504	8,078
Rakaposhi, Pakistan	25,550	7,788
Kongur Shan, China	25,325	7,719
Tirich Mir, Pakistan	25,230	7,690
Gongga Shan, China	24,790	7,556
Communism Peak, Tajikistan	24,590	7,495
Pobedy Peak, Kyrgyzstan	24,406	7,439
Chomo Lhari, Bhutan-China	23,997	7,314
Muztag, China	23,891	7,282
Cerro Aconcagua, Argentina	22,831	6,959
Ojos del Salado, Chile-Argentina	22,572	6,880
Bonete, Chile-Argentina	22,546	6,872
Tupungato, Chile-Argentina	22,310	6,800
Pissis, Argentina	22,241	6,779
Mercedario, Argentina	22,211	6,770
Huascarán, Peru	22,205	6,768
Llullaillaco, Chile-Argentina	22,057	6,723
Nevada Ancohuma, Bolivia	21,489	6,550
Chimborazo, Ecuador	20,561	6,267
Pico Cristóbal Colón, Colombia	18,947	5,775
Huila, Colombia	18,865	5,750
Citlaltépetl (Orizaba), Mexico	18,701	5,700
Damavand, Iran	18,606	5,671
El'brus, Russia	18,510	5,642
St. Elias, Alaska, U.S.A.-Yukon, Canada	18,008	5,489
Dykh-tau, Russia	17,070	5,203
Batian (Kenya), Kenya	17,058	5,199
Ararat, Turkey	16,946	5,165
Vinson Massif, Antarctica	16,864	5,140
Margherita (Ruwenzori), Africa	16,795	5,119
Kazbek, Georgia-Russia	16,558	5,047
Puncak Jaya, Indonesia	16,503	5,030
Blanc, France	15,771	4,807
Klyuchevskaya Sopka, Russia	15,584	4,750
Fairweather, Br. Col., Canada	15,300	4,663
Dufourspitze (Mte. Rosa), Italy-Switzerland	15,203	4,634
Ras Dashen, Ethiopia	15,157	4620
Matterhorn, Switzerland	14,691	4,478
Whitney, California, U.S.A.	14,494	4,418
Elbert, Colorado, U.S.A.	14,433	4,399
Rainier, Washington, U.S.A.	14,410	4,392
Shasta, California, U.S.A.	14,162	4,317
Pikes Peak, Colorado, U.S.A.	14,110	4,301
Finsteraarhorn, Switzerland	14,022	4,274
Mauna Kea, Hawaii, U.S.A.	13,796	4,205
Mauna Loa, Hawaii, U.S.A.	13,677	4,169
Jungfrau, Switzerland	13,642	4,158
Grossglockner, Austria	12,457	3,797
Fujiyama, Japan	12,389	3,776
Cook, New Zealand	12,349	3,764
Etna, Italy	10,902	3,323
Kosciusko, Australia	7,310	2,228
Mitchell, North Carolina, U.S.A.	6,684	2,037

Name	Length in: Miles	Kms.
Nile, Africa	4,145	6,671
Amazon, S. America	3,915	6,300
Chang Jiang (Yangtze), China	3,900	6,276
Mississippi-Missouri-Red Rock, U.S.A.	3,741	6,019
Ob'-Irtysh-Black Irtysh, Russia-Kazakhstan	3,362	5,411
Yenisey-Angara, Russia	3,100	4,989
Huang He (Yellow), China	2,877	4,630
Amur-Shilka-Onon, Asia	2,744	4,416
Lena, Russia	2,734	4,400
Congo (Zaire), Africa	2,718	4,374
Mackenzie-Peace-Finlay, Canada	2,635	4,241
Mekong, Asia	2,610	4,200
Missouri-Red Rock, U.S.A.	2,564	4,125
Niger, Africa	2,548	4,101
Paraná-La Plata, S. America	2,450	3,943
Mississippi, U.S.A.	2,348	3,778
Murray-Darling, Australia	2,310	3,718
Volga, Russia	2,194	3,531
Madeira, S. America	2,013	3,240
Purus, S. America	1,995	3,211
Yukon, Alaska-Canada	1,979	3,185
St. Lawrence, Canada-U.S.A.	1,900	3,058
Rio Grande, Mexico-U.S.A.	1,885	3,034
Syrdar'ya-Naryn, Asia	1,859	2,992
Kama, Russia	1,811	2,914
Indus, Asia	1,800	2,897
Danube, Europe	1,775	2,857
Salween, Asia	1,770	2,849
Brahmaputra, Asia	1,700	2,736
Euphrates, Asia	1,700	2,736
Tocantins, Brazil	1,677	2,699
Xi (Si), China	1,650	2,601
Amudar'ya, Asia	1,616	2,601
Nelson-Saskatchewan, Canada	1,600	2,575
Orinoco, S. America	1,600	2,575
Zambezi, Africa	1,600	2,575
Paraguay, S. America	1,584	2,549
Kolyma, Russia	1,562	2,514
Ganges, Asia	1,550	2,494
Ural, Russia-Kazakhstan	1,509	2,428
Japurá, S. America	1,500	2,414
Arkansas, U.S.A.	1,450	2,334
Colorado, U.S.A.-Mexico	1,450	2,334
Negro, S. America	1,400	2,253
Dnieper, Russia-Belarus-Ukraine	1,368	2,202
Orange, Africa	1,350	2,173
Irrawaddy, Burma	1,325	2,132
Brazos, U.S.A.	1,309	2,107
Ohio-Allegheny, U.S.A.	1,306	2,102
Kama, Russia	1,252	2,031
Don, Russia	1,222	1,967
Red, U.S.A.	1,222	1,966
Columbia, U.S.A.-Canada	1,214	1,953
Saskatchewan, Canada	1,205	1,939
Peace-Finlay, Canada	1,195	1,923
Tigris, Asia	1,181	1,901
Darling, Australia	1,160	1,867
Angara, Russia	1,135	1,827
Sungari, Asia	1,130	1,819
Pechora, Russia	1,124	1,809
Snake, U.S.A.	1,038	1,670
Churchill, Canada	1,000	1,609
Pilcomayo, S. America	1,000	1,609
Uruguay, S. America	994	1,600
Platte-N. Platte, U.S.A.	990	1,593
Ohio, U.S.A.	981	1,578
Magdalena, Colombia	956	1,538
Pecos, U.S.A.	926	1,490
Oka, Russia	918	1,477
Canadian, U.S.A.	906	1,458
Colorado, Texas, U.S.A.	894	1,439
Dniester, Ukraine-Moldova	876	1,410
Fraser, Canada	850	1,369
Rhine, Europe	820	1,319
Northern Dvina, Russia	809	1,302

Name	Area in: Sq. Miles	Sq. Kms.	Max. Depth in: Feet	Meters
Caspian Sea, Asia	143,243	370,999	3,264	995
Lake Superior, U.S.A.-Canada	31,820	82,414	1,329	405
Lake Victoria, Africa	26,724	69,215	270	82
Lake Huron, U.S.A.-Canada	23,010	59,596	748	228
Lake Michigan, U.S.A.	22,400	58,016	923	281
Aral Sea, Kazakhstan-Uzbekistan	15,830	41,000	213	65
Lake Tanganyika, Africa	12,650	32,764	4,700	1,433
Lake Baykal, Russia	12,162	31,500	5,316	1,620
Great Bear Lake, Canada	12,096	31,328	1,356	413
Lake Nyasa (Malawi), Africa	11,555	29,928	2,320	707
Great Slave Lake, Canada	11,031	28,570	2,015	614
Lake Erie, U.S.A.-Canada	9,940	25,745	210	64
Lake Winnipeg, Canada	9,417	24,390	60	18
Lake Ontario, U.S.A.-Canada	7,540	19,529	775	244
Lake Ladoga, Russia	7,104	18,399	738	225
Lake Balkhash, Kazakhstan	7,027	18,200	87	27
Lake Maracaibo, Venezuela	5,120	13,261	100	31
Lake Chad, Africa	4,000-10,000	10,360-25,900	25	8
Lake Onega, Russia	3,710	9,609	377	115
Lake Eyre, Australia	3,500-0	9,000-0	–	–
Lake Titicaca, Peru-Bolivia	3,200	8,288	1,000	305
Lake Nicaragua, Nicaragua	3,100	8,029	230	70
Lake Athabasca, Canada	3,064	7,936	400	122
Reindeer Lake, Canada	2,568	6,651	–	–
Lake Turkana (Rudolf), Africa	2,463	6,379	240	73
Issyk-Kul', Kyrgyzstan	2,425	6,281	2,303	702
Lake Torrens, Australia	2,230	5,776	–	–
Vänern, Sweden	2,156	5,584	328	100
Nettilling Lake, Canada	2,140	5,543	–	–
Lake Winnipegosis, Canada	2,075	5,374	38	12
Lake Mobutu Sese Seko (Albert), Africa	2,075	5,374	160	49
Kariba Lake, Zambia-Zimbabwe	2,050	5,310	295	90
Lake Nipigon, Canada	1,872	4,848	540	165
Lake Mweru, Zaire-Zambia	1,800	4,662	60	18
Lake Manitoba, Canada	1,799	4,659	12	4
Lake Taymyr, Russia	1,737	4,499	85	26
Lake Khanka, China-Russia	1,700	4,403	33	10
Lake Kioga, Uganda	1,700	4,403	25	8
Lake of the Woods, U.S.A.-Canada	1,679	4,349	70	21.2

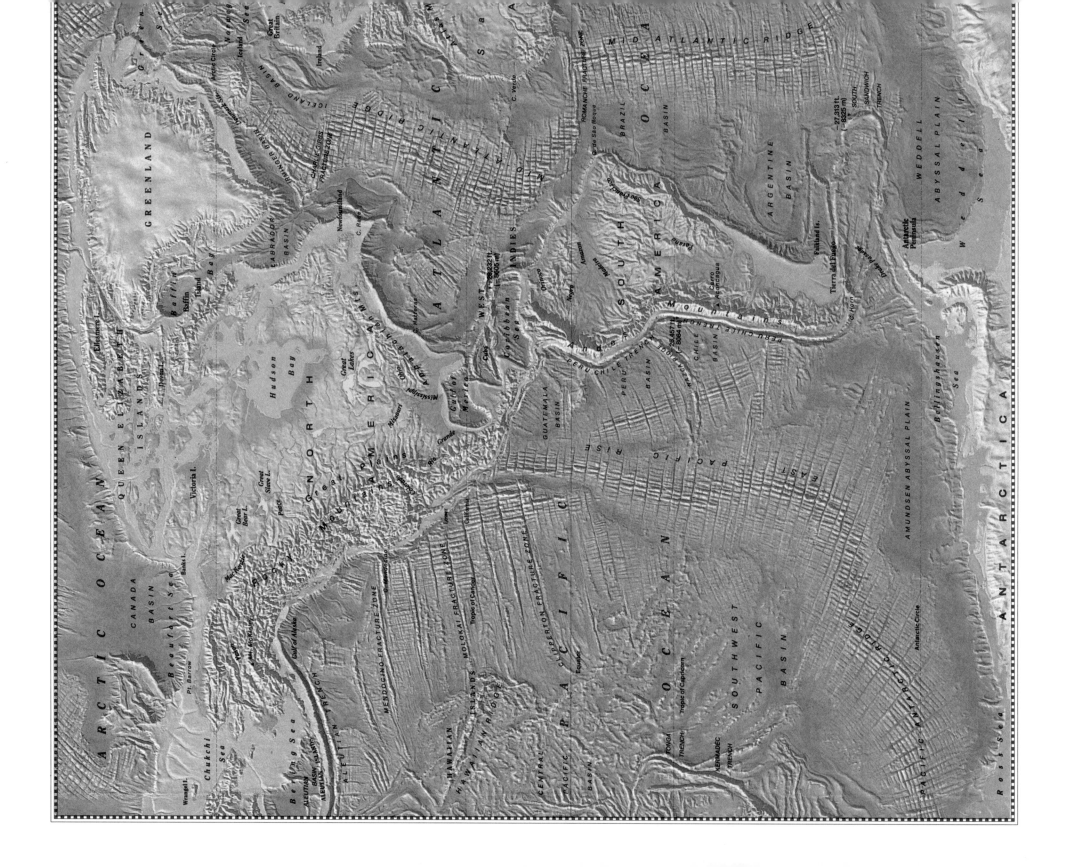

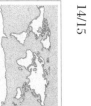

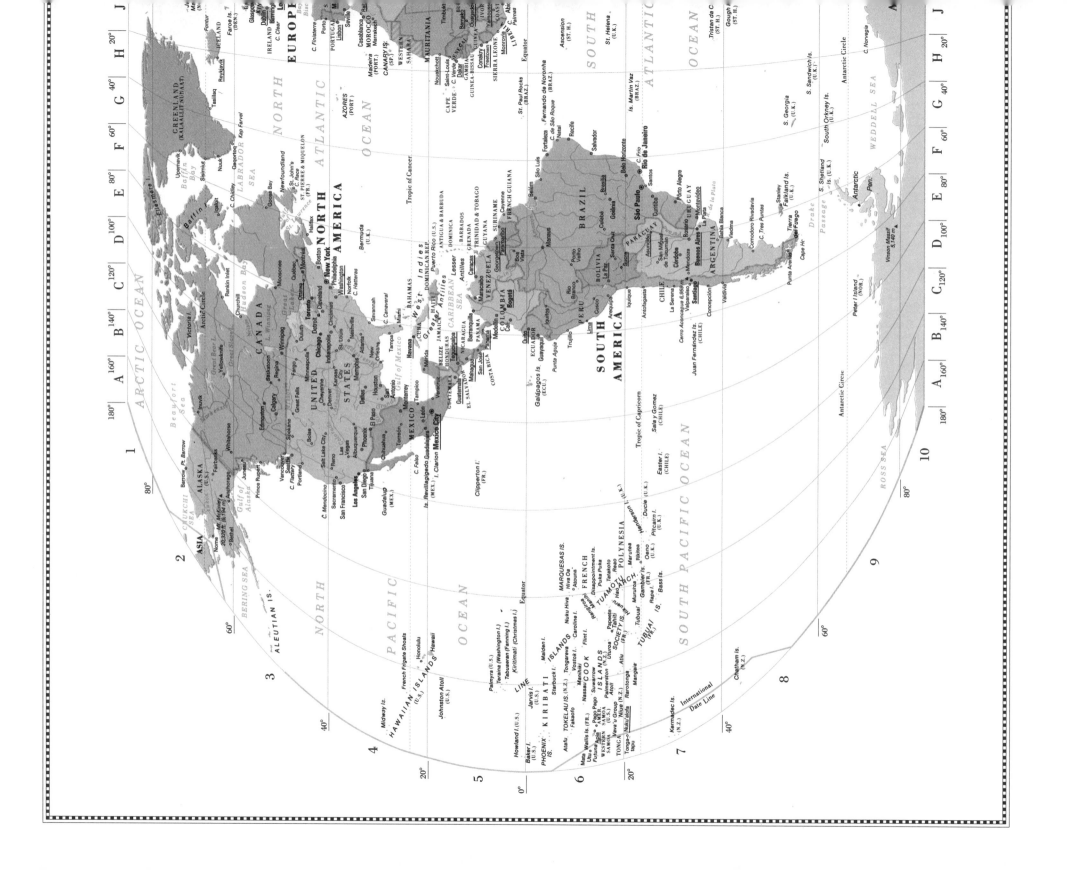

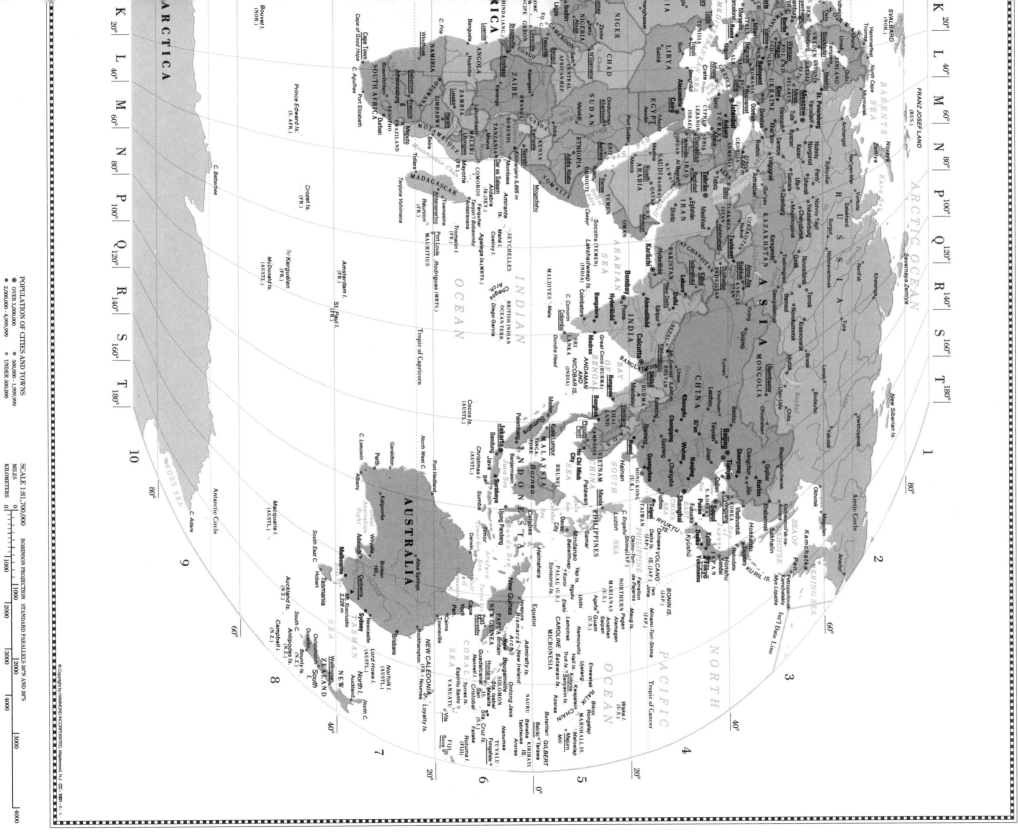

World

16/17

POPULATION OF CITIES AND TOWNS

⊛ OVER 5,000,000
⊛ 2,000,000 - 4,999,999
◉ 500,000 - 1,999,999
○ UNDER 500,000

SCALE 1:81,700,000   ROBINSON PROJECTION   STANDARD PARALLELS 38°N AND 38°S

MILES
KILOMETERS

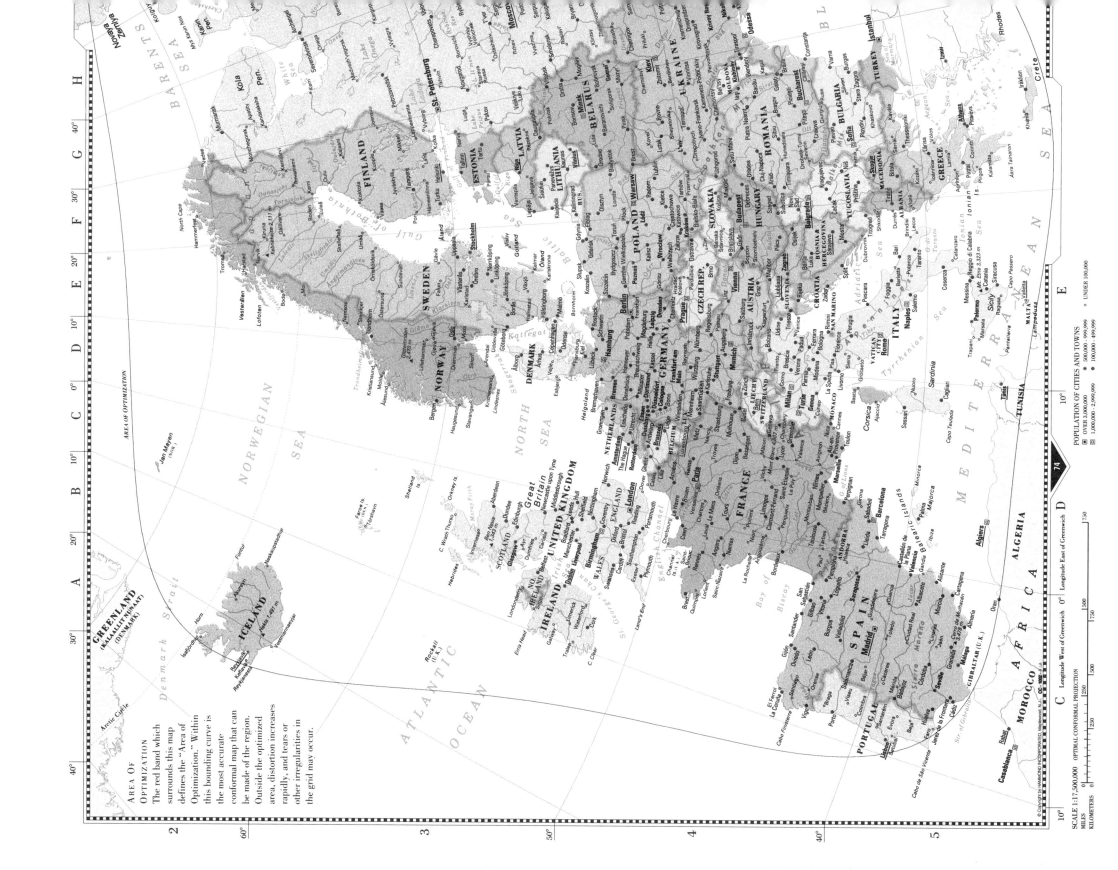

AREA OF OPTIMIZATION

The red band which surrounds this map defines the "Area of Optimization." Within this bounding curve is the most accurate conformal map that can be made of the region. Outside the optimized area, distortion increases rapidly, and tears or other irregularities in the grid may occur.

SCALE 1:17,500,000   OPTIMAL CONFORMAL PROJECTION

MILES

KILOMETERS

C   Longitude West of Greenwich   0°   Longitude East of Greenwich   D   74   E

POPULATION OF CITIES AND TOWNS

OVER 3,000,000   500,000 - 999,999   100,000 - 499,999

1,000,000 - 2,999,999   UNDER 100,000

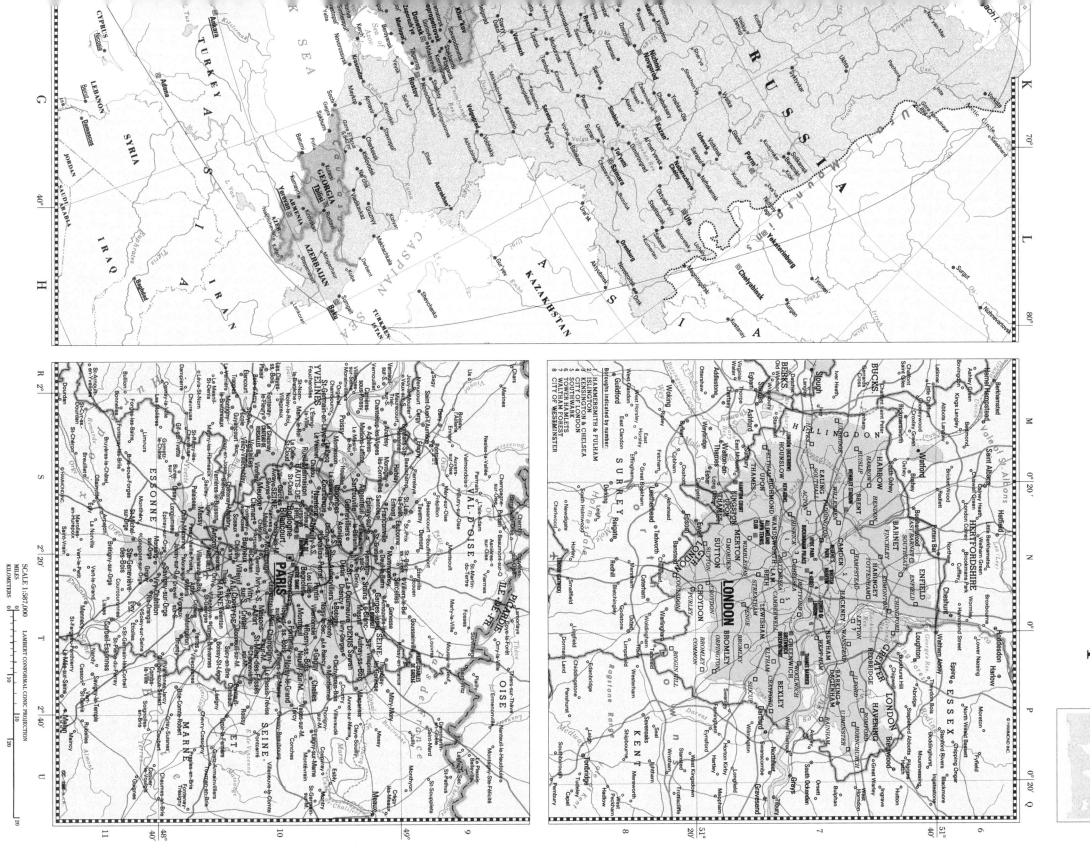

Europe

18/19

Scandinavia and Finland, Iceland

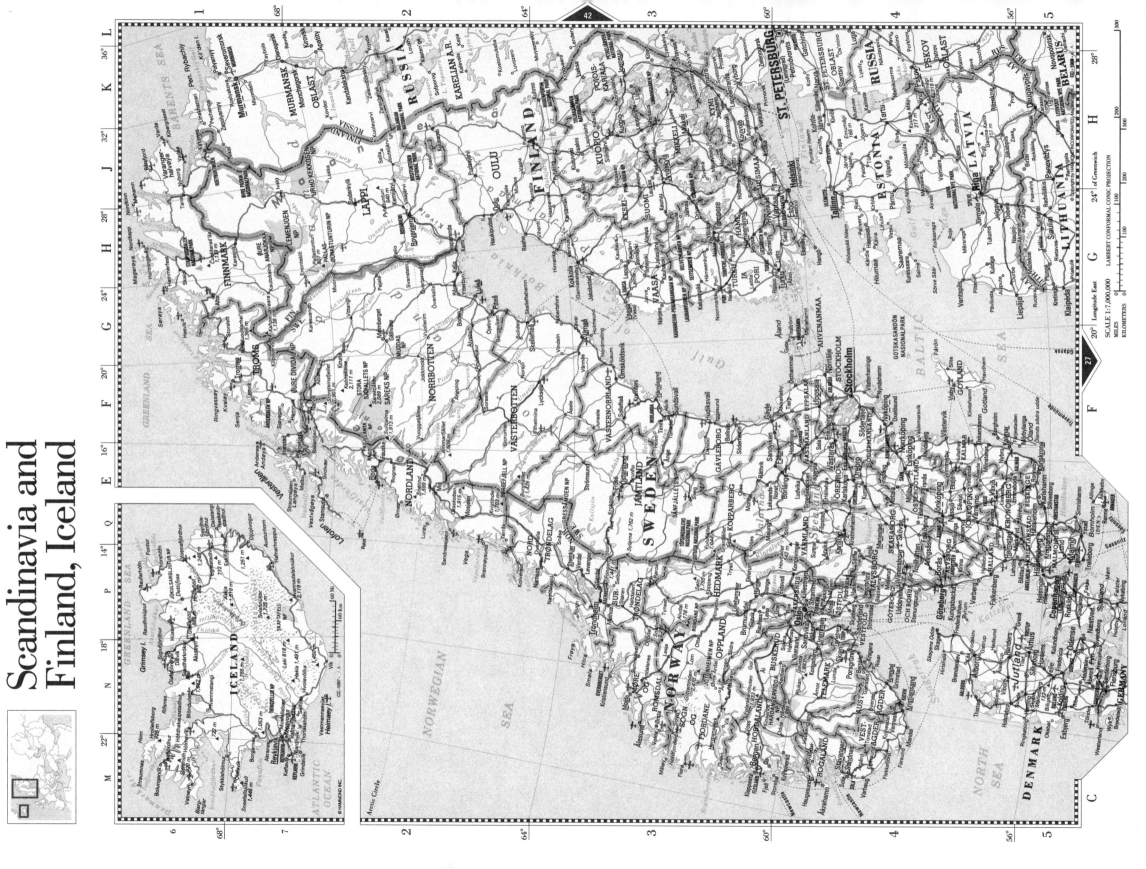

United Kingdom, Ireland

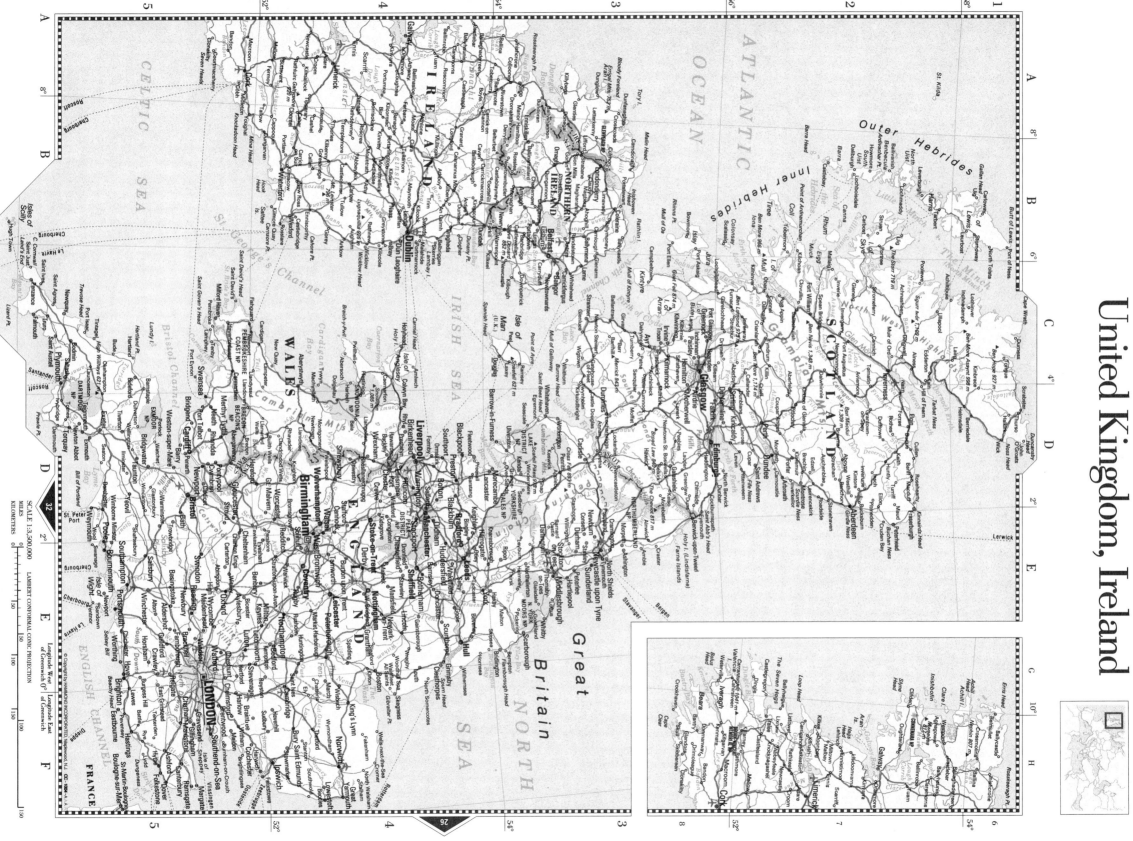

SCALE 1:3,500,000

LAMBERT CONFORMAL CONIC PROJECTION

MILES
KILOMETERS

Longitude West of Greenwich 0° | Longitude East of Greenwich

21

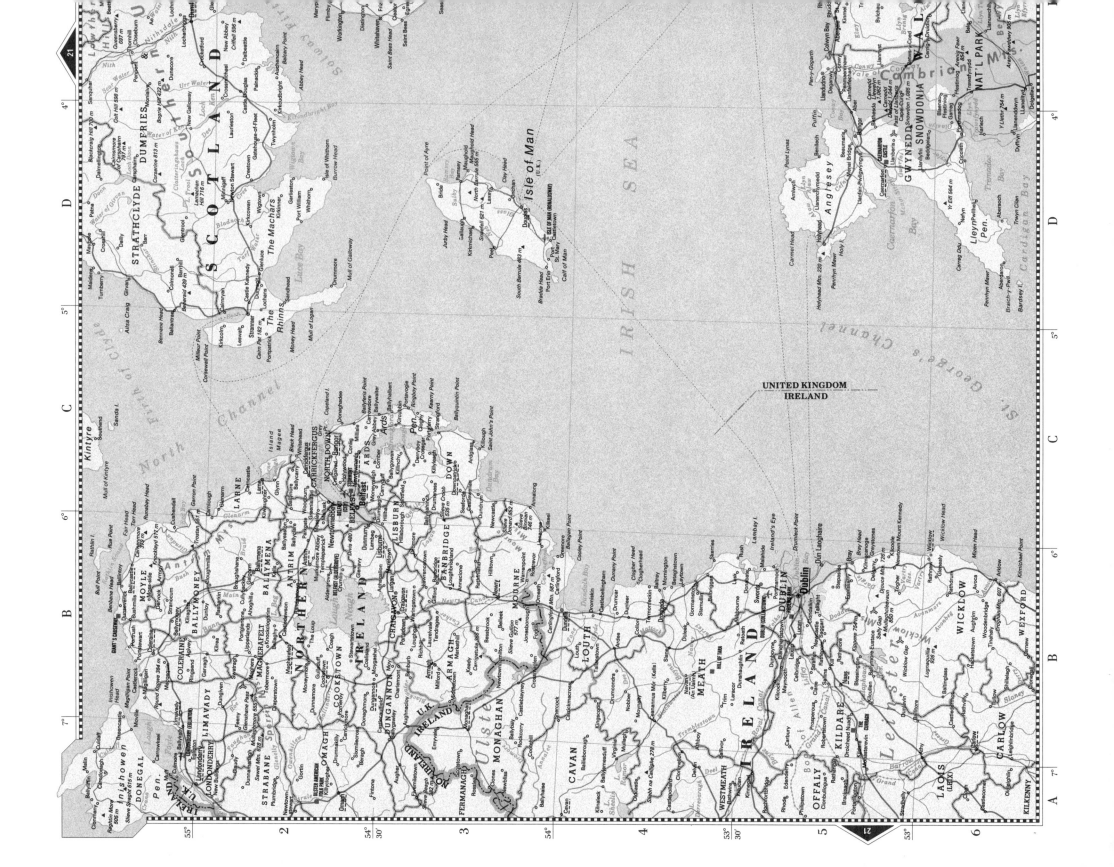

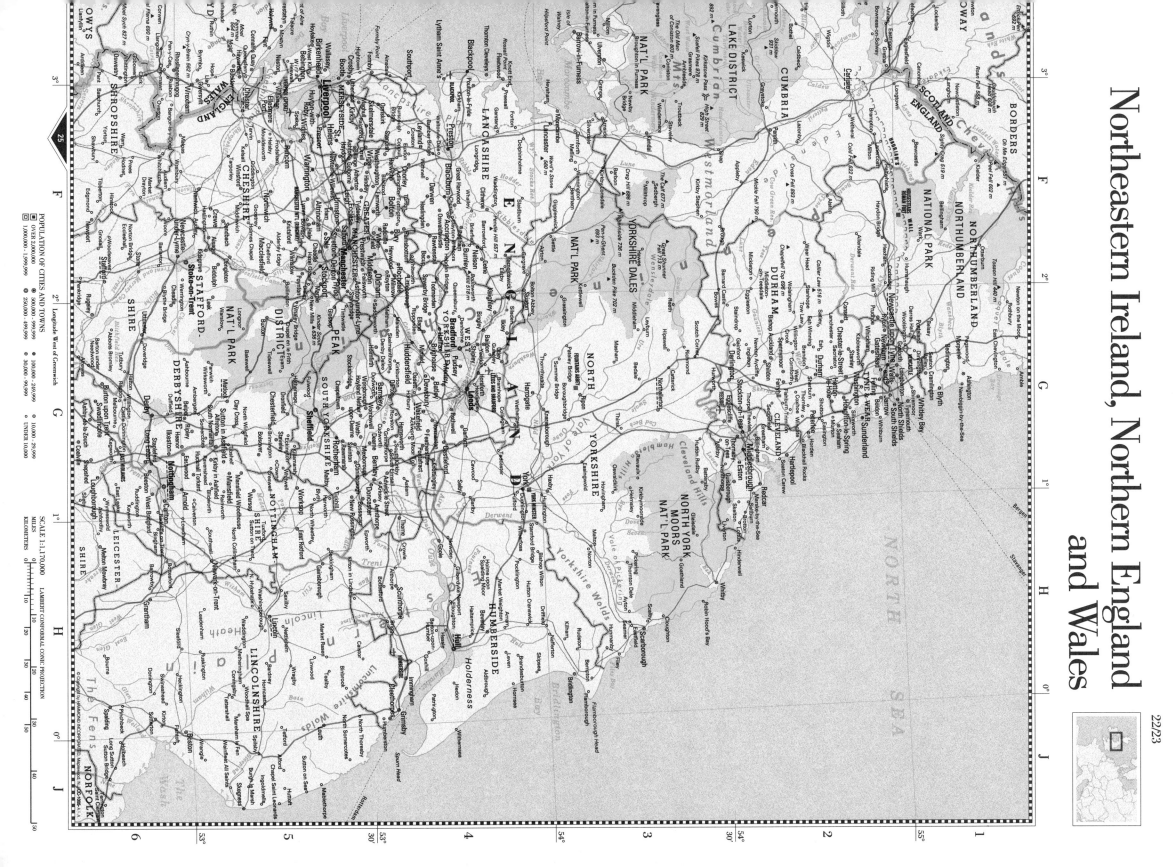

Northeastern Ireland, Northern England and Wales

POPULATION OF CITIES AND TOWNS

☐ OVER 2,000,000
◻ 1,000,000 – 1,999,999
● 500,000 – 999,999
◐ 250,000 – 499,999
○ 100,000 – 249,999
◦ 30,000 – 99,999
◦ 10,000 – 29,999
· UNDER 10,000

Longitude West of Greenwich

SCALE 1:1,170,000

LAMBERT CONFORMAL CONIC PROJECTION

MILES
KILOMETERS

Southern England and Wales

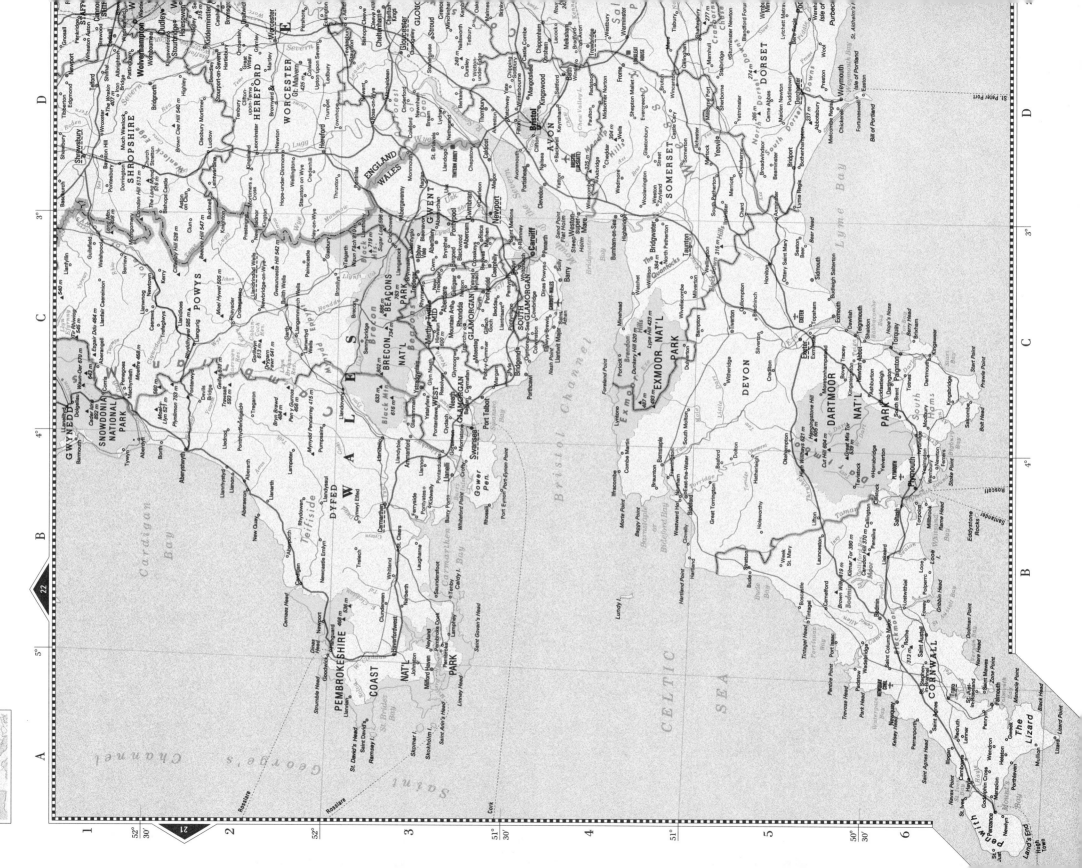

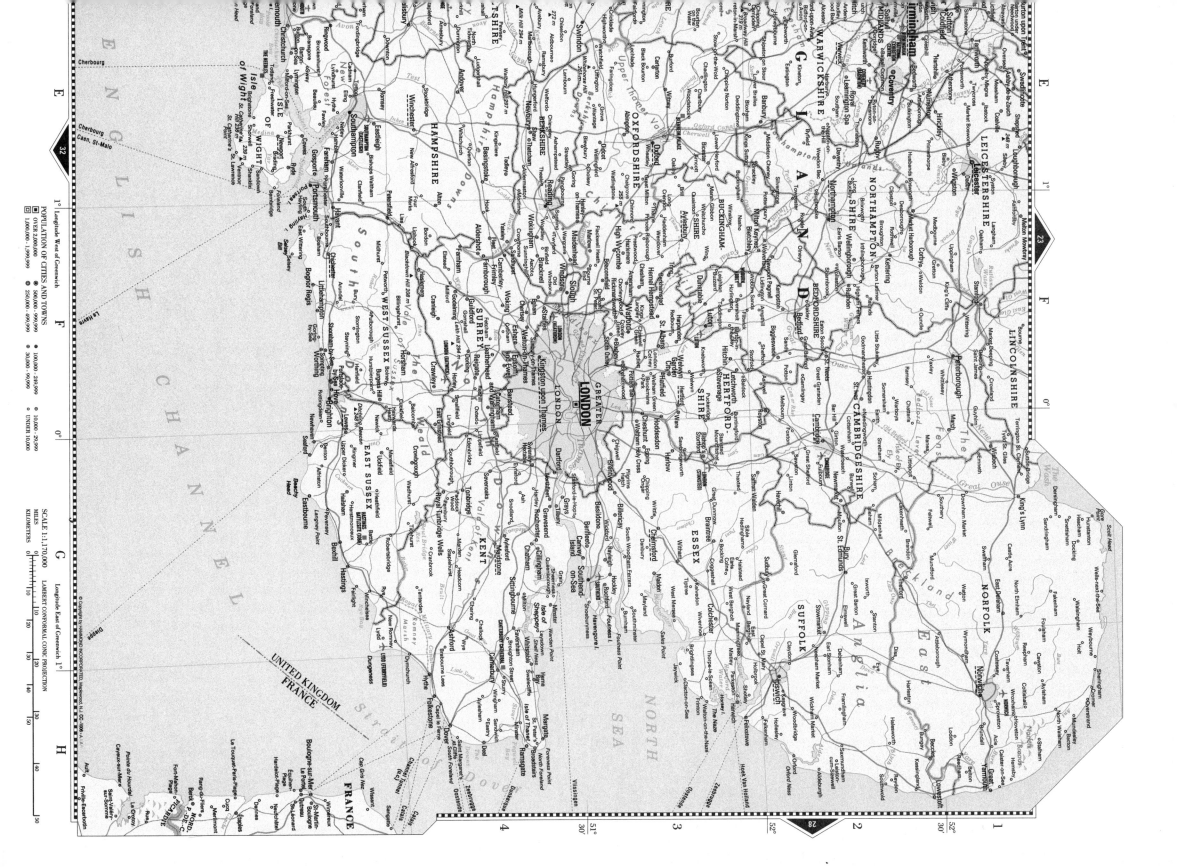

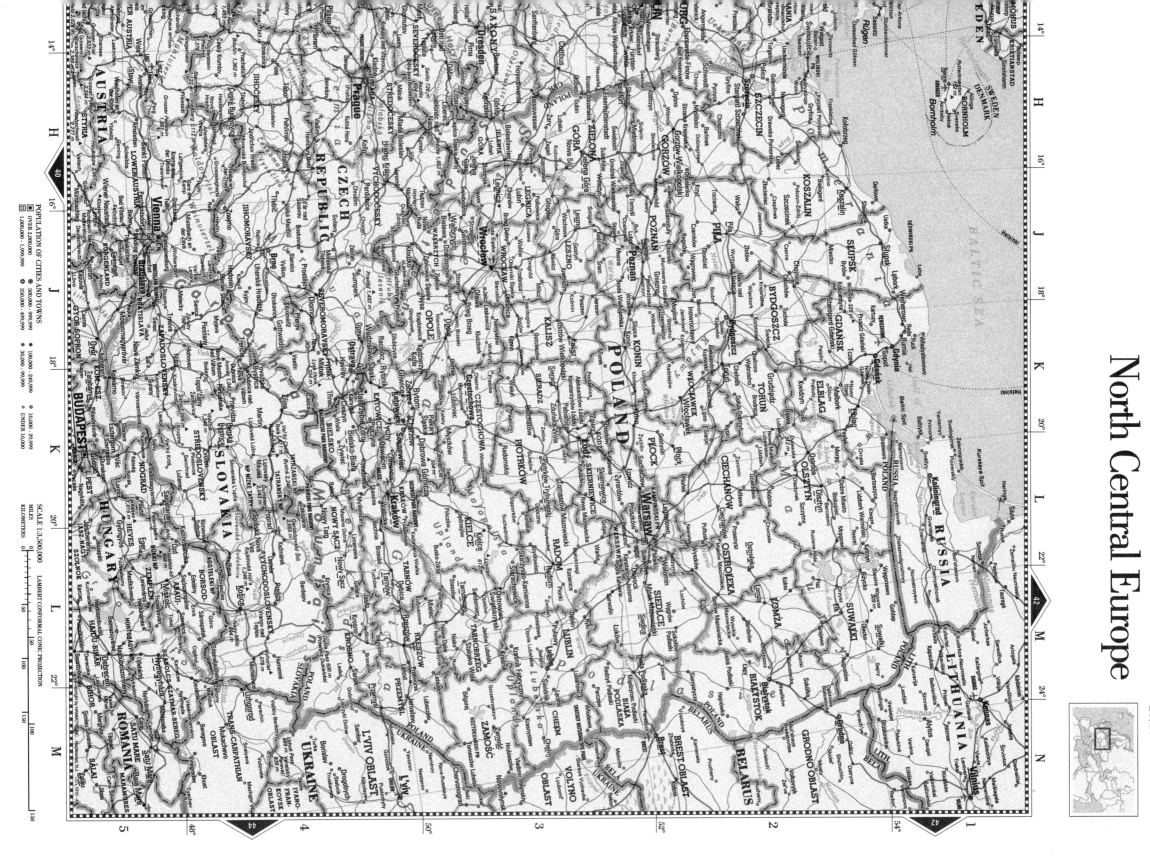

North Central Europe

Netherlands, Northwestern Germany

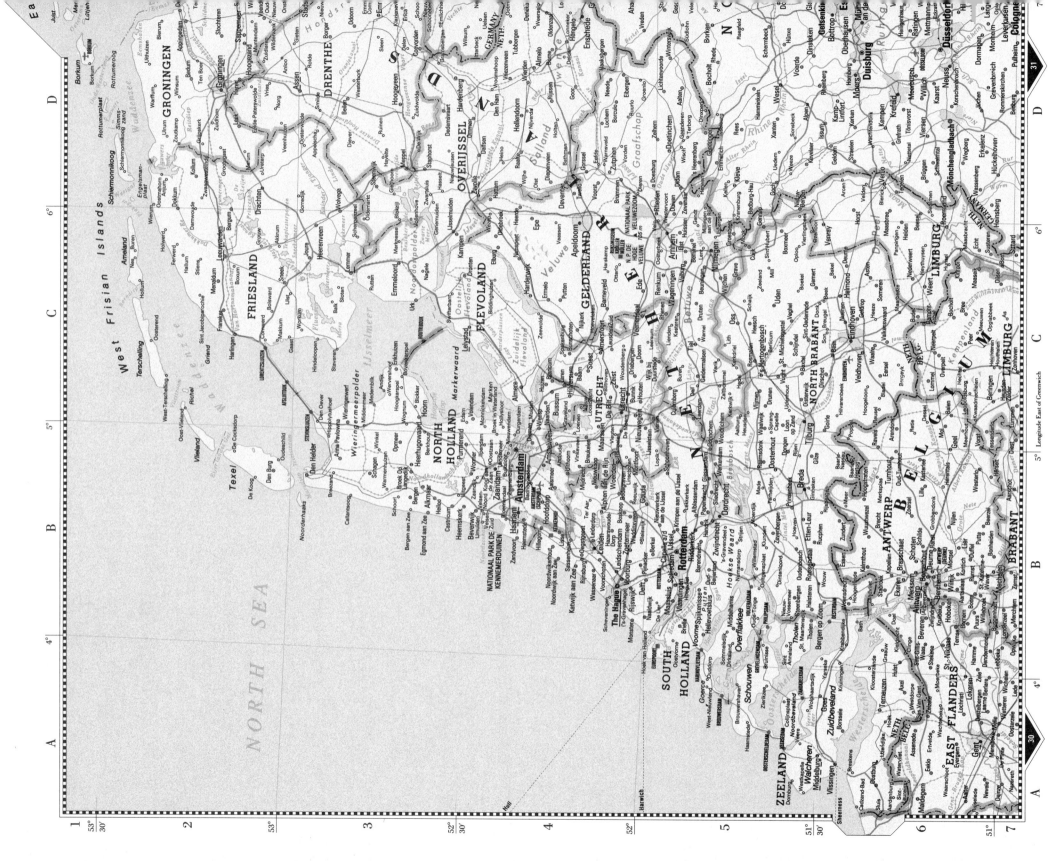

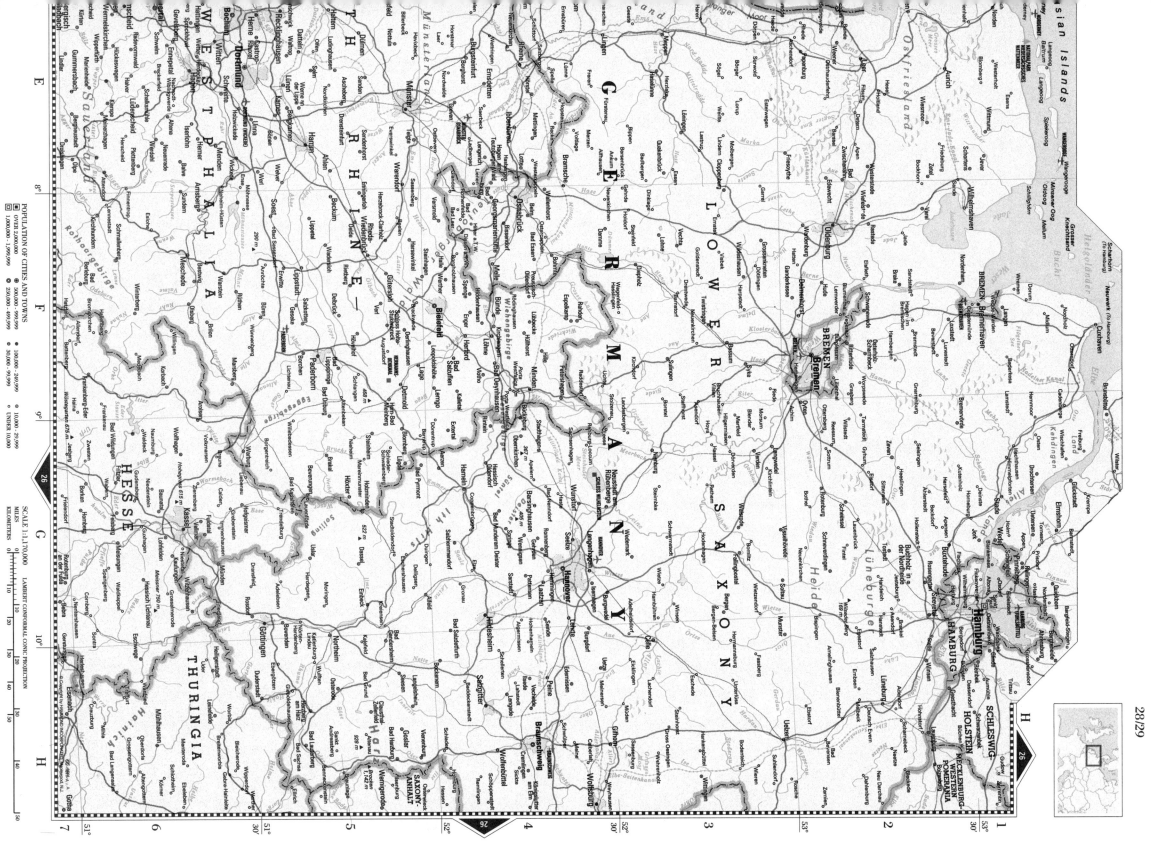

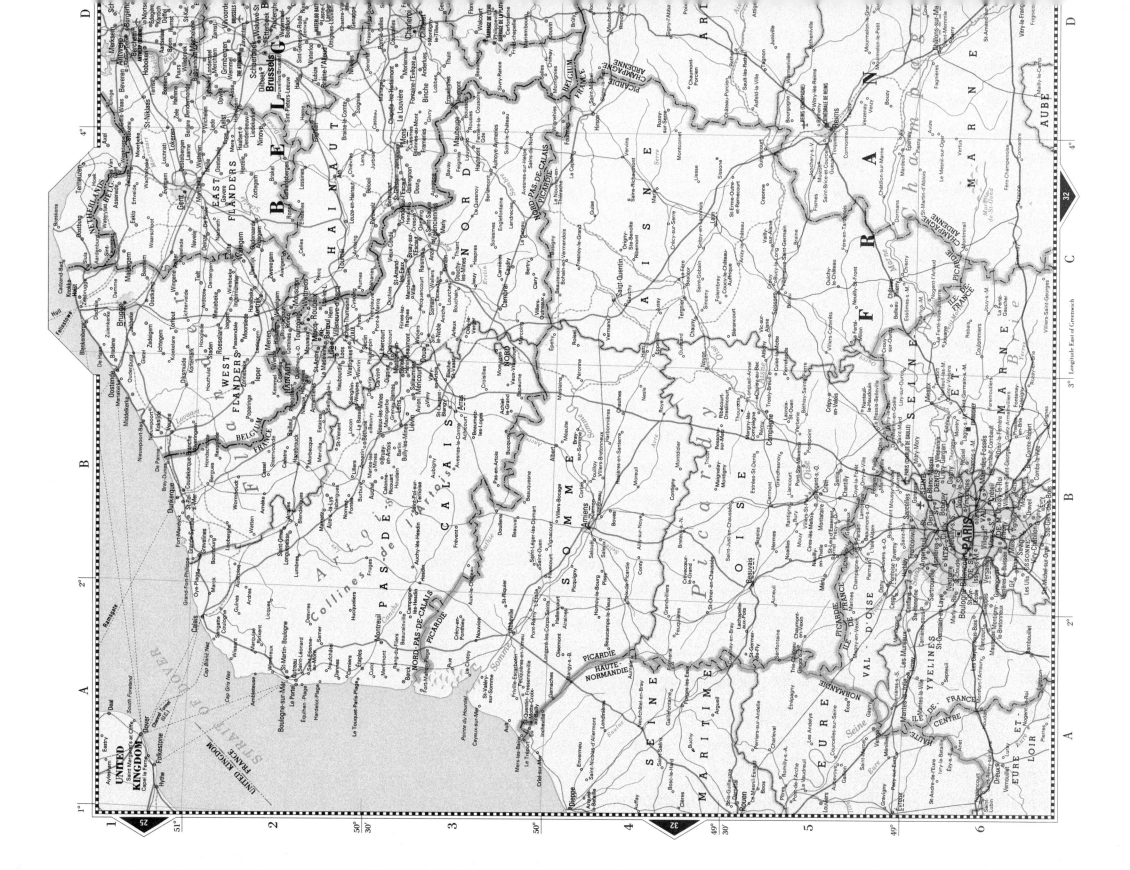

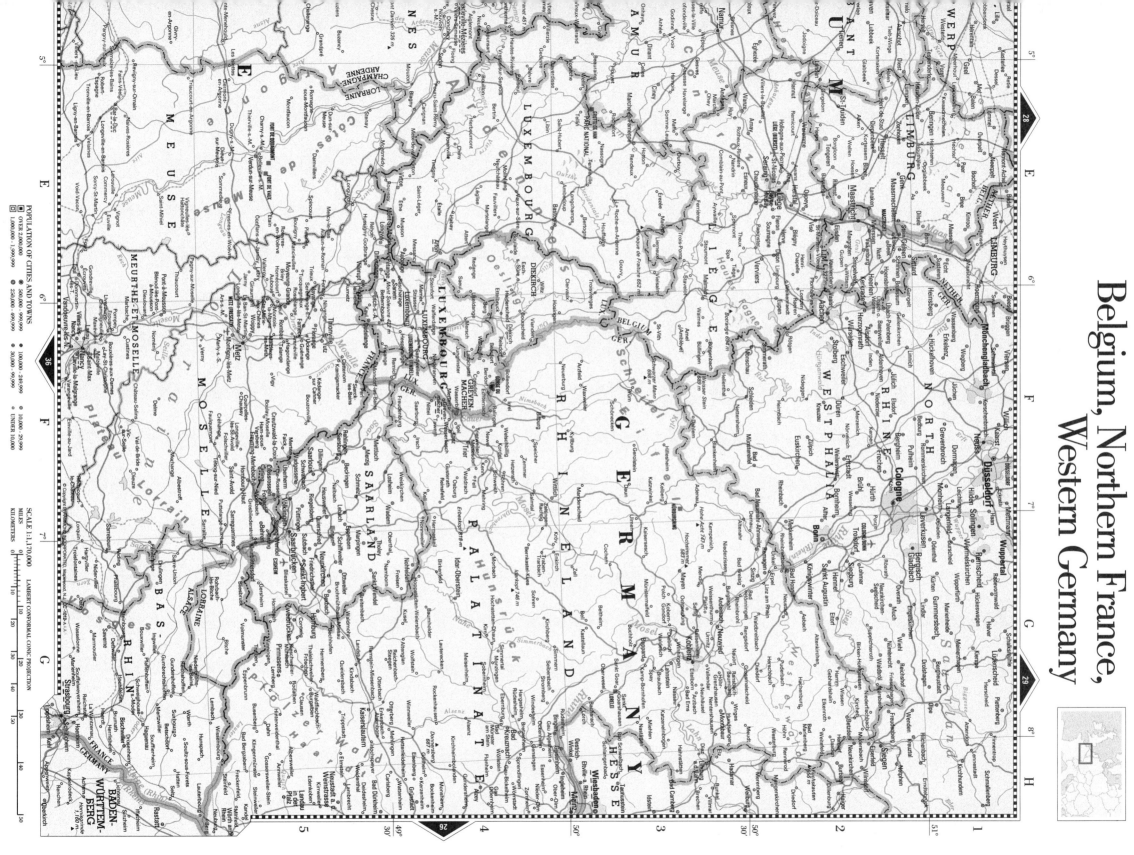

Belgium, Northern France, Western Germany

30/31

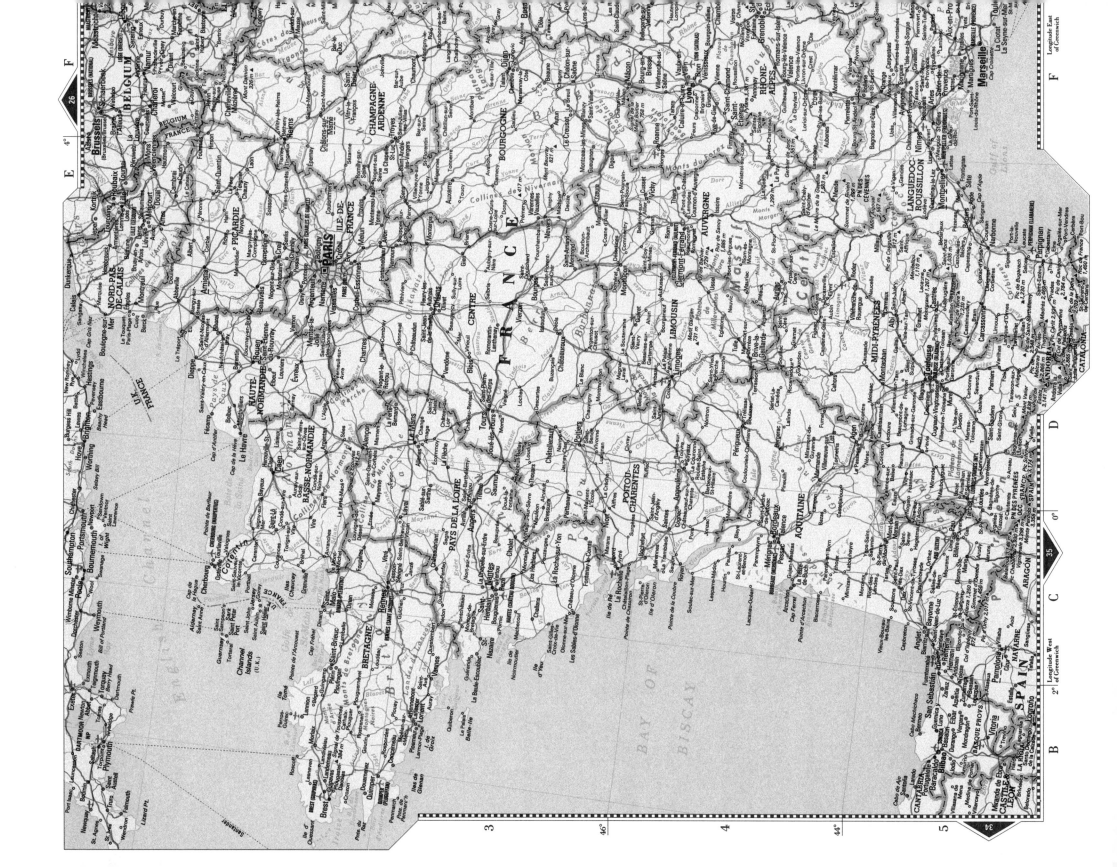

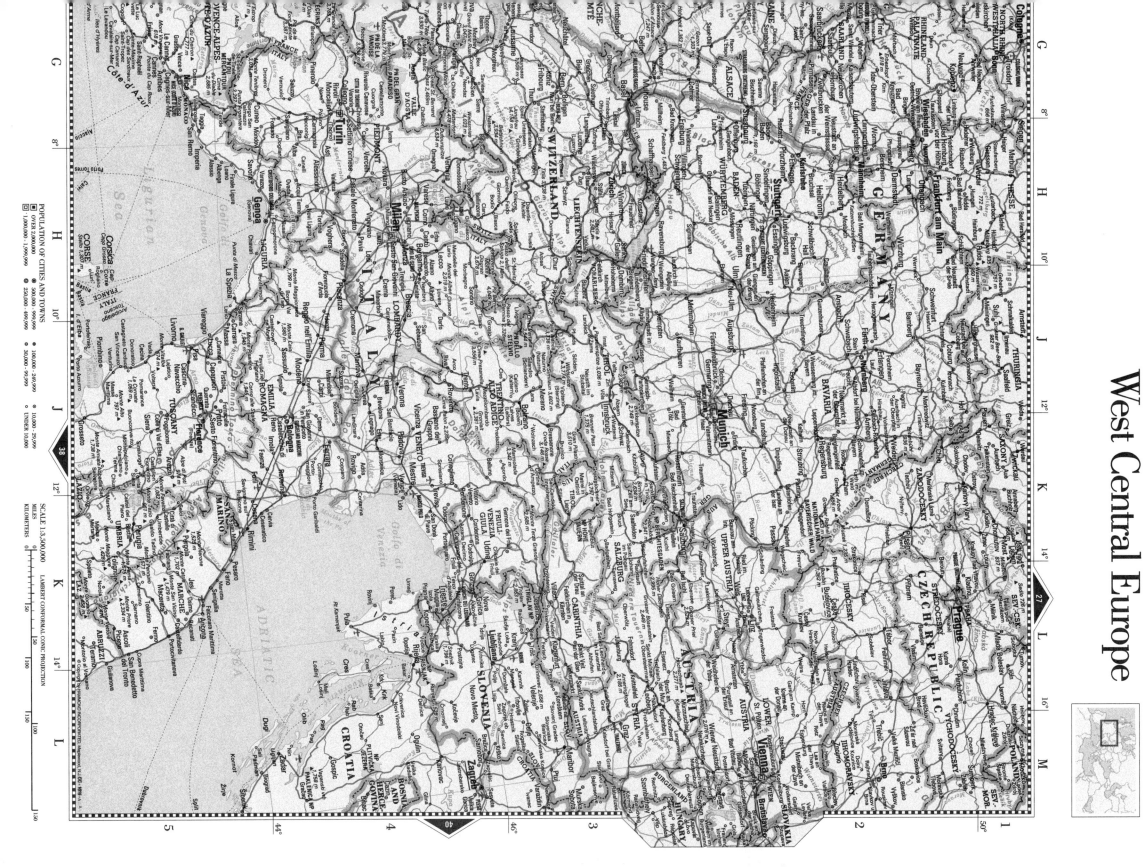

POPULATION OF CITIES AND TOWNS
- OVER 2,000,000
- 1,000,000 - 1,999,999
- 500,000 - 999,999
- 250,000 - 499,999
- 100,000 - 249,999
- 30,000 - 99,999
- 10,000 - 29,999
- UNDER 10,000

SCALE 1:3,500,000
MILES
KILOMETERS
LAMBERT CONFORMAL CONIC PROJECTION
© Copyright DIAMOND INCORPORATED, Maplewood, N.J. U.S.A. 1999

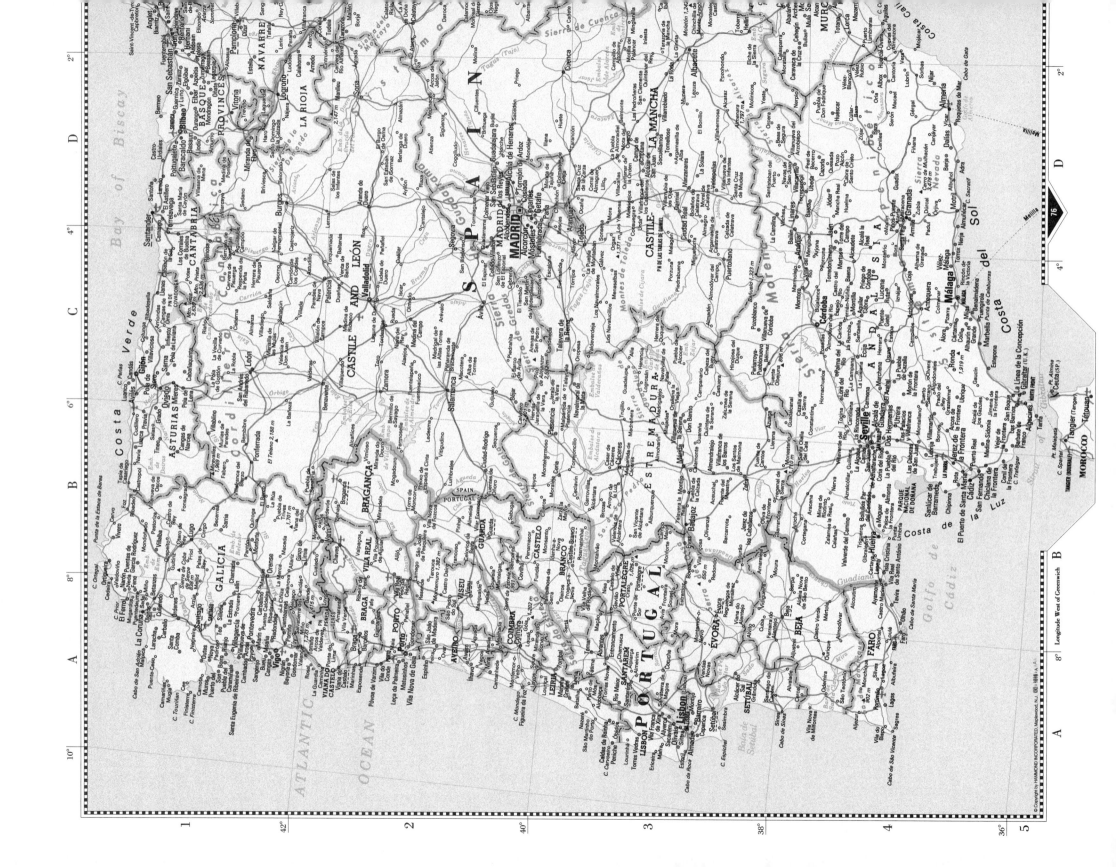

Spain, Portugal

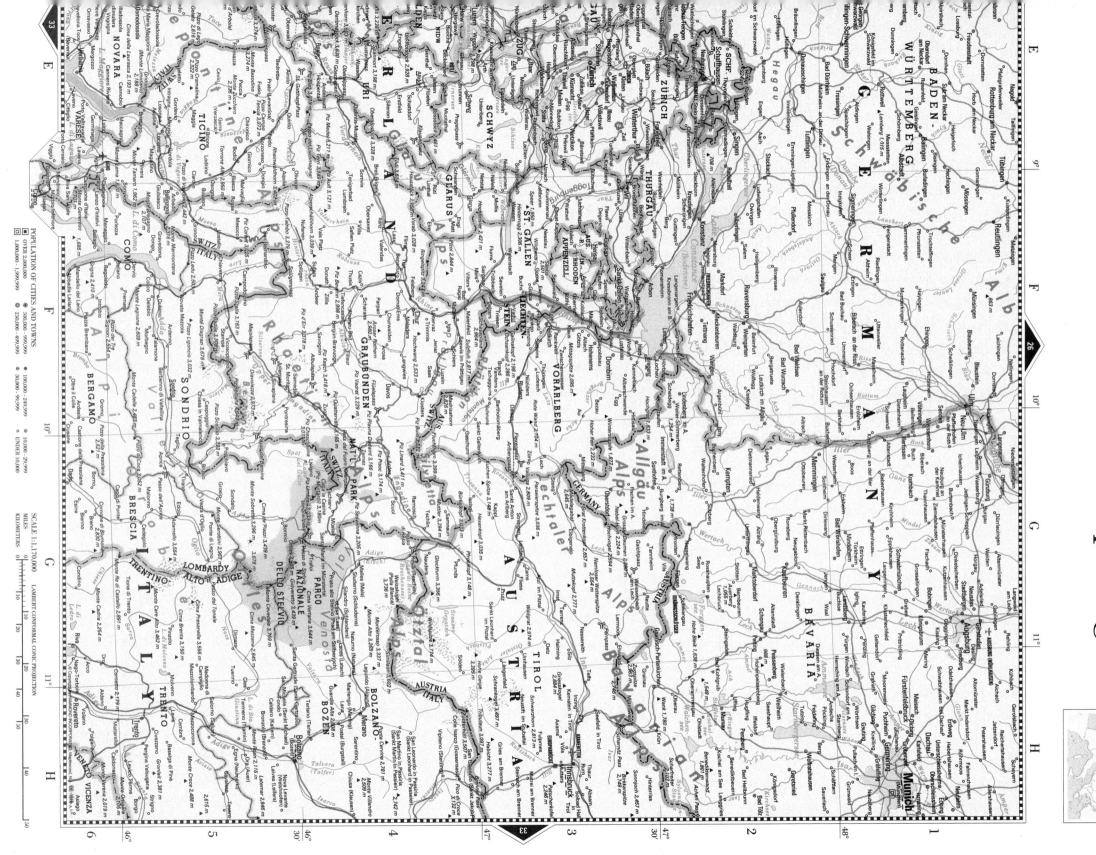

POPULATION OF CITIES AND TOWNS

- OVER 2,000,000
- 1,000,000 - 1,999,999
- 500,000 - 999,999
- 250,000 - 499,999
- 100,000 - 249,999
- 30,000 - 99,999
- 10,000 - 29,999
- UNDER 10,000

SCALE 1:1,170,000
LAMBERT CONFORMAL CONIC PROJECTION
MILES
KILOMETERS

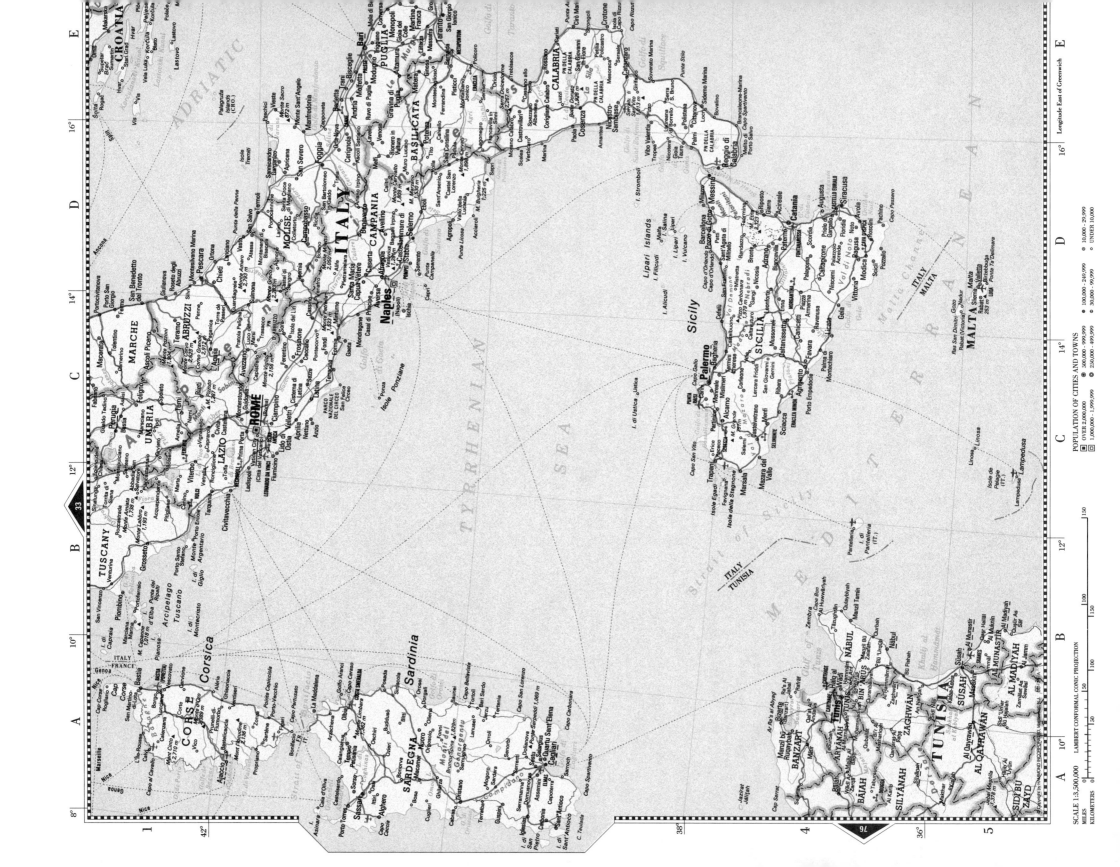

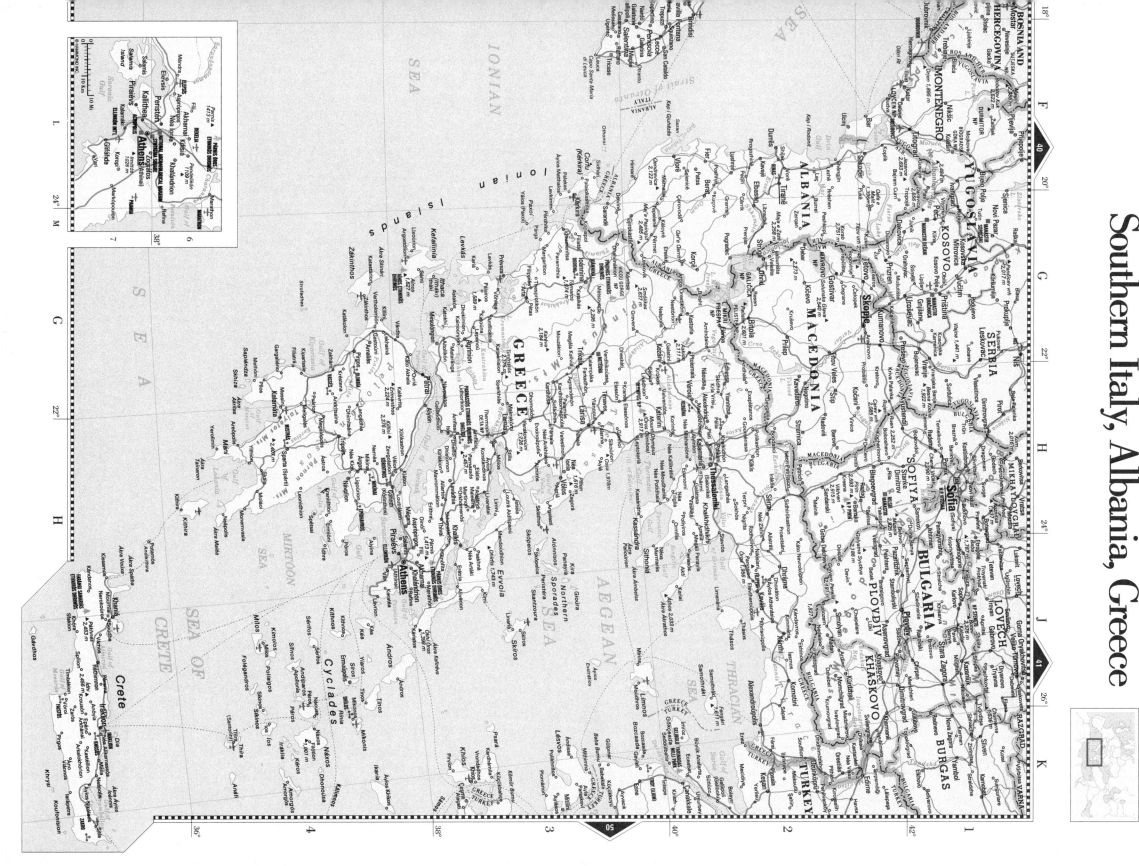

Southern Italy, Albania, Greece

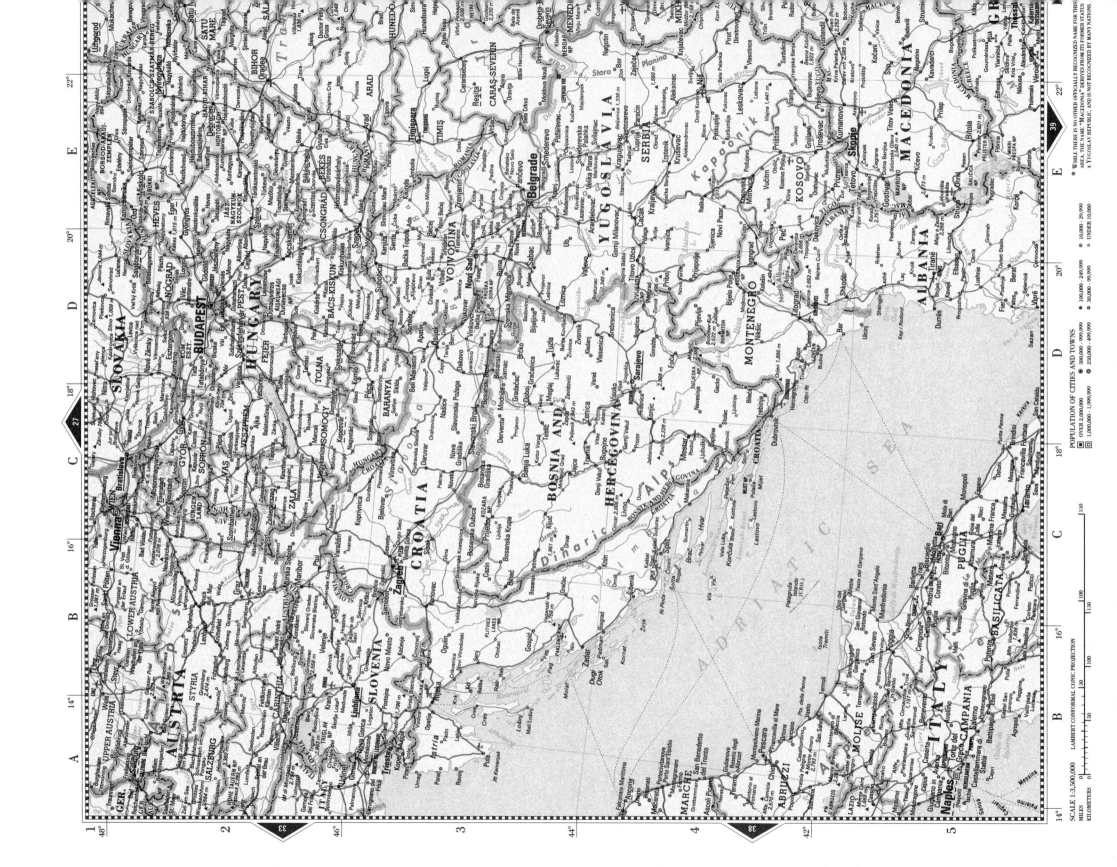

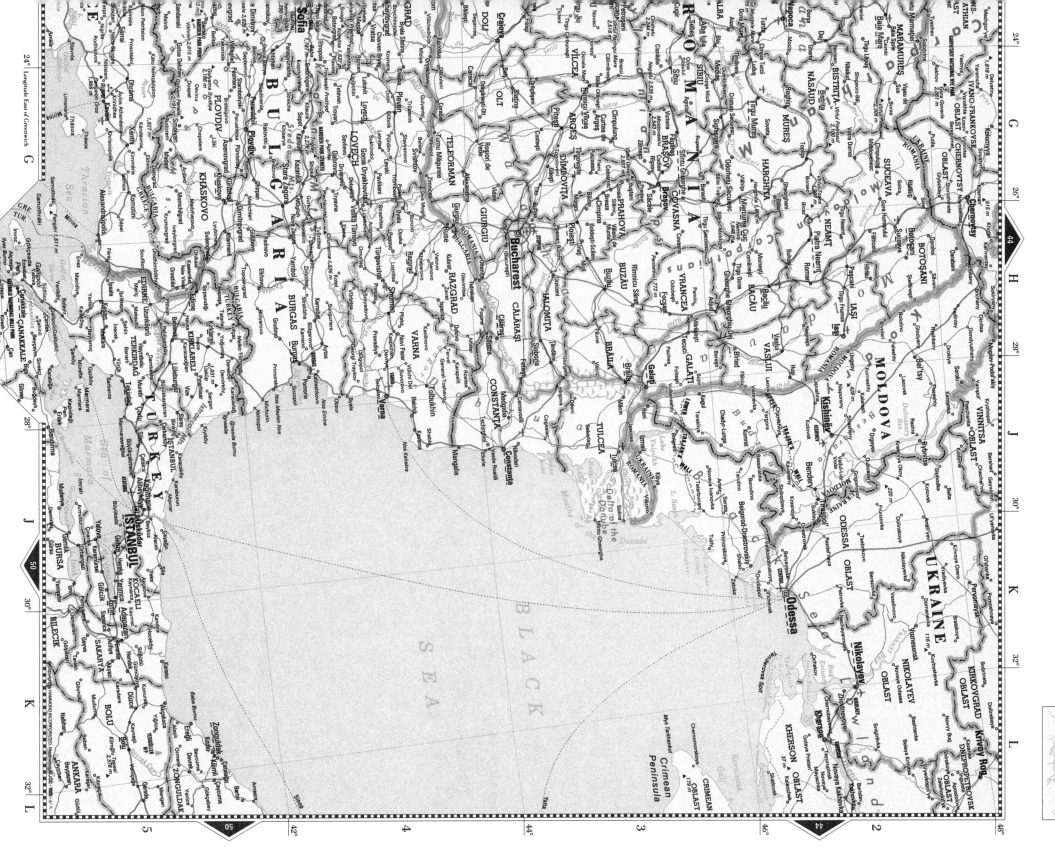

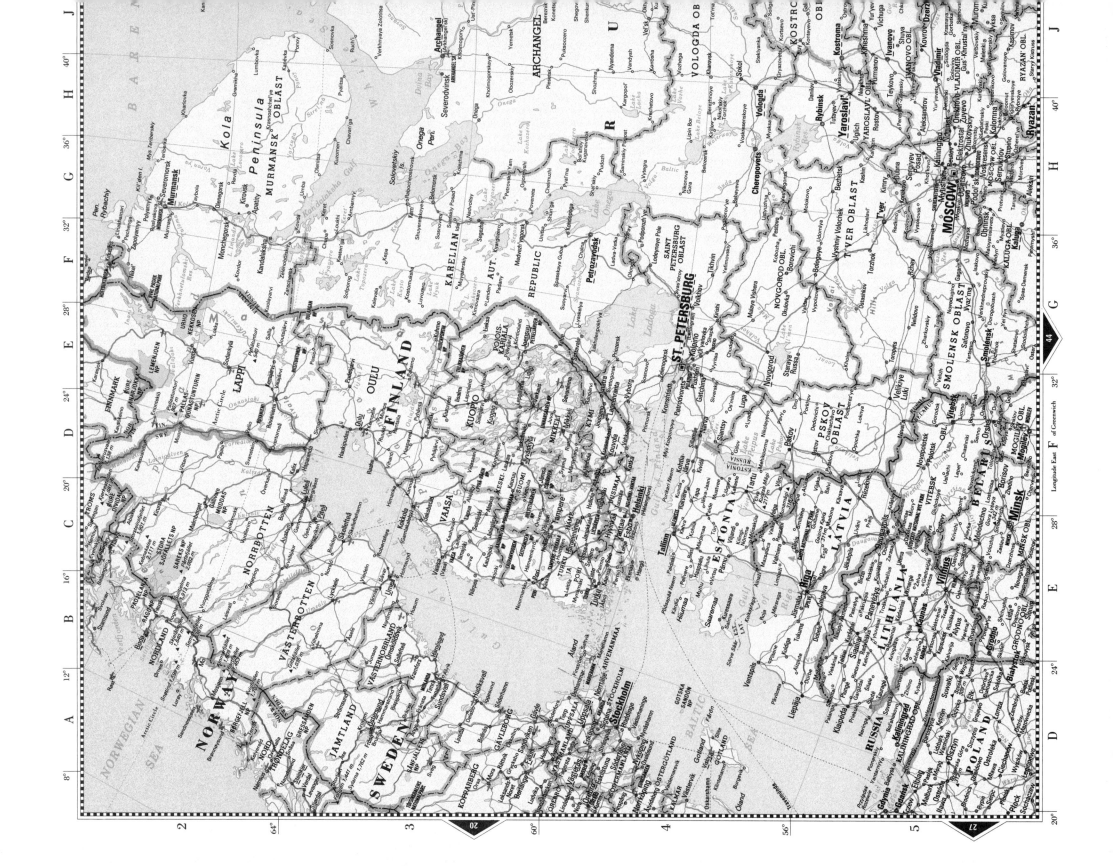

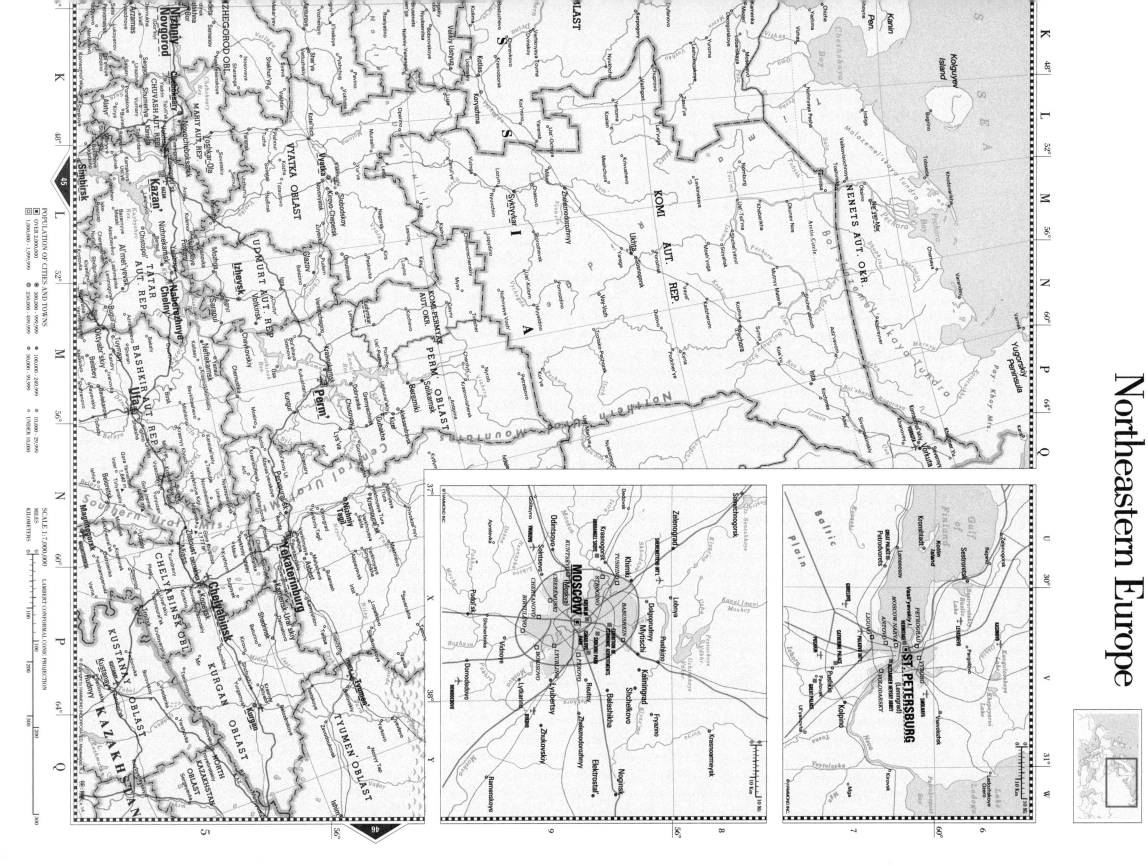

Northeastern Europe

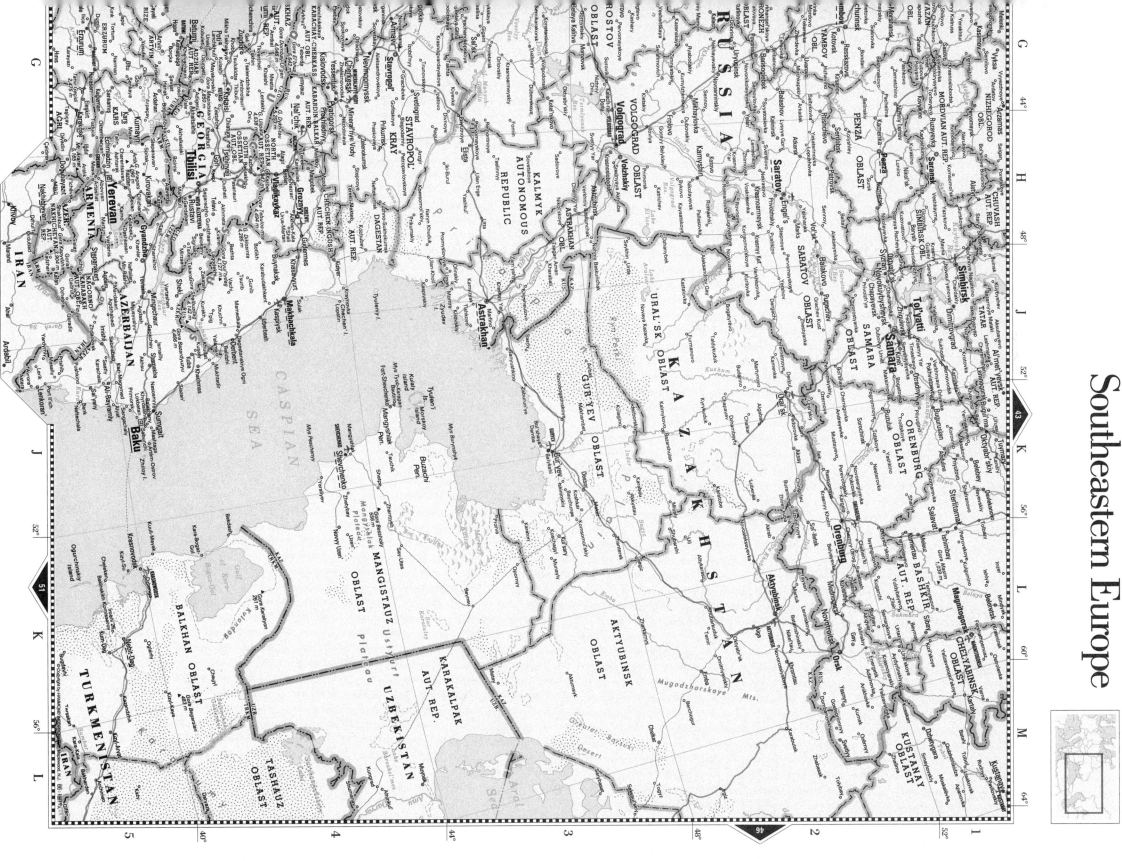

44/45

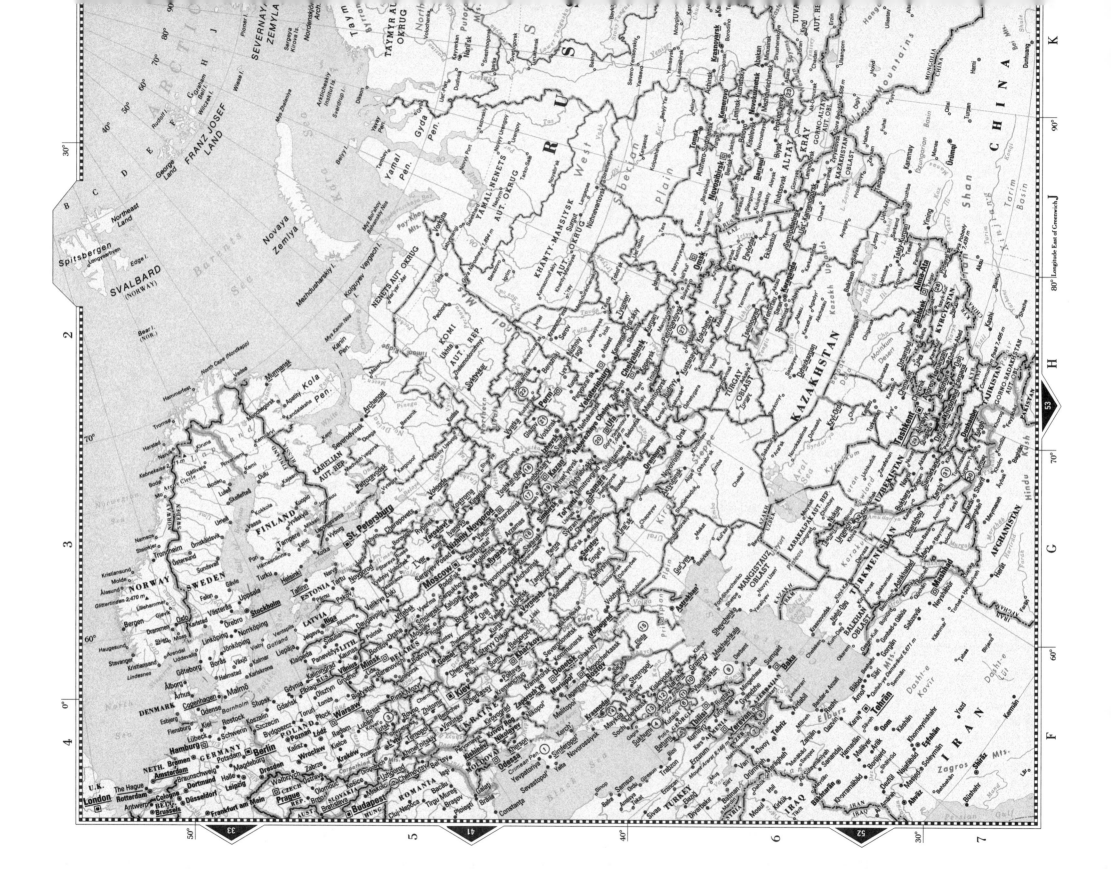

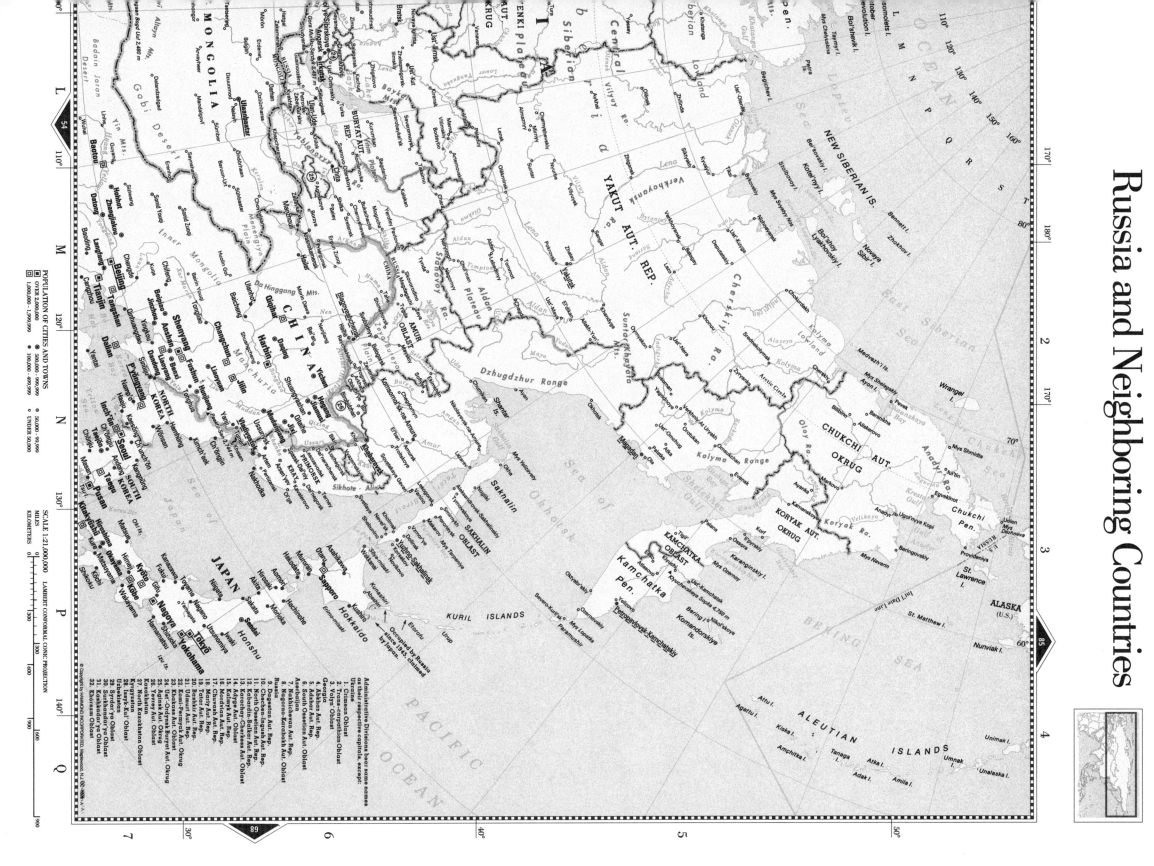

Russia and Neighboring Countries

46/47

POPULATION OF CITIES AND TOWNS
⊙ OVER 2,000,000
⊡ 1,000,000 - 1,999,999
● 500,000 - 999,999
◉ 100,000 - 499,999
• 50,000 - 99,999
• UNDER 50,000

SCALE 1:21,000,000
MILES
KILOMETERS
LAMBERT CONFORMAL CONIC PROJECTION

Administrative Divisions bear same names
as their respective capitals, except:
1. Crimean Oblast
2. Trans-carpathian Oblast
3. Volyn' Oblast
Georgia
4. Abkhaz Aut. Rep.
5. Adzhar Aut. Rep.
6. South Ossetian Aut. Oblast
Azerbaijan
7. Nakhichevan Aut. Rep.
8. Nagorno-Karabakh Aut. Oblast
Russia
9. Dagestan Aut. Rep.
10. Chechen-Ingush Aut. Rep.
11. North Ossetian Aut. Rep.
12. Kabardin-Balkar Aut. Rep.
13. Kalmyk Aut. Rep.
14. Karachai-Cherkess Aut. Oblast
15. Kalmyk Aut. Rep.
16. Mordvian Aut. Rep.
17. Chuvash Aut. Rep.
18. Mariy Aut. Rep.
19. Tatar Aut. Rep.
20. Bashkir Aut. Rep.
21. Udmurt Aut. Rep.
22. Khakass Aut. Oblast
23. Komi-Permyak Aut. Okrug
24. Ust'-Ordynski Buryat Aut. Okrug
25. Aginsk Aut. Okrug
26. Yevrey Aut. Oblast
Kazakhstan
27. Northern Kazakhstan Oblast
Kyrgyzstan
28. Issyk-Kul' Oblast
Uzbekistan
29. Syrdar'ya Oblast
30. Surkhandar'ya Oblast
31. Kashkadar'ya Oblast
32. Khorezm Oblast

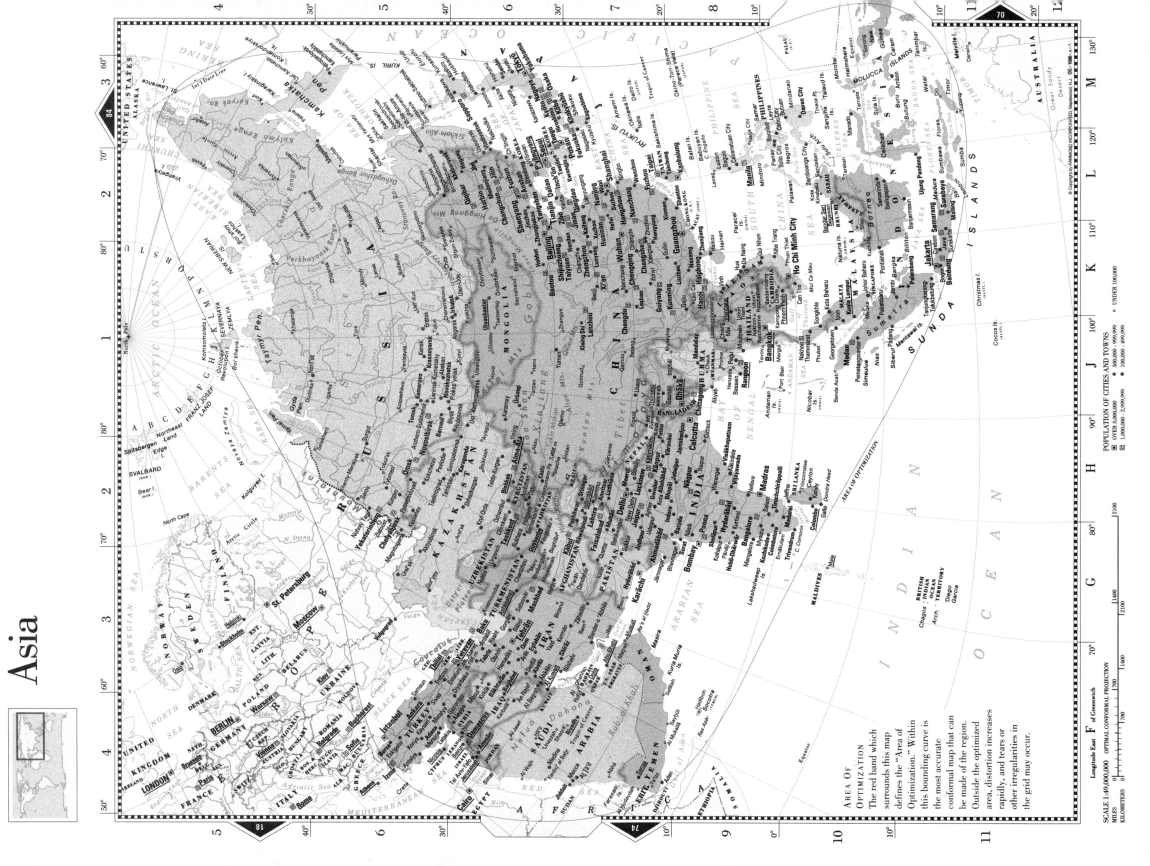

Asia

48

POPULATION OF CITIES AND TOWNS

⬛ OVER 3,000,000	⬛ 500,000-999,999	○ UNDER 100,000
⬛ 1,000,000-2,999,999	● 100,000-499,999	

AREA OF OPTIMIZATION The red band which surrounds this map defines the "Area of Optimization." Within this bounding curve is the most accurate conformal map that can be made of the region. Outside the optimized area, distortion increases rapidly, and tears or other irregularities in the grid may occur.

SCALE 1:49,000,000 OPTIMAL CONFORMAL PROJECTION

Longitude East F of Greenwich

Eastern Mediterranean Region

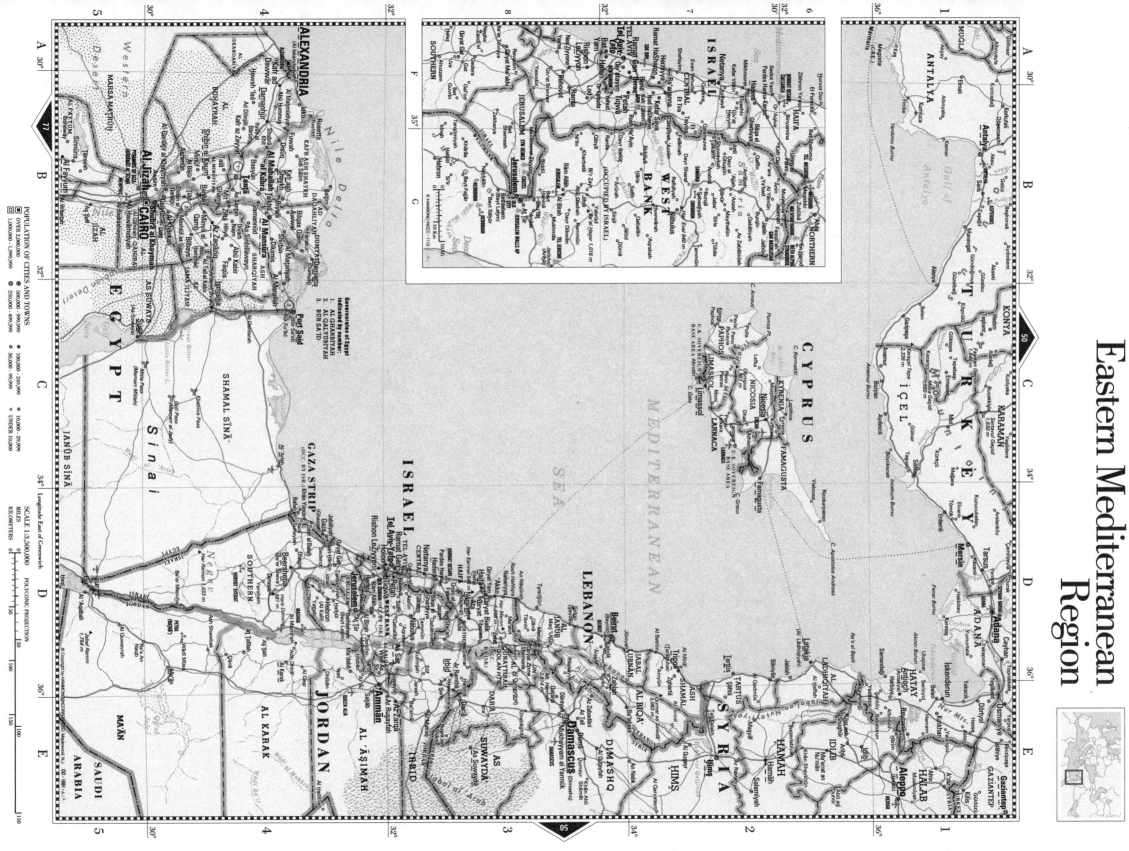

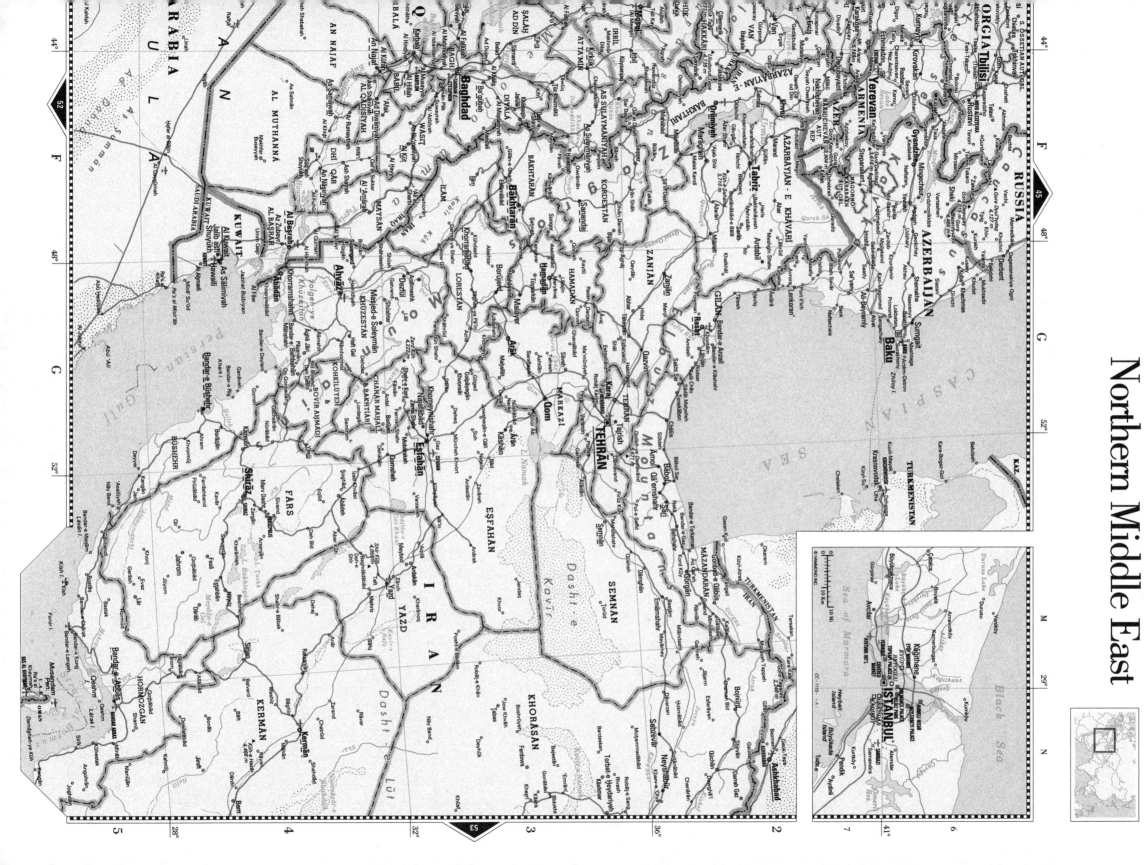

Northern Middle East

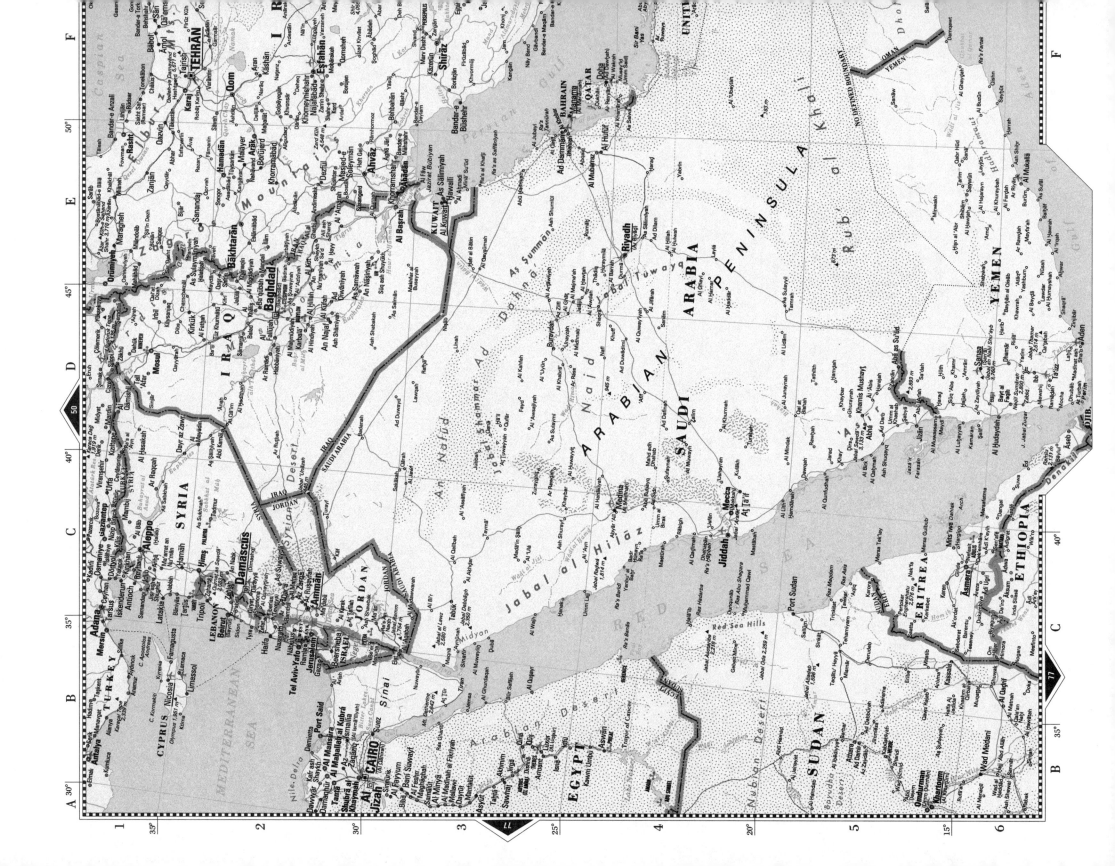

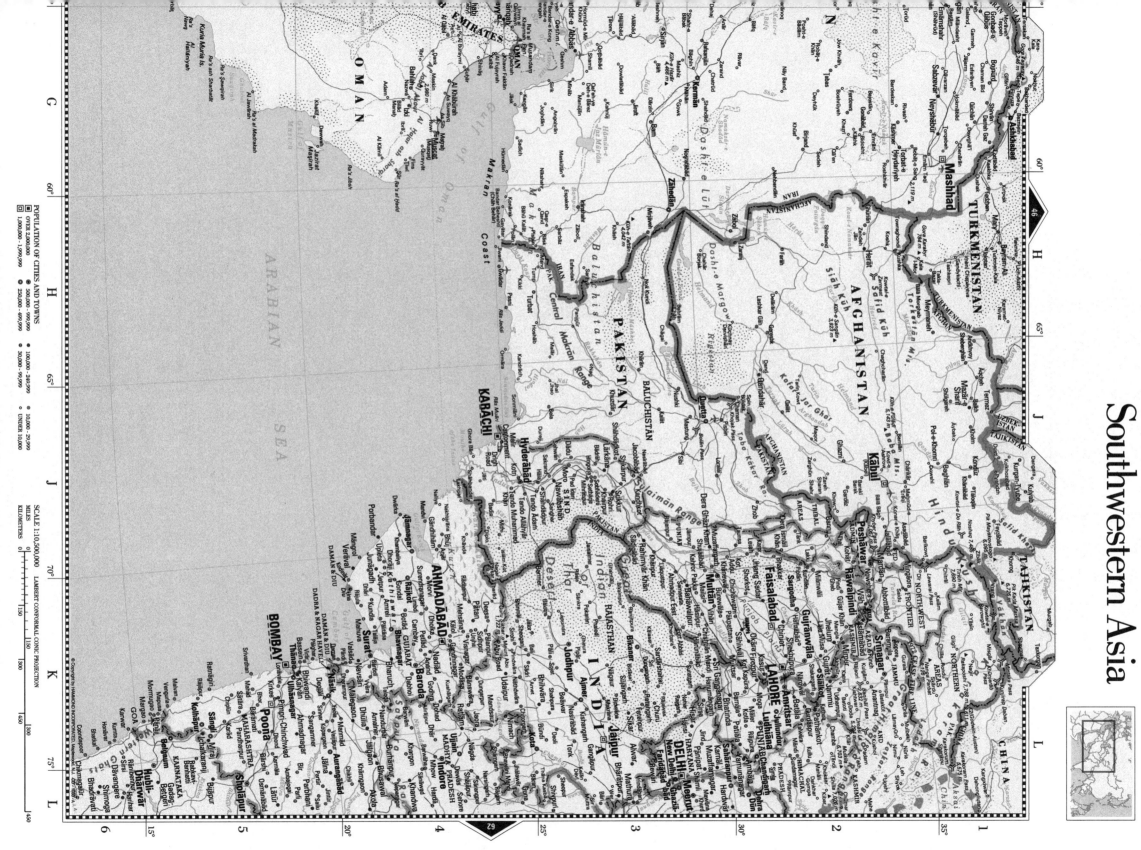

Southwestern Asia

52/53

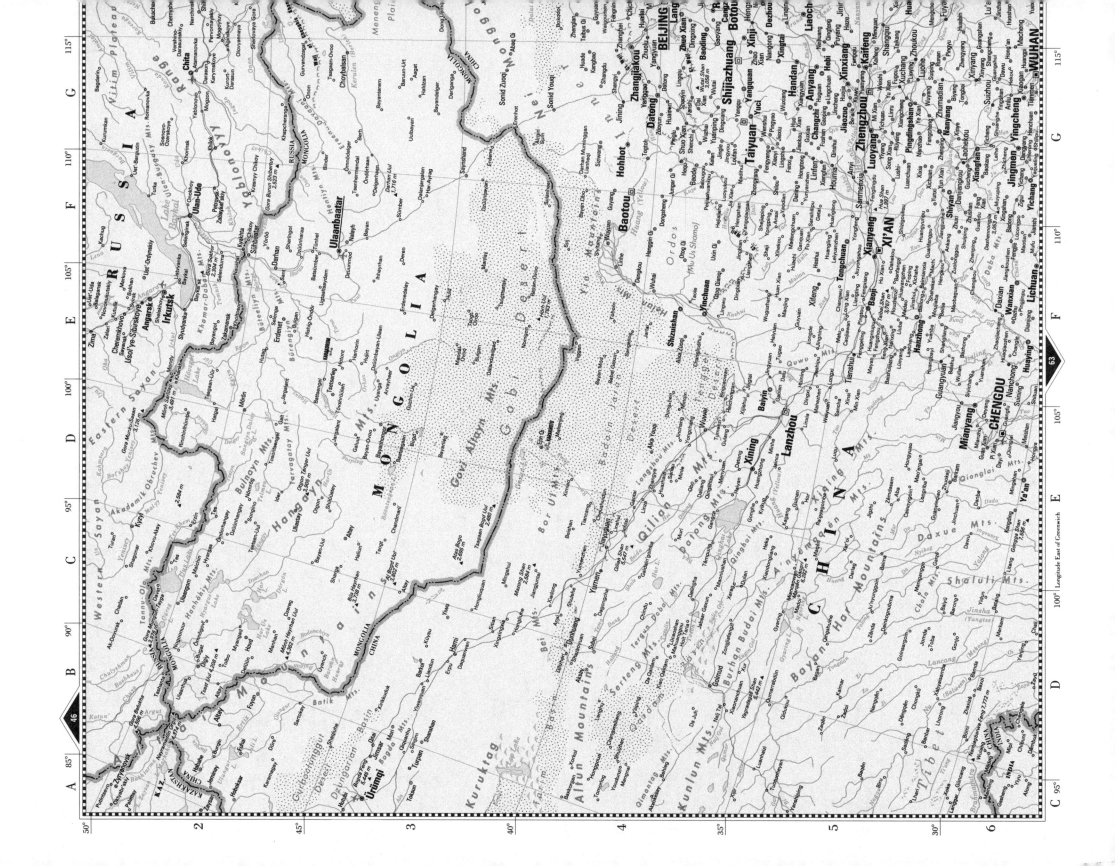

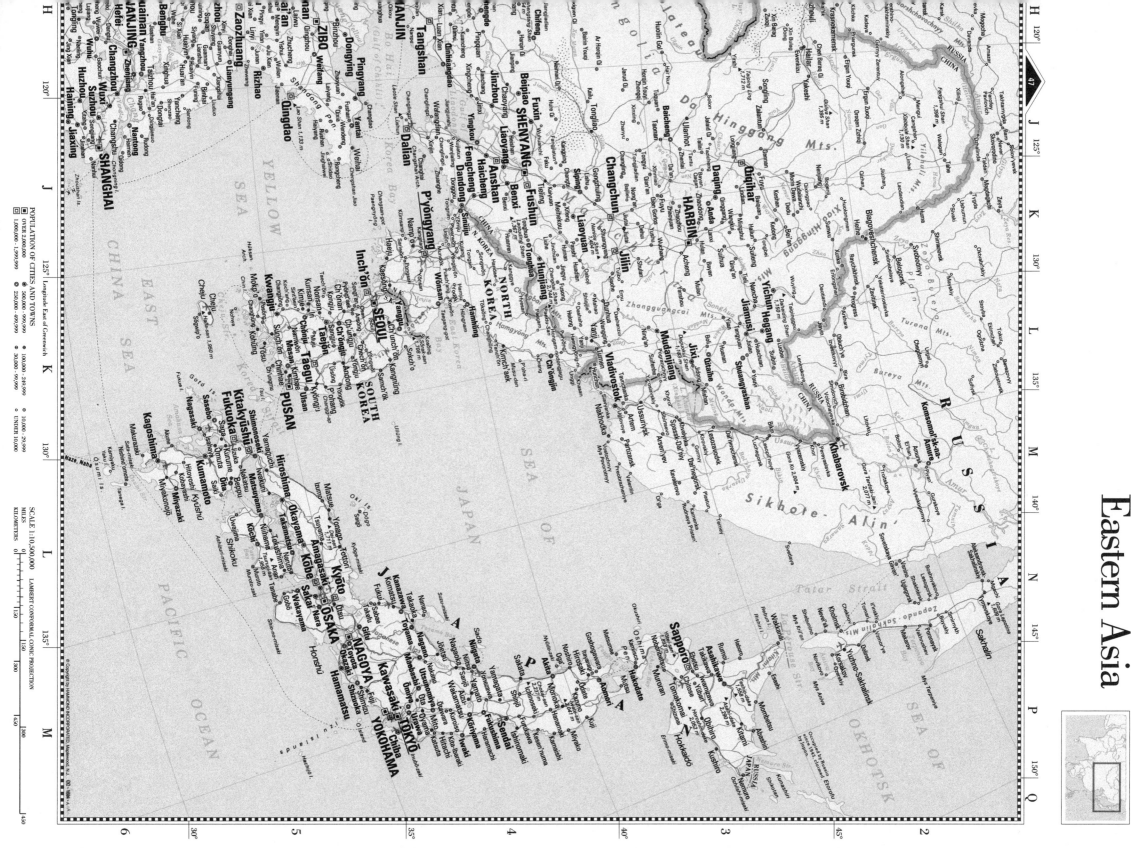

Eastern Asia

POPULATION OF CITIES AND TOWNS

- ■ OVER 2,000,000
- ● 1,000,000 - 1,999,999
- ⊙ 500,000 - 999,999
- ◉ 250,000 - 499,999
- ◎ 100,000 - 249,999
- ● 30,000 - 99,999
- ○ 10,000 - 29,999
- ○ UNDER 10,000

SCALE 1:10,500,000
LAMBERT CONFORMAL CONIC PROJECTION

MILES
KILOMETERS

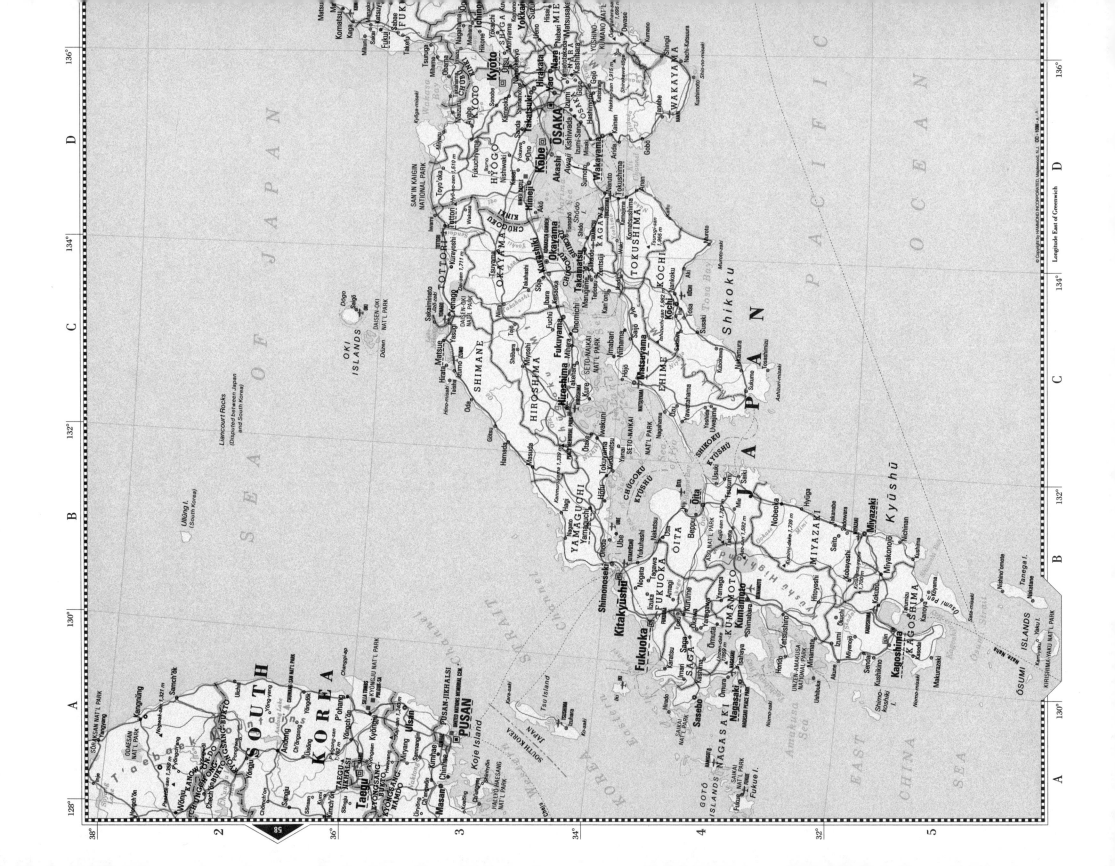

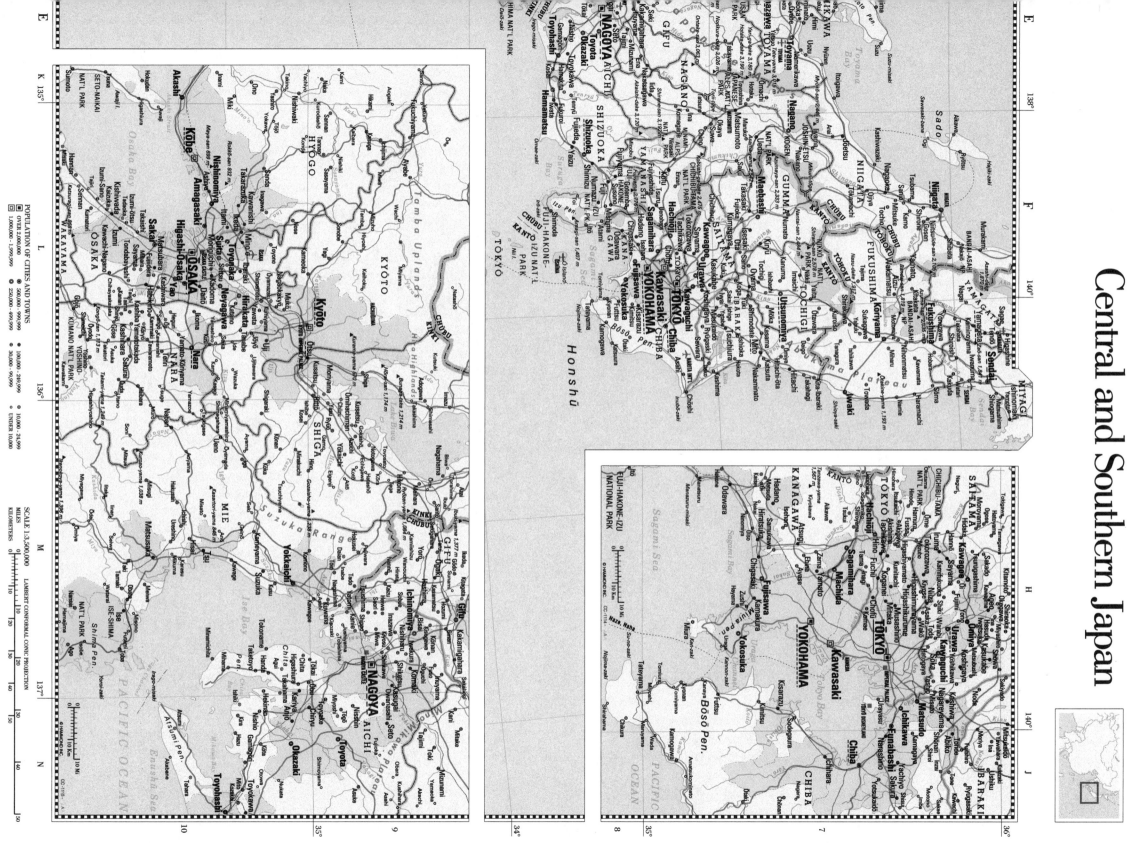

Central and Southern Japan

POPULATION OF CITIES AND TOWNS

☐ OVER 2,000,000
☐ 1,000,000 - 1,999,999

● 500,000 - 999,999
● 250,000 - 499,999
● 100,000 - 249,999
● 30,000 - 99,999
○ 10,000 - 24,999
○ UNDER 10,000

SCALE 1:3,500,000

LAMBERT CONFORMAL CONIC PROJECTION

MILES
KILOMETERS

FUJI-HAKONE-IZU
NATIONAL PARK

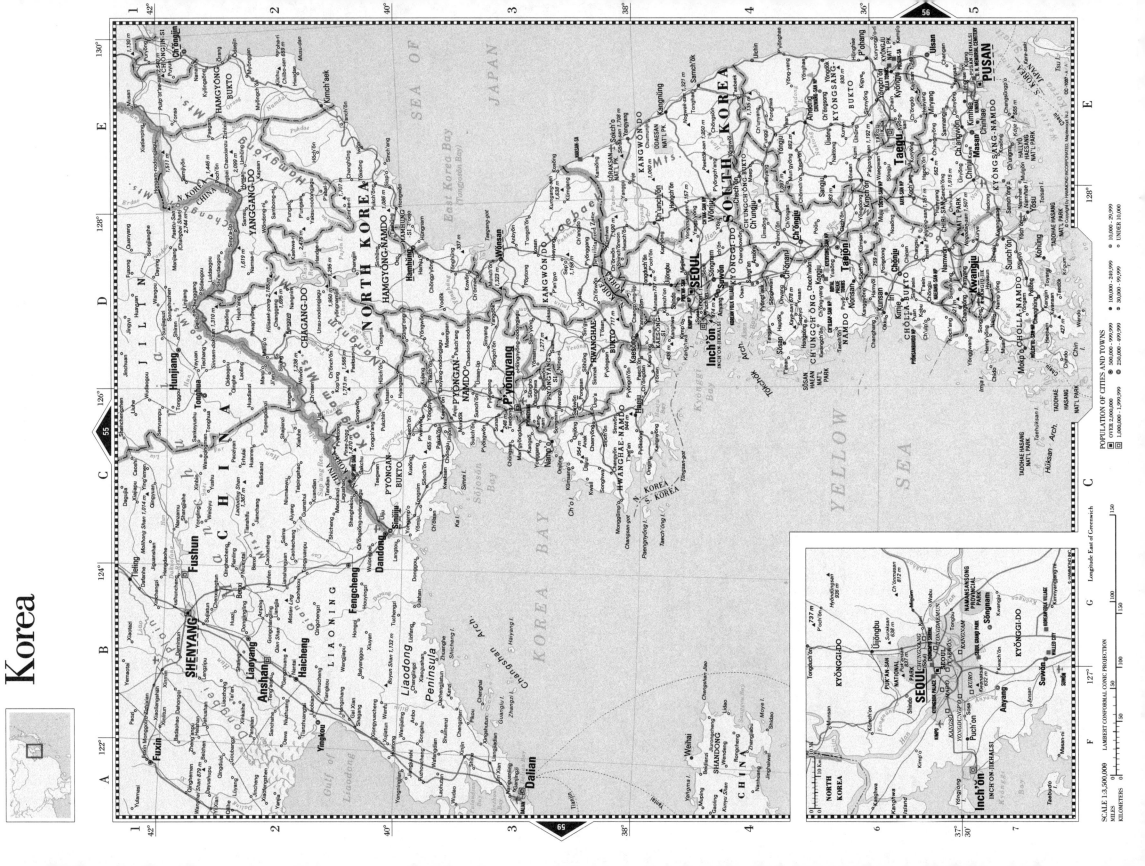

Korea

58

SCALE 1:3,500,000   LAMBERT CONFORMAL CONIC PROJECTION

POPULATION OF CITIES AND TOWNS

Northeastern China

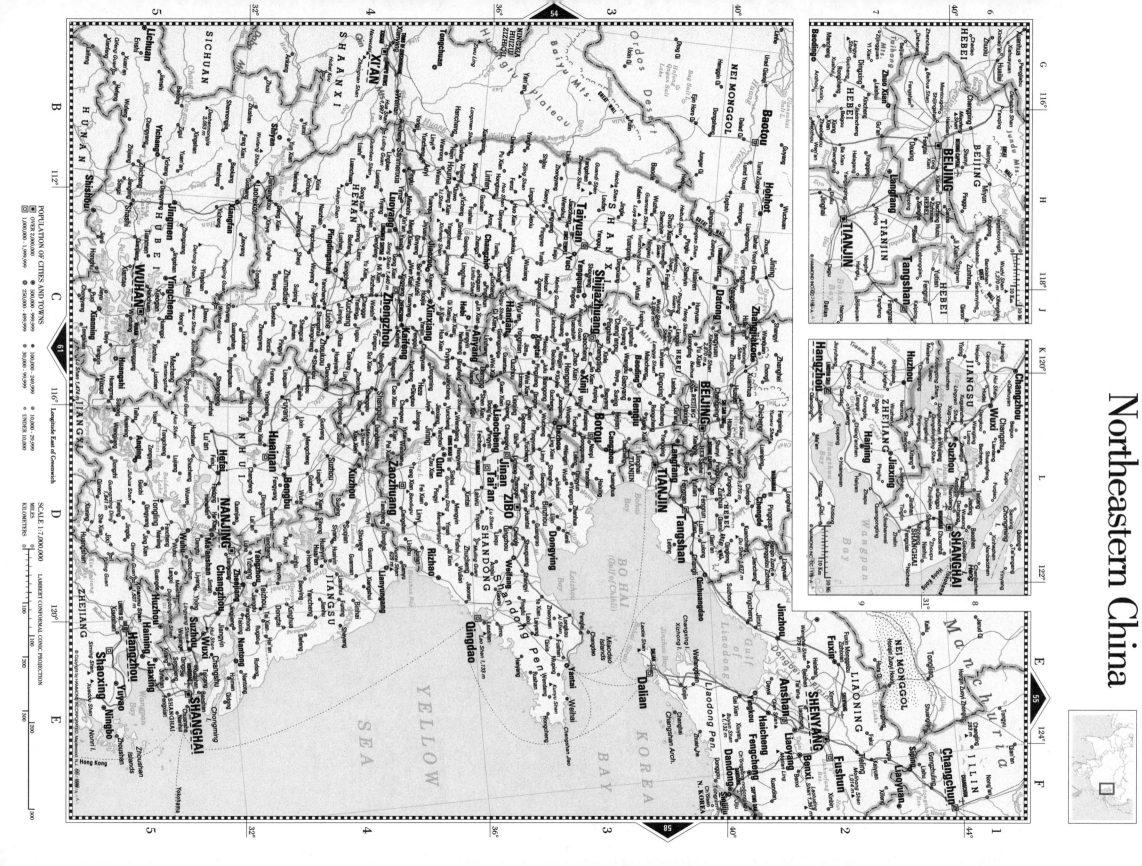

POPULATION OF CITIES AND TOWNS

- ◉ OVER 2,000,000
- ■ 1,000,000 - 1,999,999
- ● 500,000 - 999,999
- ● 250,000 - 499,999
- ● 100,000 - 249,999
- ● 50,000 - 99,999
- ● 30,000 - 99,999
- ○ 10,000 - 29,999
- □ UNDER 10,000

116° Longitude East of Greenwich

SCALE 1:7,000,000

LAMBERT CONFORMAL CONIC PROJECTION

© Copyright by HAMMOND INCORPORATED, Maplewood, N.J.

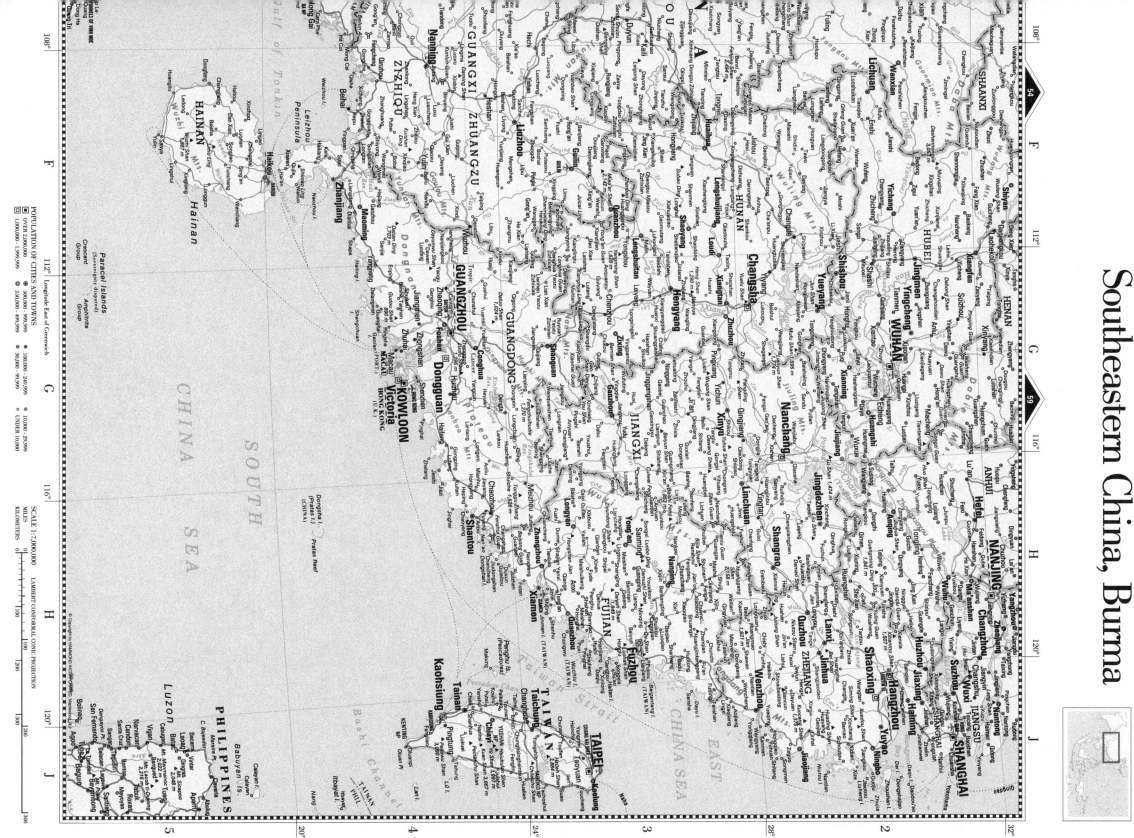

Southeastern China, Burma

SCALE 1:7,000,000

LAMBERT CONFORMAL CONIC PROJECTION

POPULATION OF CITIES AND TOWNS

- ▣ OVER 2,000,000
- ◉ 1,000,000 - 1,999,999
- ◉ 250,000 - 499,999
- ● 500,000 - 999,999
- ● 100,000 - 249,999
- ● 30,000 - 99,999
- ◉ 10,000 - 29,999
- ◦ UNDER 10,000

112° Longitude East of Greenwich

Parcel Islands
(Sovereignty disputed)
Crescent Group
Amphitrite Group

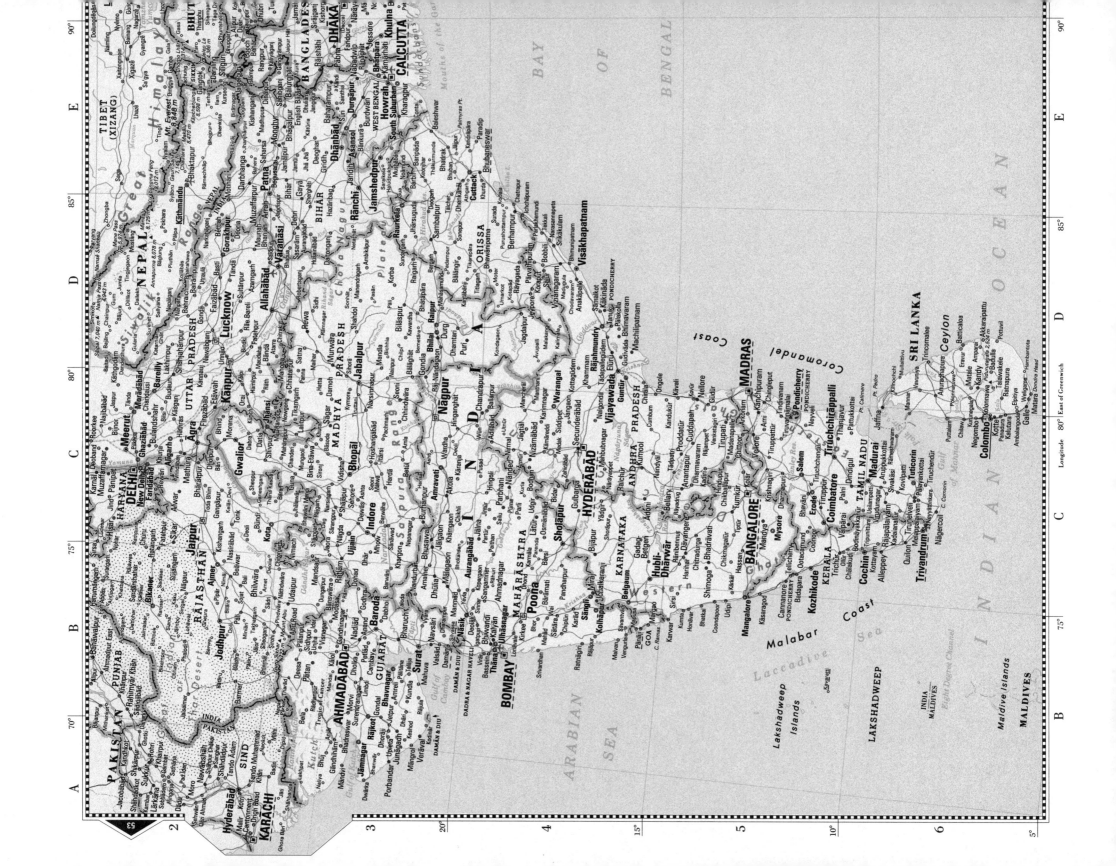

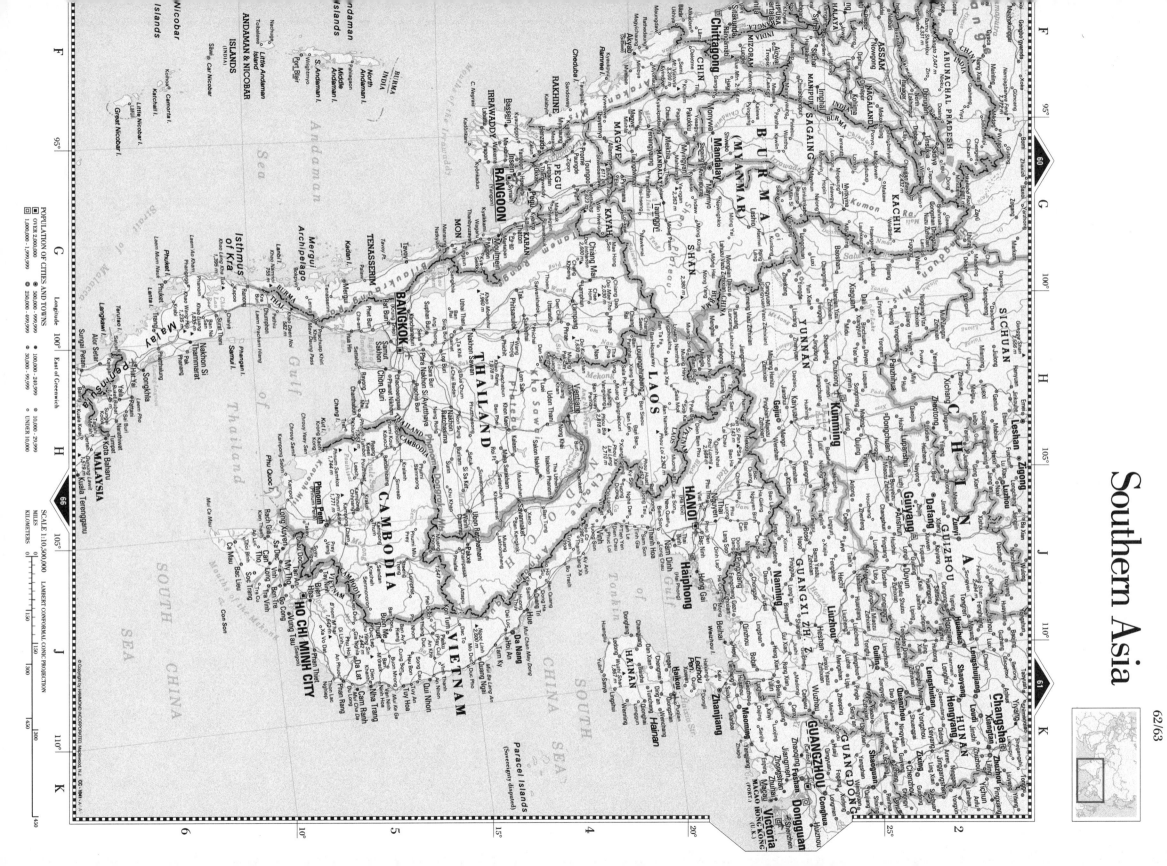

Southern Asia

POPULATION OF CITIES AND TOWNS
- OVER 2,000,000
- 1,000,000 - 1,999,999
- 500,000 - 999,999
- 250,000 - 499,999
- 100,000 - 249,999
- 30,000 - 99,999
- 10,000 - 29,999
- UNDER 10,000

Longitude 100° East of Greenwich

SCALE 1:10,500,000   LAMBERT CONFORMAL CONIC PROJECTION

MILES
KILOMETERS

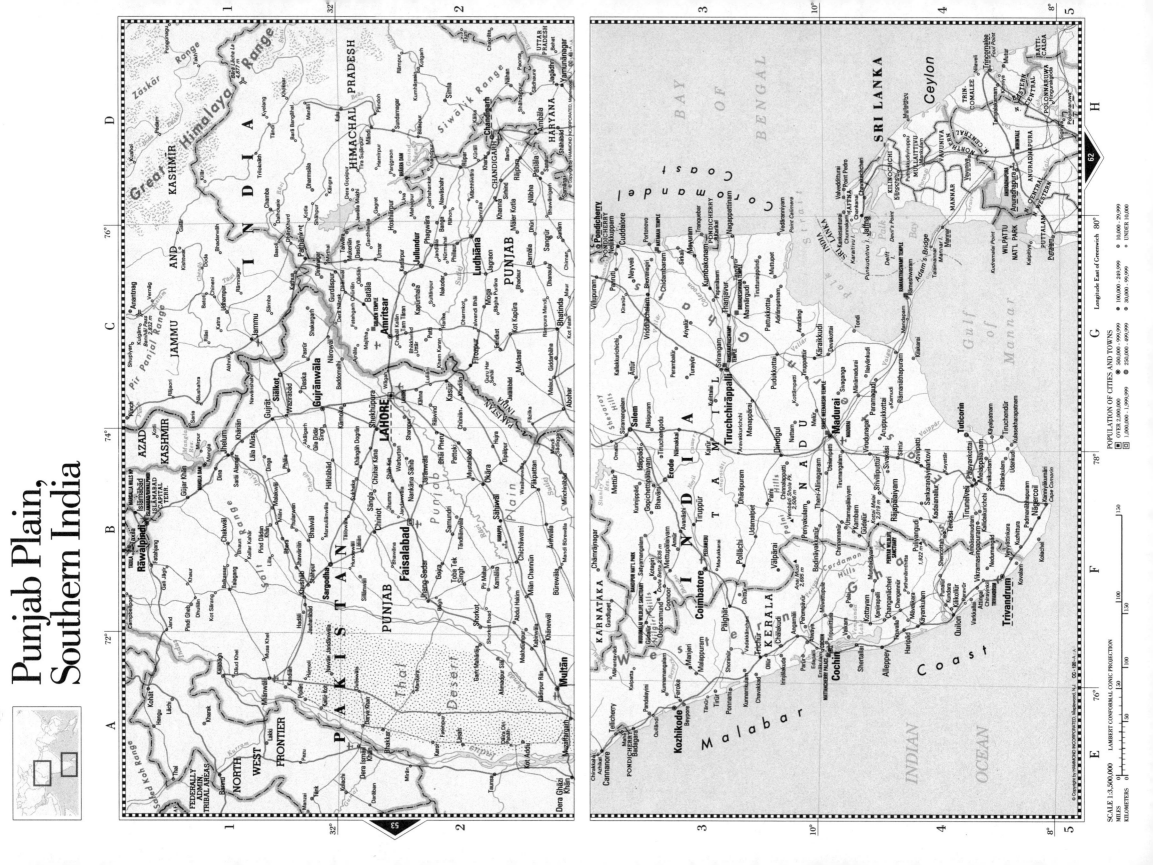

Punjab Plain, Southern India

SCALE 1:3,500,000   LAMBERT CONFORMAL CONIC PROJECTION

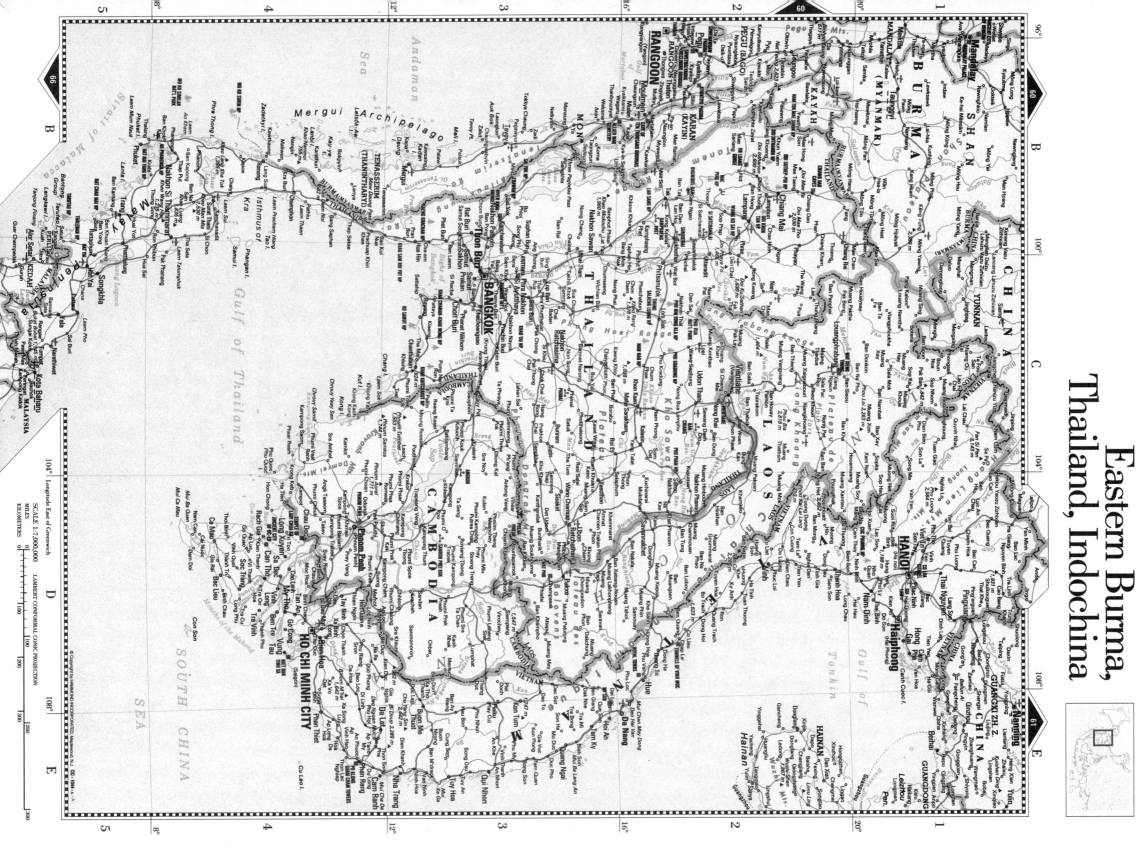

Eastern Burma, Thailand, Indochina

SCALE 1:7,000,000
MILES
KILOMETERS
LAMBERT CONFORMAL CONIC PROJECTION

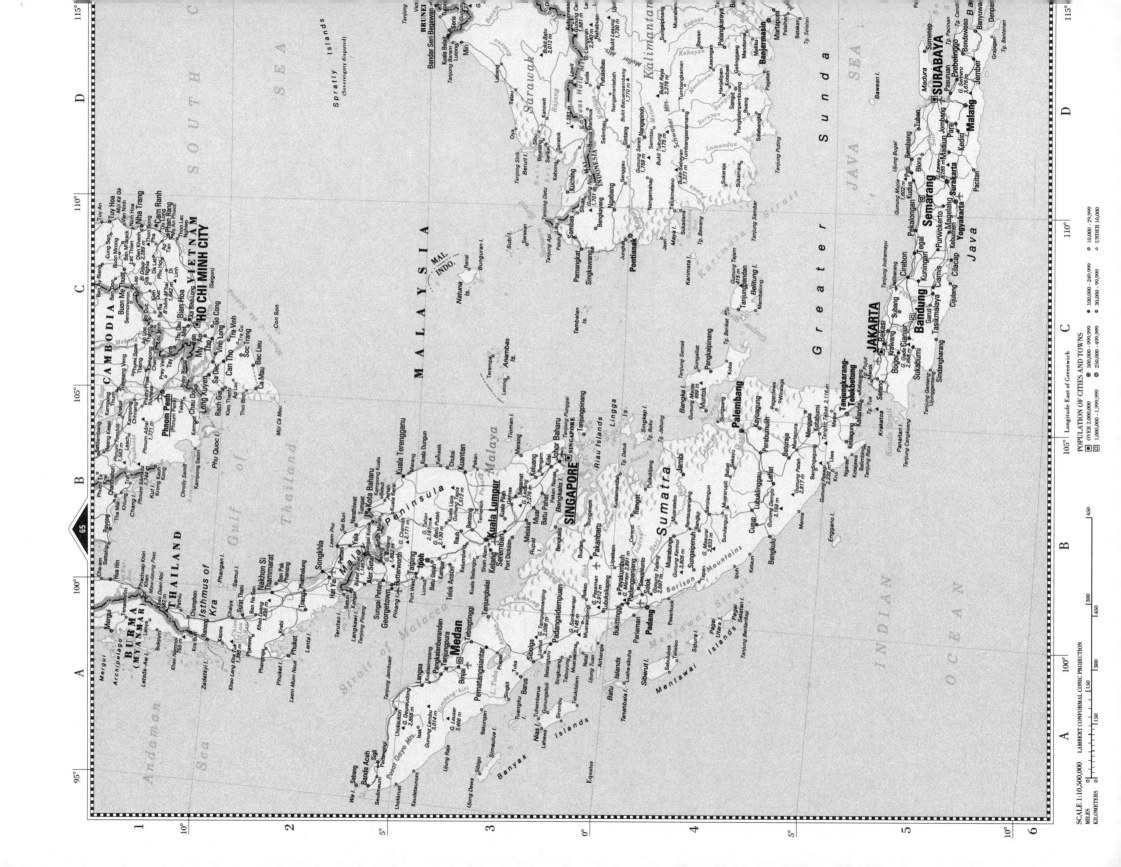

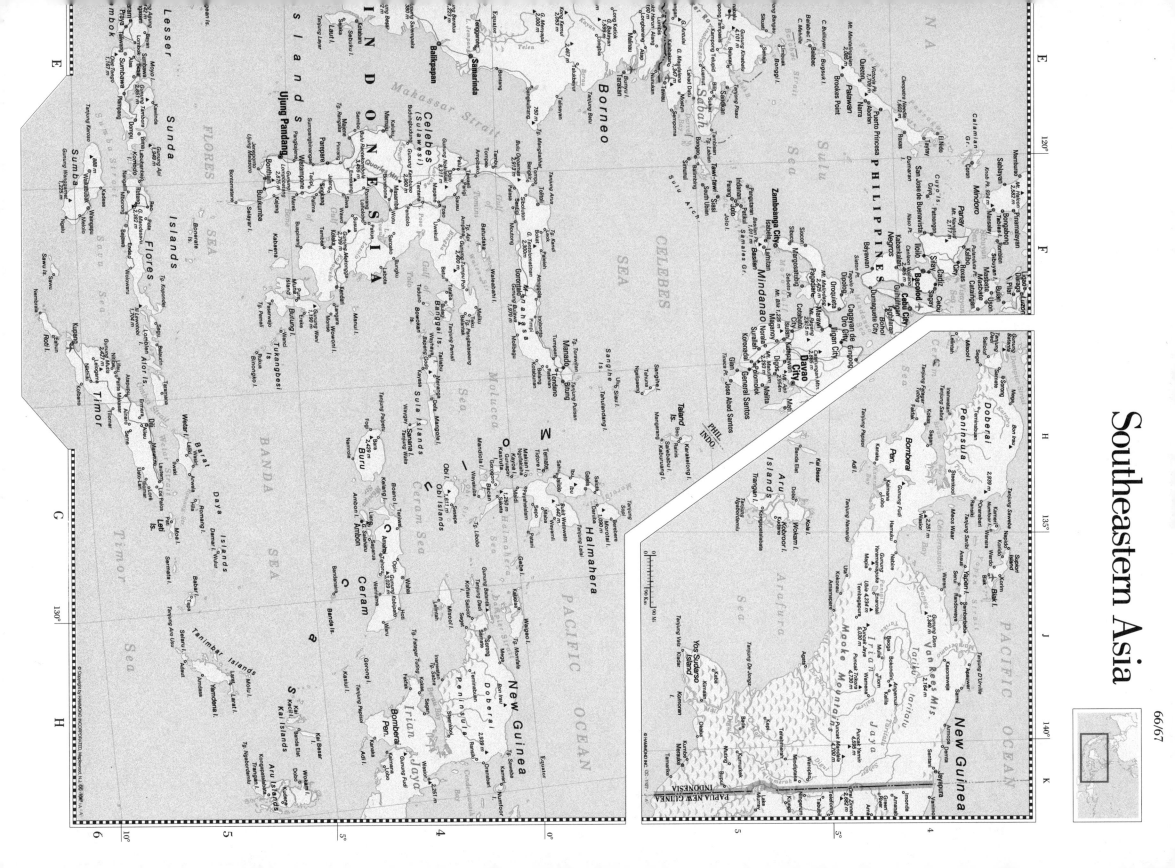

Southeastern Asia

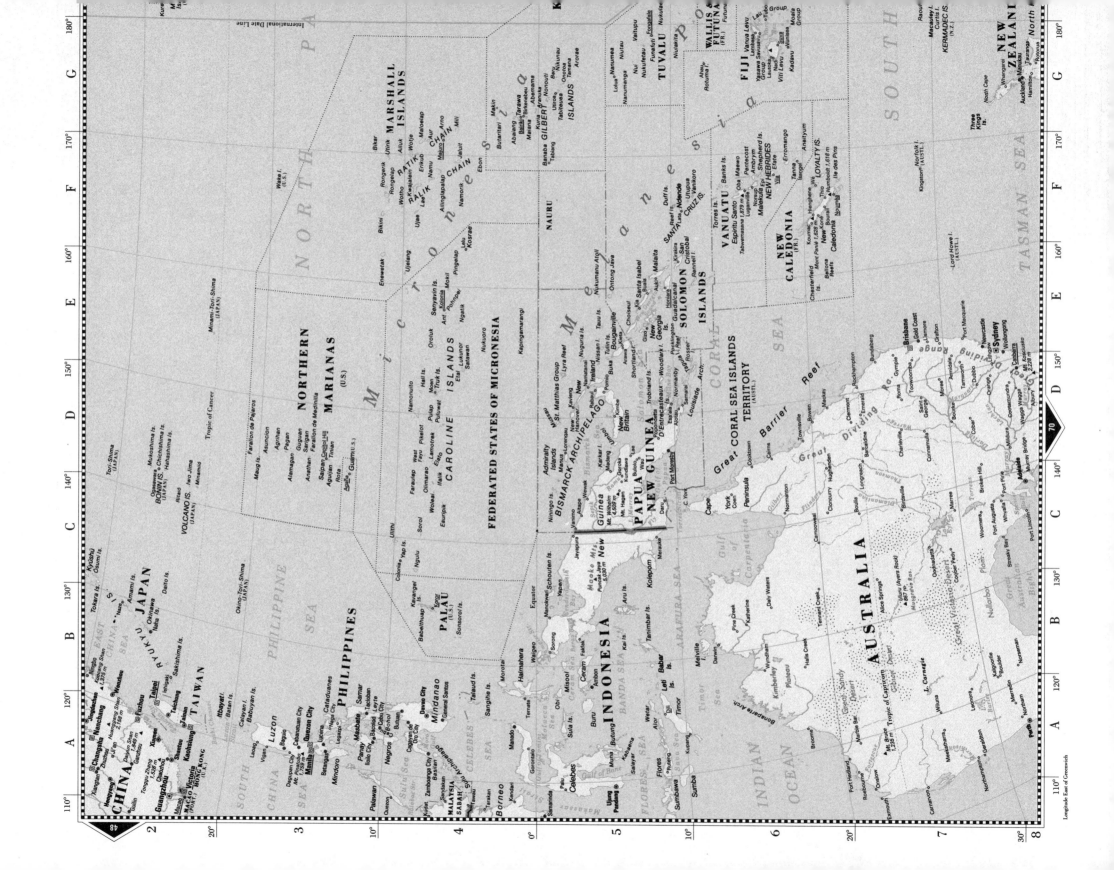

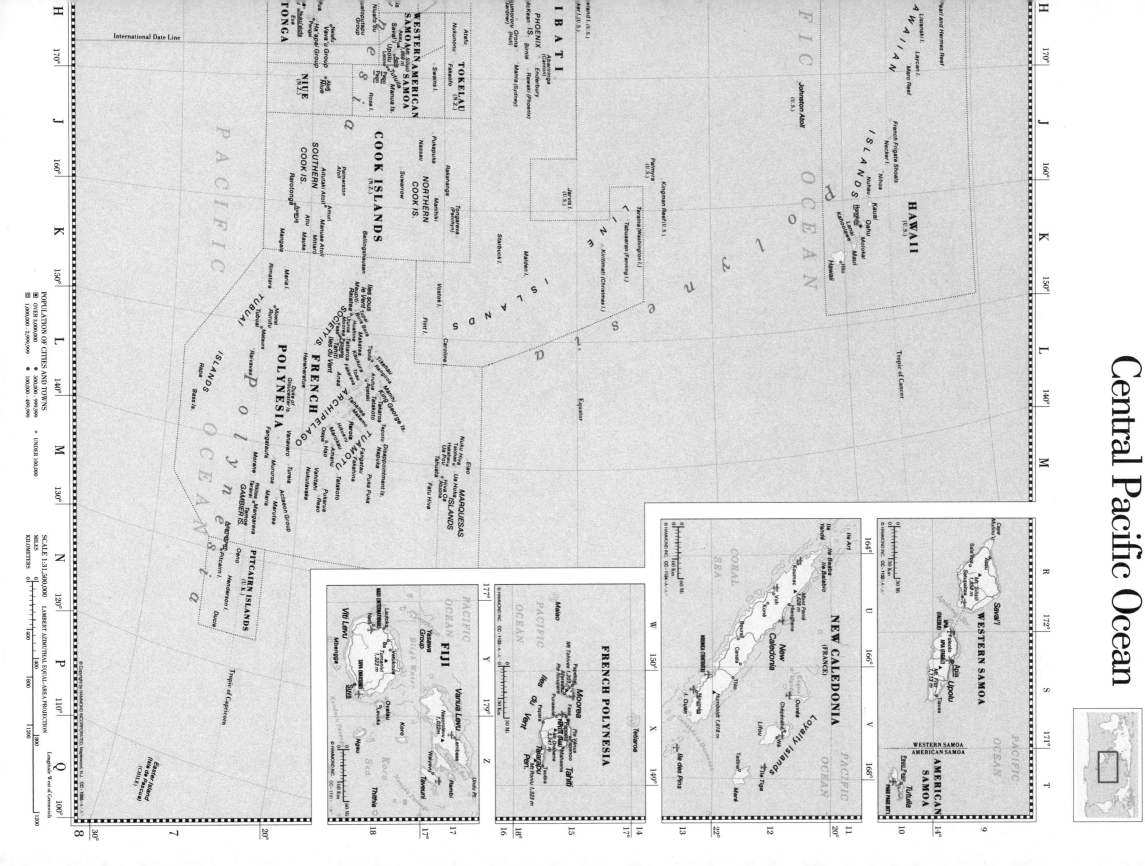

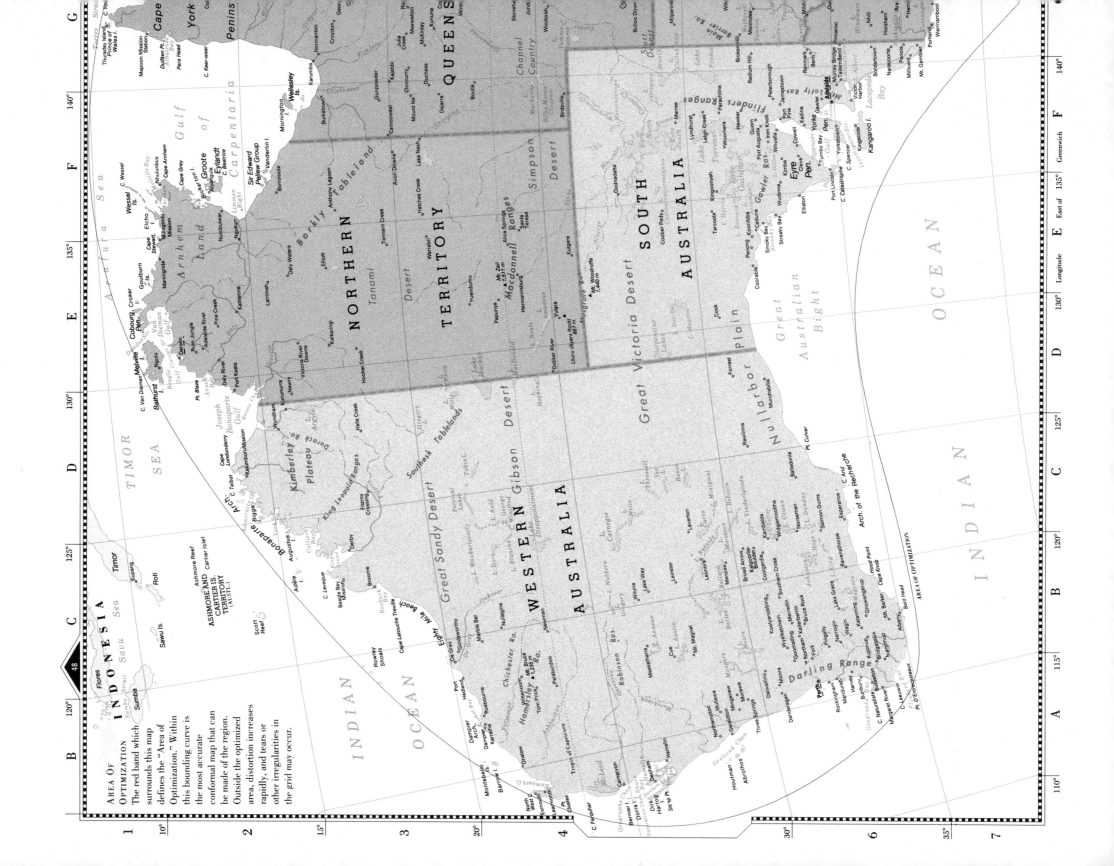

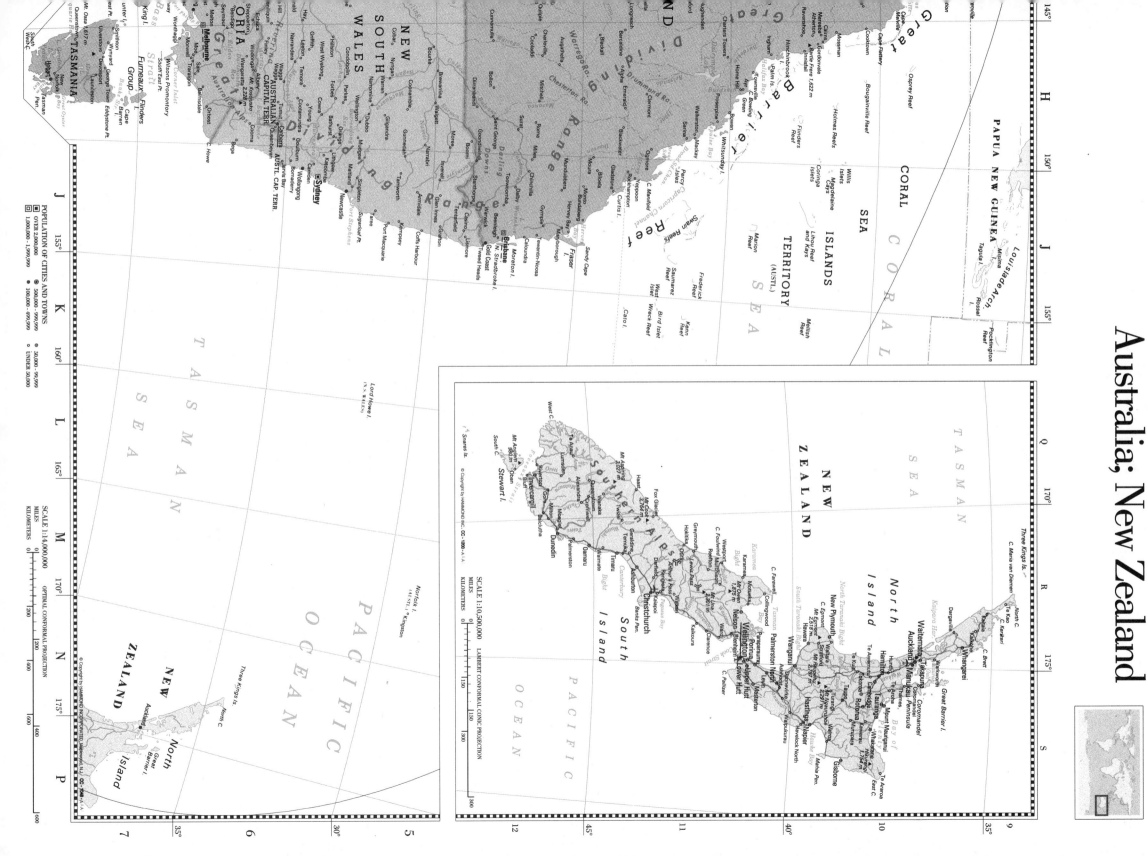

Australia; New Zealand

POPULATION OF CITIES AND TOWNS

- ■ OVER 2,000,000
- ■ 1,000,000 - 1,999,999
- ● 500,000 - 999,999
- ● 100,000 - 499,999
- ● 30,000 - 99,999
- ○ UNDER 30,000

SCALE 1:14,000,000
OPTIMAL CONFORMAL PROJECTION
MILES
KILOMETERS

SCALE 1:10,500,000
LAMBERT CONFORMAL CONIC PROJECTION
MILES
KILOMETERS

TASMANIA

VICTORIA

NEW SOUTH WALES

AUSTRALIAN CAPITAL TERR.

PAPUA NEW GUINEA

CORAL SEA

CORAL SEA ISLANDS TERRITORY (AUSTL.)

NEW ZEALAND

North Island

South Island

Southern Alps

TASMAN SEA

PACIFIC OCEAN

Northeastern Australia

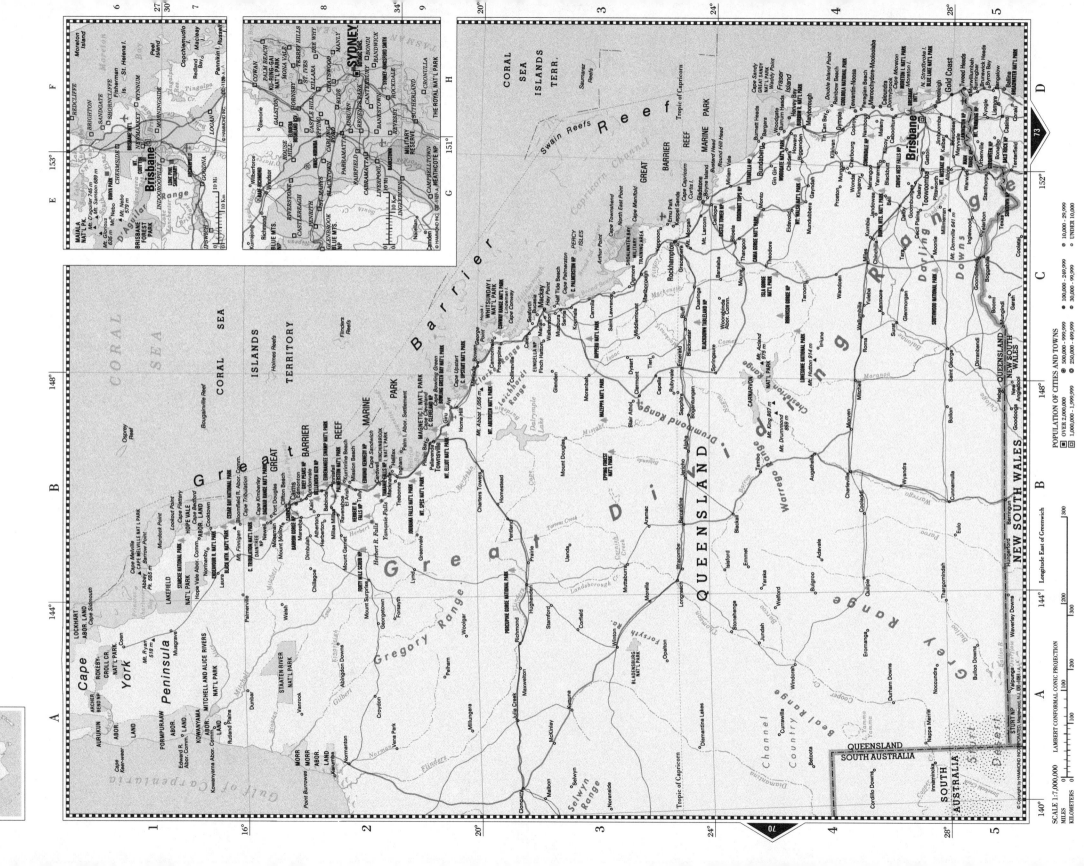

SCALE 1:7,000,000   LAMBERT CONFORMAL CONIC PROJECTION

© Copyright by HAMMOND INCORPORATED, Maplewood, N.J. 08-H9B1-A-A

MILES
KILOMETERS

Longitude East of Greenwich

POPULATION OF CITIES AND TOWNS

Symbol	Population
■ OVER 2,000,000	● 500,000 - 999,999	● 100,000 - 249,999	● 10,000 - 29,999
▣ 1,000,000 - 1,999,999	● 250,000 - 499,999	● 30,000 - 99,999	○ UNDER 10,000

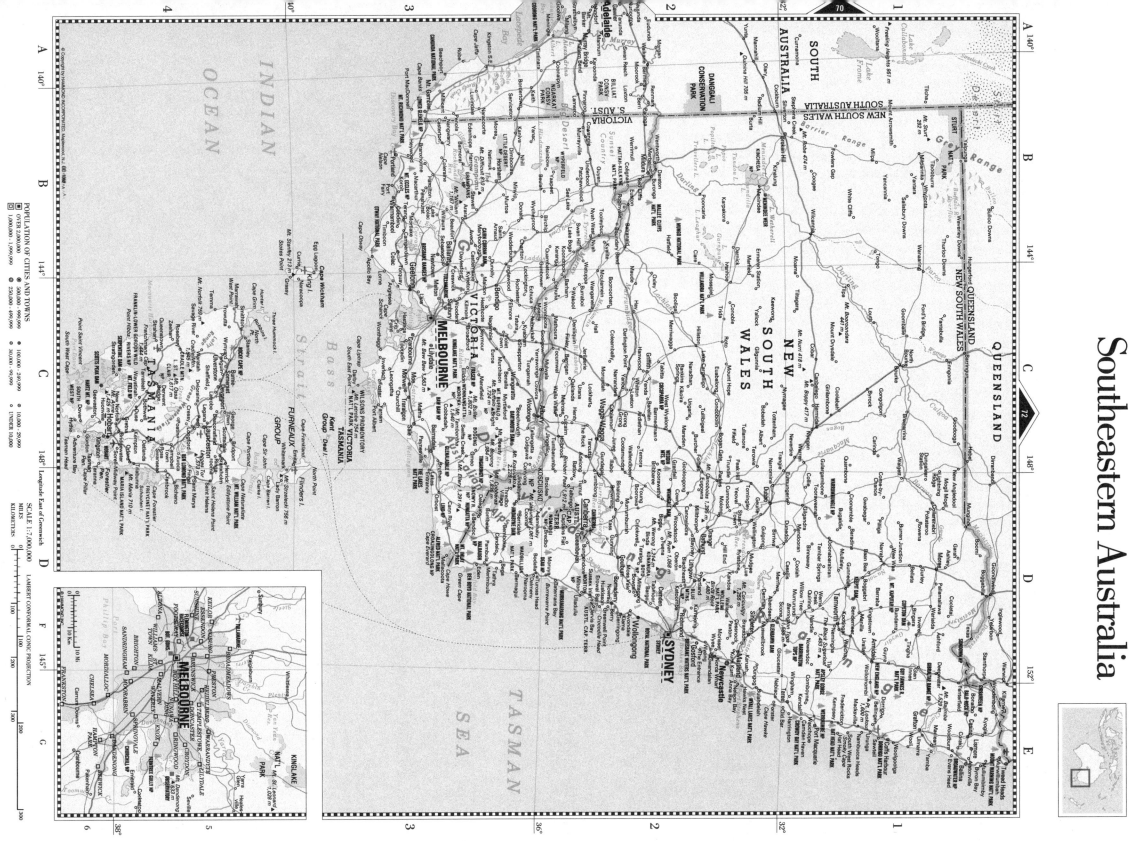

Southeastern Australia

POPULATION OF CITIES AND TOWNS
- ◉ OVER 2,000,000
- ◉ 1,000,000 - 1,999,999
- ◉ 500,000 - 999,999
- ◉ 250,000 - 499,999
- ◉ 100,000 - 249,999
- ◉ 30,000 - 99,999
- ○ 10,000 - 29,999
- ○ UNDER 10,000

SCALE 1:7,000,000
MILES
KILOMETERS

LAMBERT CONFORMAL CONIC PROJECTION

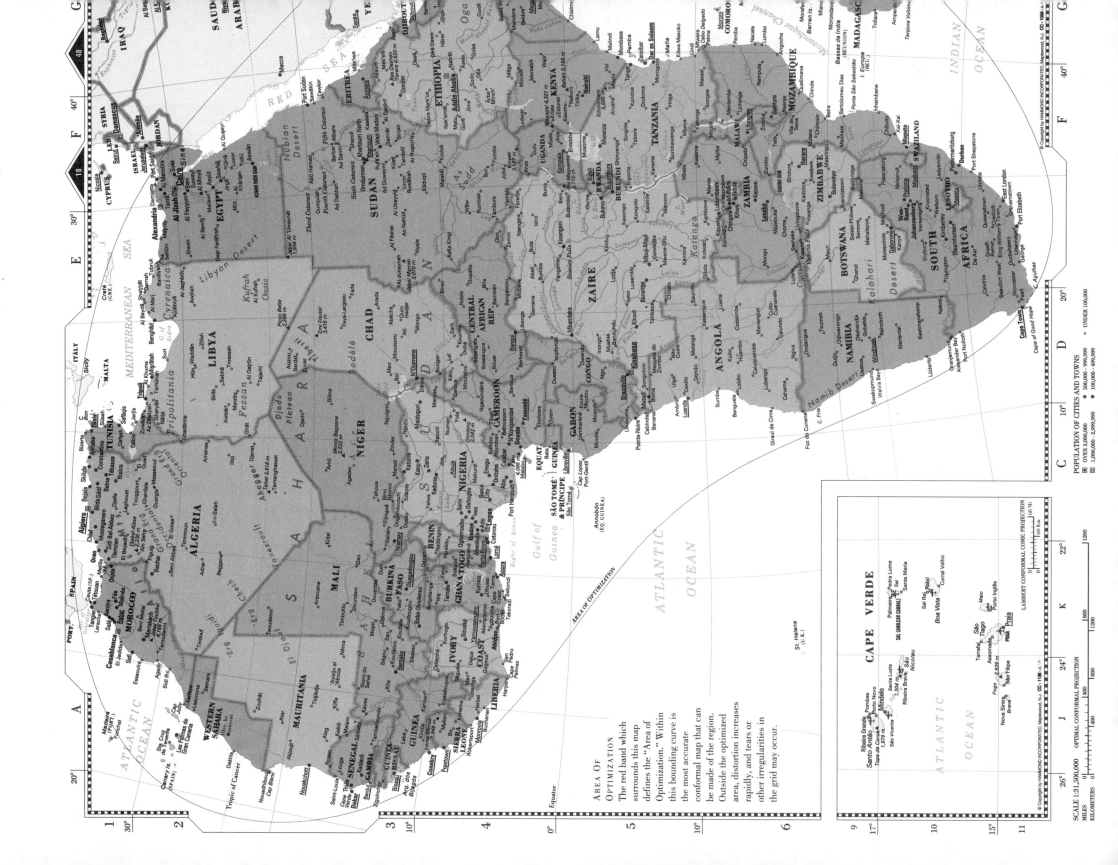

AREA OF
OPTIMIZATION
The red band which
surrounds this map
defines the "Area of
Optimization." Within
this bounding curve is
the most accurate
conformal map that can
be made of the region.
Outside the optimized
area, distortion increases
rapidly, and tears or
other irregularities in
the grid may occur.

POPULATION OF CITIES AND TOWNS

● OVER 3,000,000   ◉ 500,000 - 999,999   ● UNDER 100,000
● 1,000,000 - 2,999,999   ● 100,000 - 499,999

CAPE VERDE

LAMBERT CONFORMAL CONIC PROJECTION

SCALE 1:31,500,000   OPTIMAL CONFORMAL PROJECTION

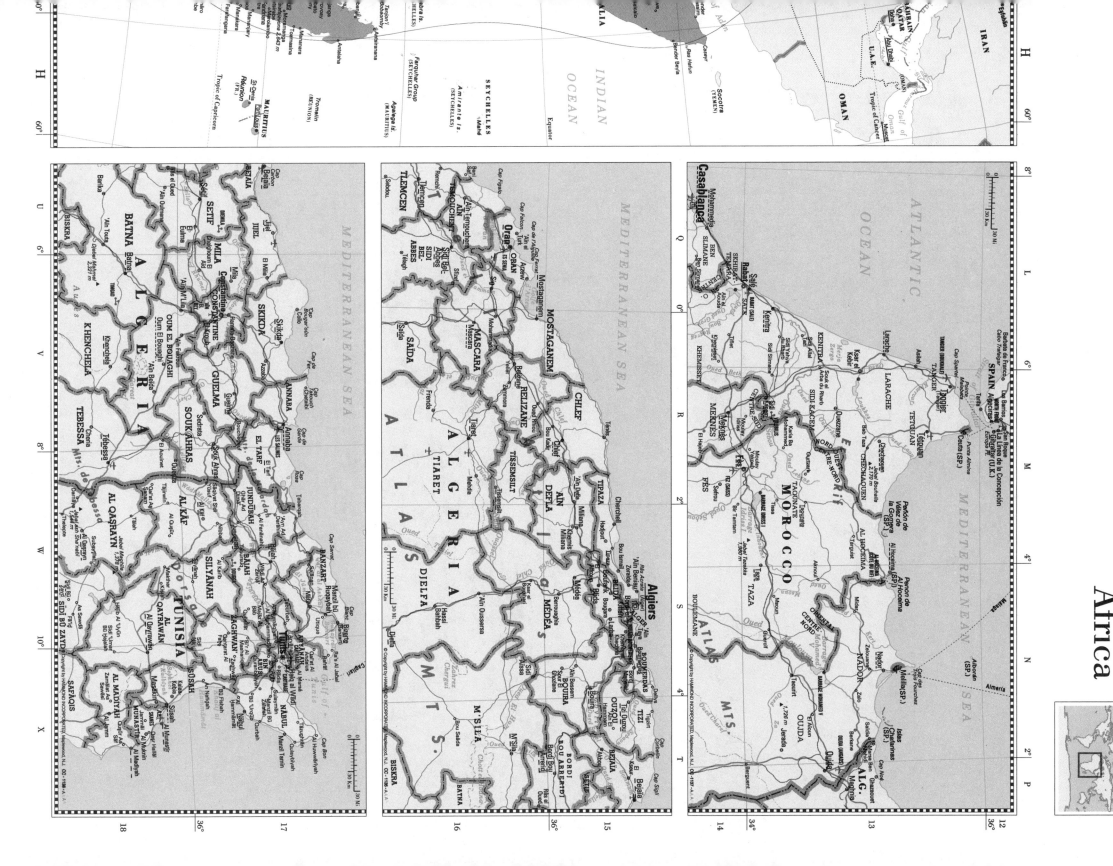

Africa

74/75

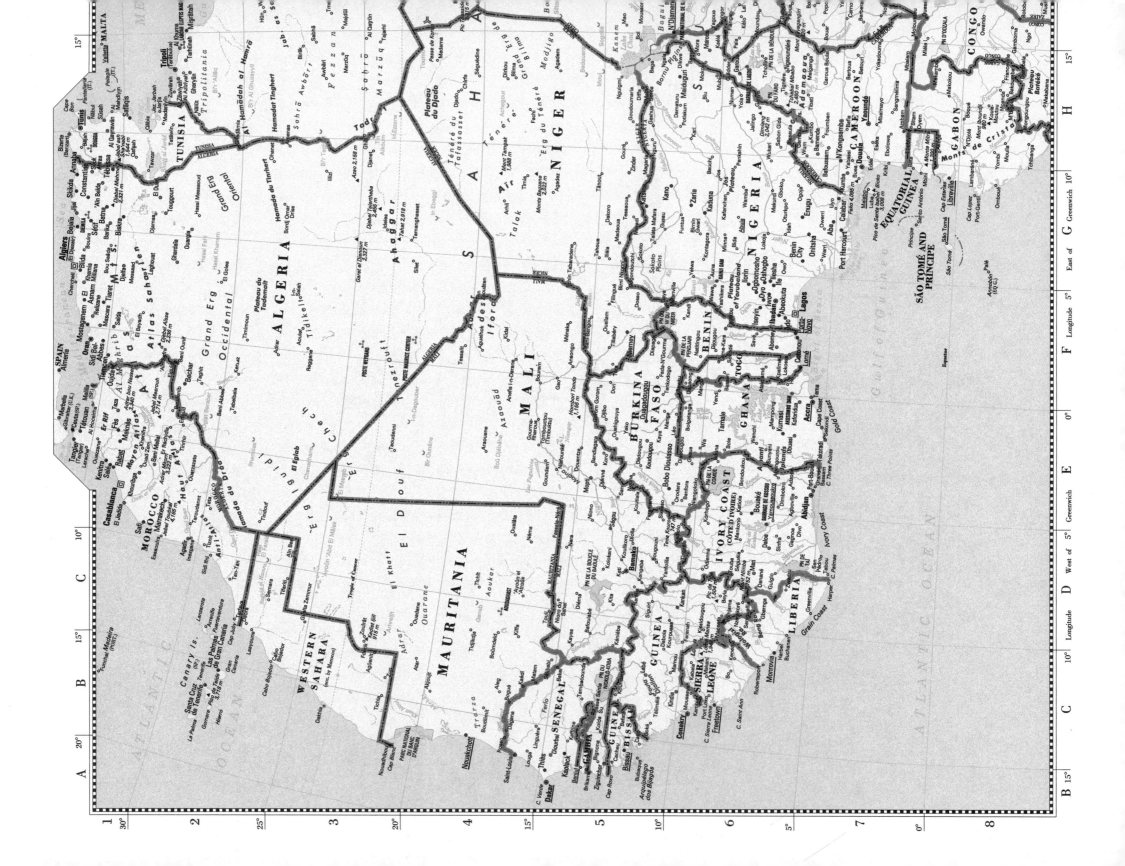

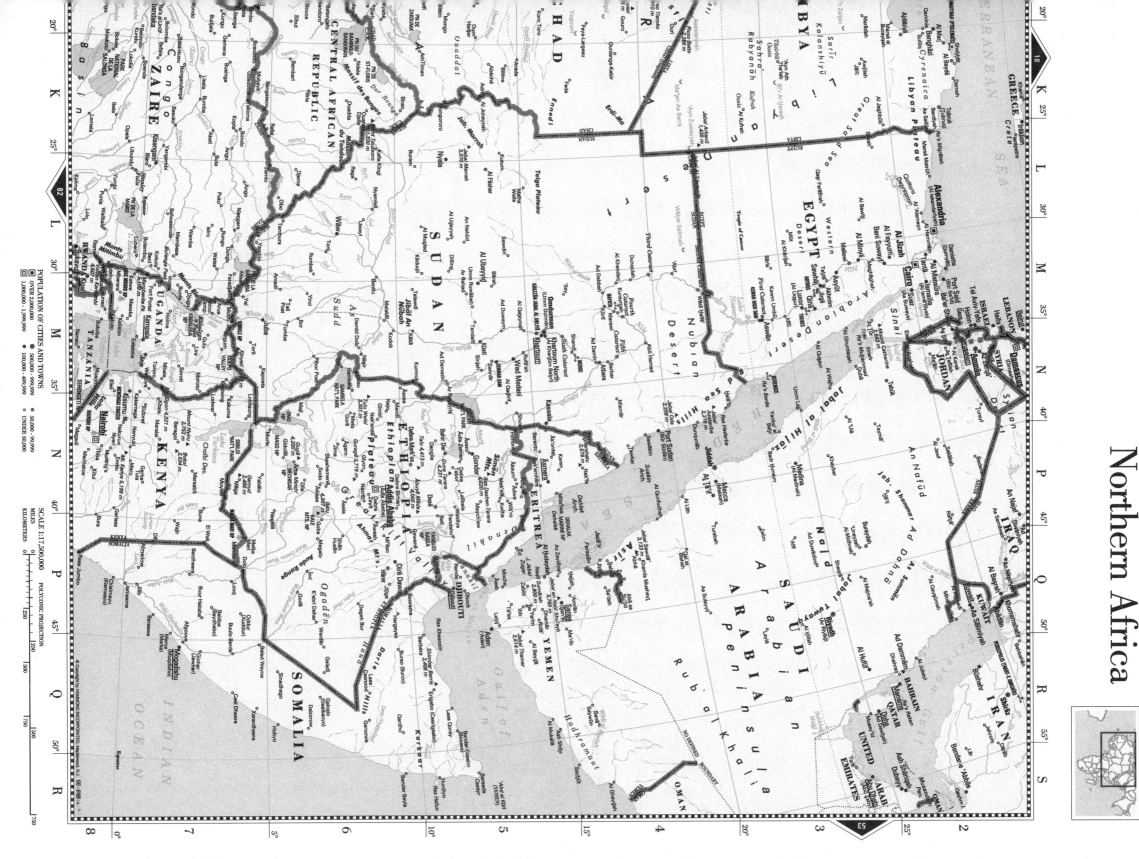

Northern Africa

76/77

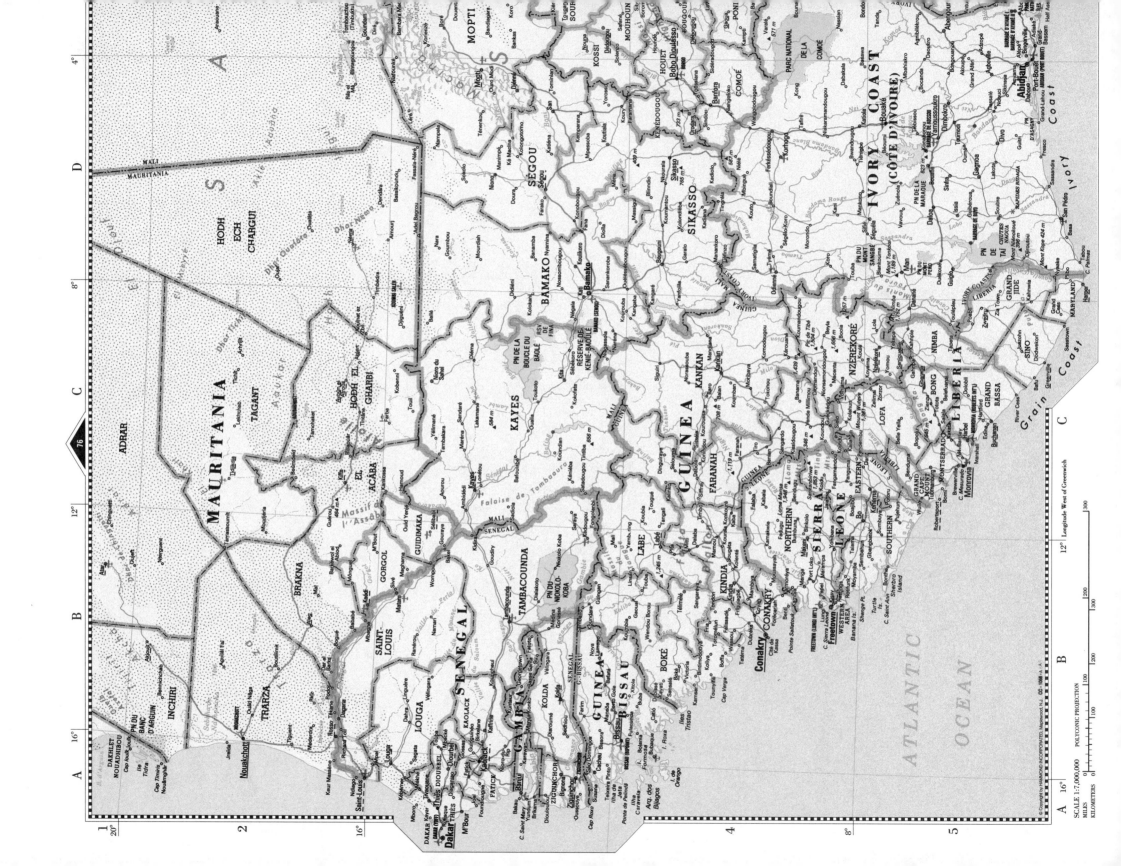

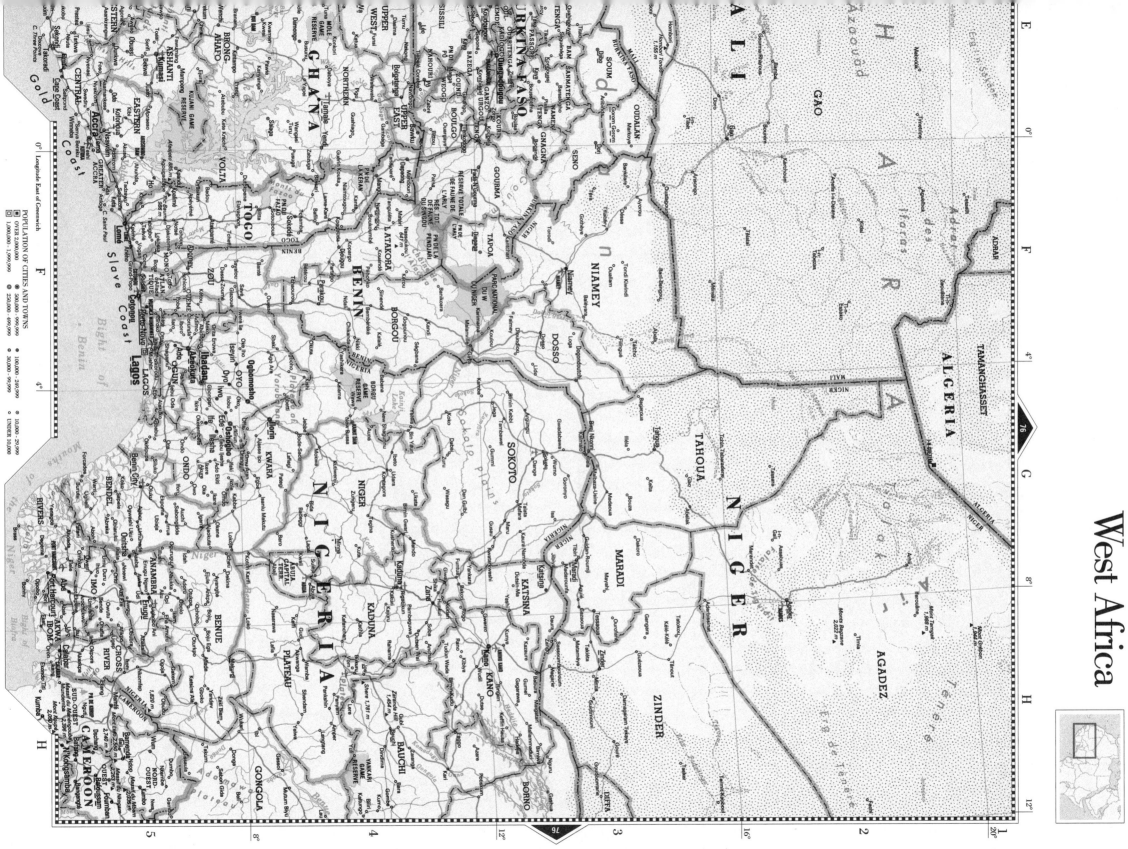

West Africa

78/79

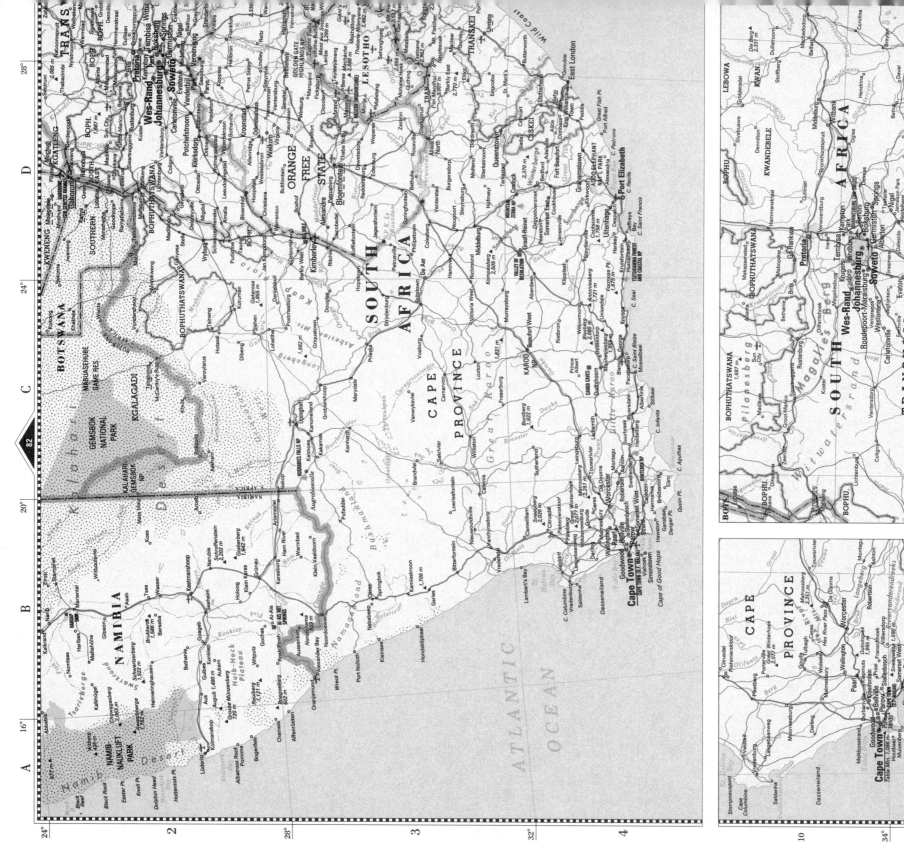

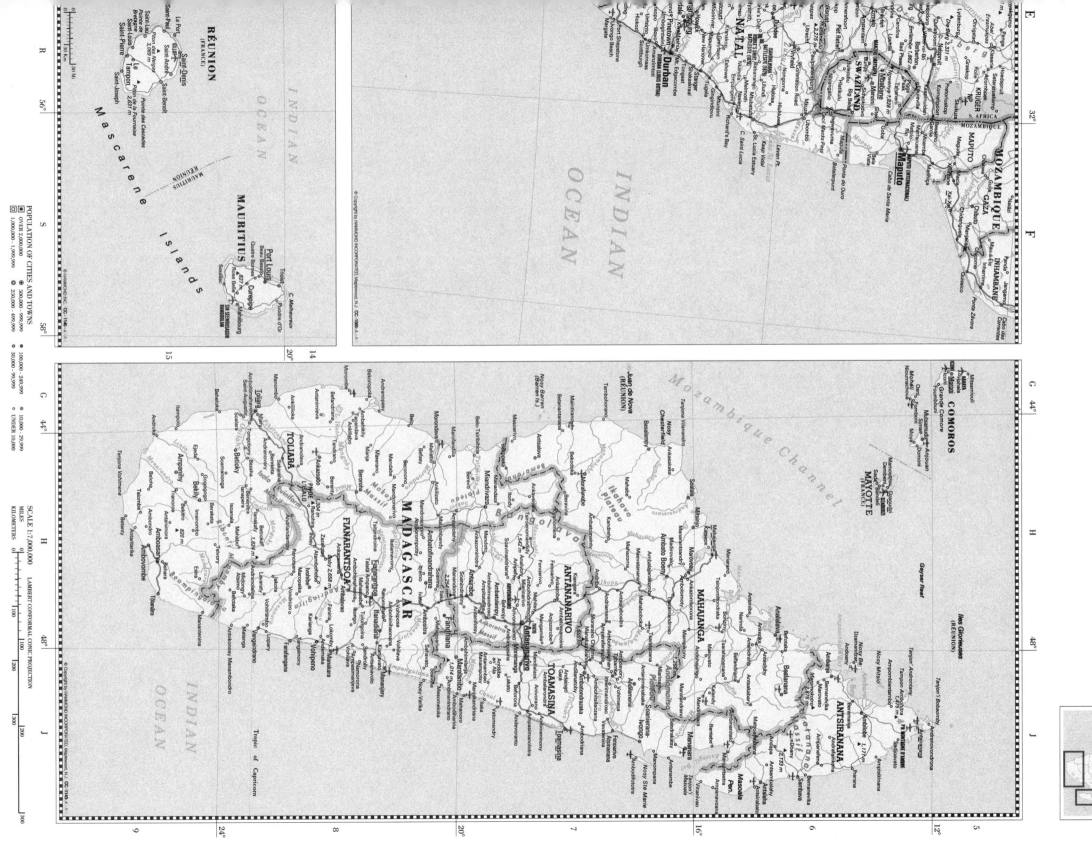

South Africa

80/81

POPULATION OF CITIES AND TOWNS

□ OVER 2,000,000
⊙ 1,000,000 – 1,999,999
● 500,000 – 999,999
⊙ 250,000 – 499,999
● 100,000 – 249,999
● 30,000 – 99,999
○ 10,000 – 29,999
○ UNDER 10,000

SCALE 1:7,000,000

MILES
KILOMETERS

LAMBERT CONFORMAL CONIC PROJECTION

RÉUNION
(FRANCE)

MAURITIUS

Mascarene Islands

INDIAN OCEAN

INDIAN OCEAN

MADAGASCAR

COMOROS

MOZAMBIQUE

Mozambique Channel

NATAL

SWAZILAND

Maputo

Durban

Southern Africa

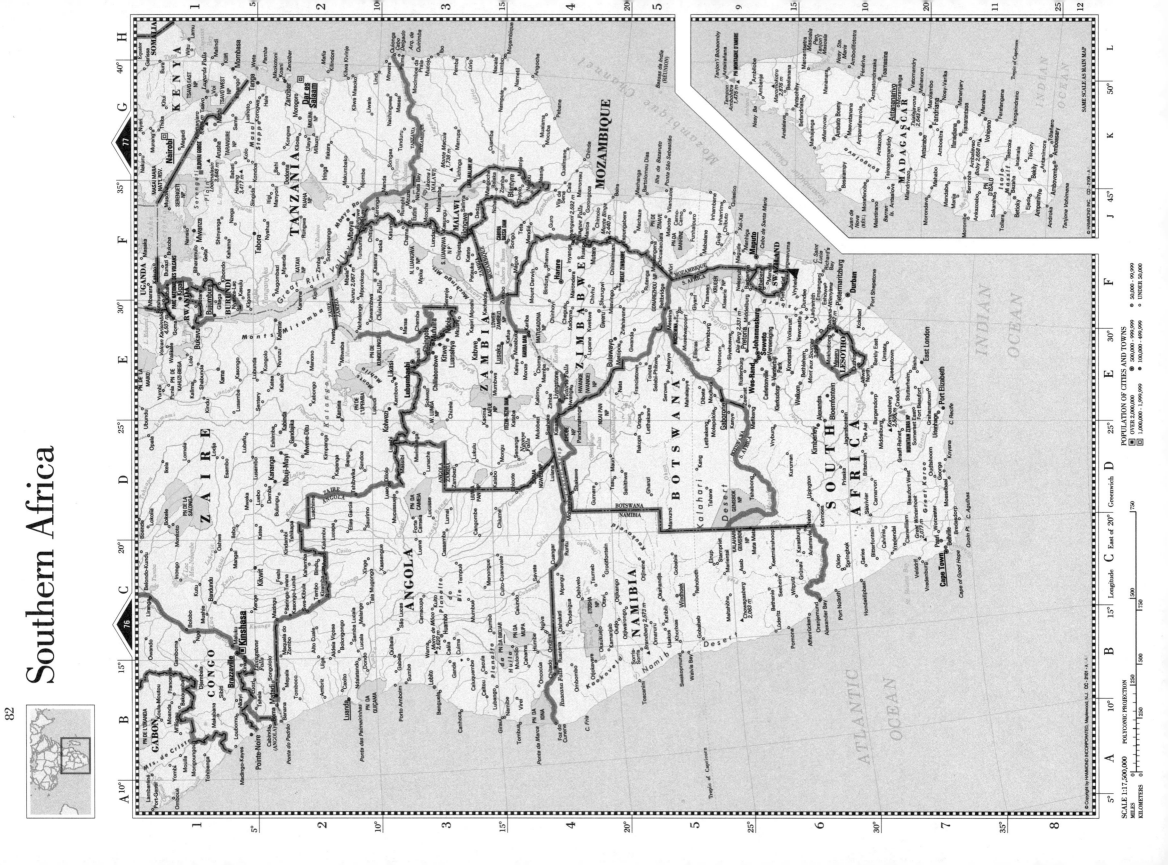

SCALE 1:17,500,000
POLYCONIC PROJECTION

POPULATION OF CITIES AND TOWNS
- ☐ OVER 2,000,000
- ● 1,000,000 - 1,999,999
- ● 500,000 - 999,999
- ● 100,000 - 499,999
- ● 50,000 - 99,999
- ● UNDER 50,000

SAME SCALE AS MAIN MAP

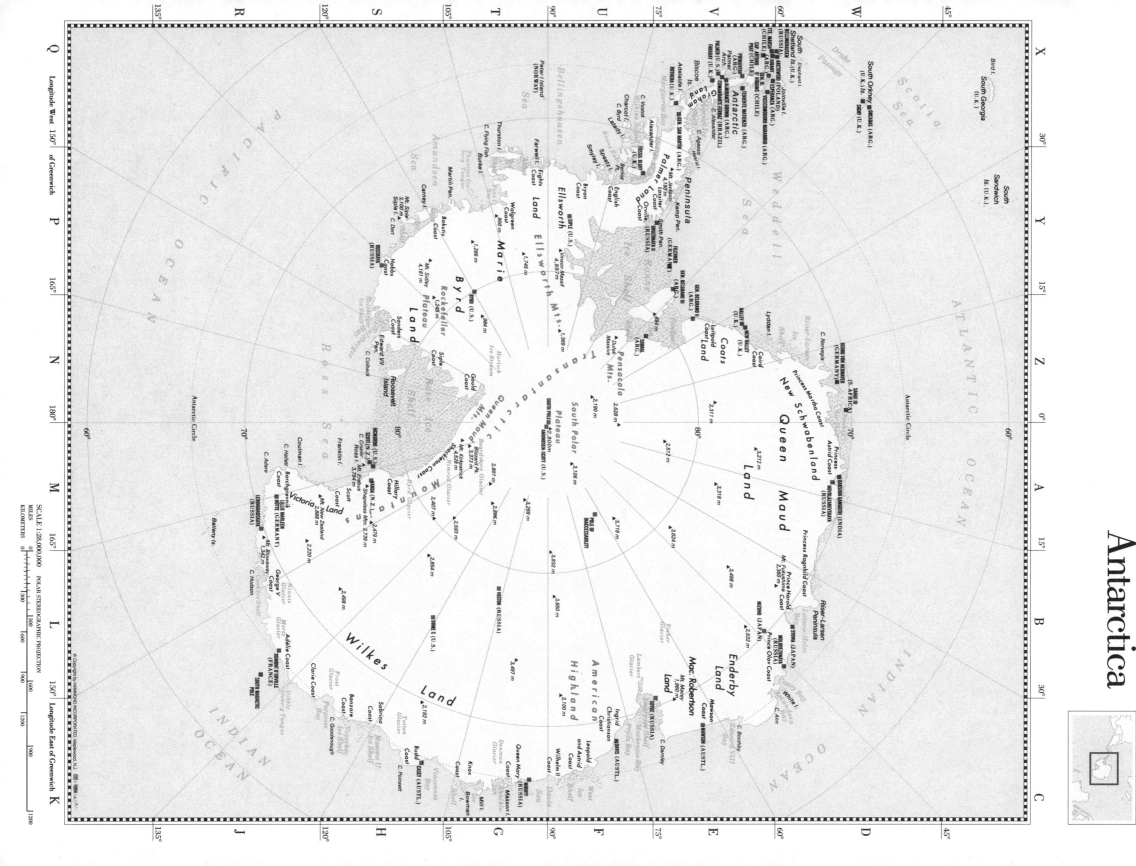

Antarctica

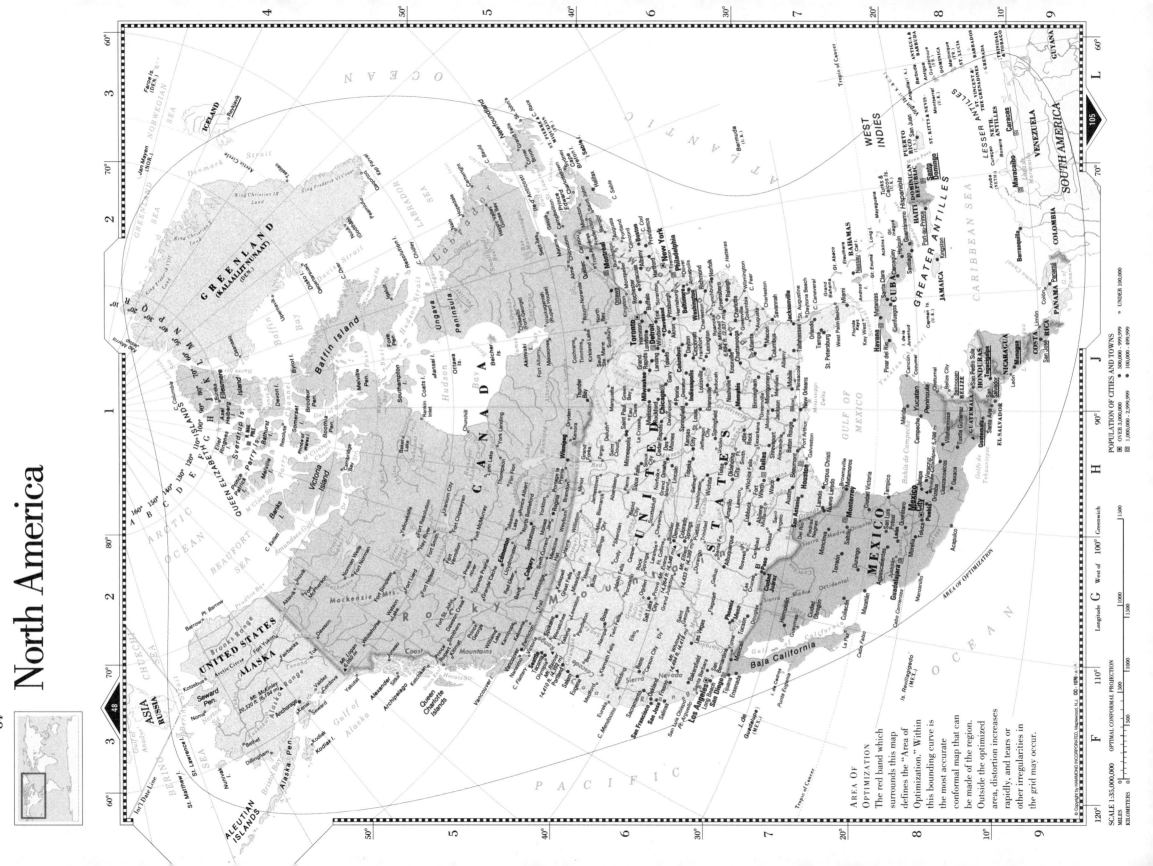

North America

AREA OF
OPTIMIZATION
The red band which
surrounds this map
defines the "Area of
Optimization." Within
this bounding curve is
the most accurate
conformal map that can
be made of the region.
Outside the optimized
area, distortion increases
rapidly, and tears or
other irregularities in
the grid may occur.

POPULATION OF CITIES AND TOWNS

☐ OVER 3,000,000   ● 500,000 - 999,999   ○ UNDER 100,000
☐ 1,000,000 - 2,999,999   ● 100,000 - 499,999

SCALE 1:35,000,000   OPTIMAL CONFORMAL PROJECTION
Longitude G West of 100° Greenwich
MILES
KILOMETERS

© Copyright by HAMMOND INCORPORATED, Maplewood, N.J.

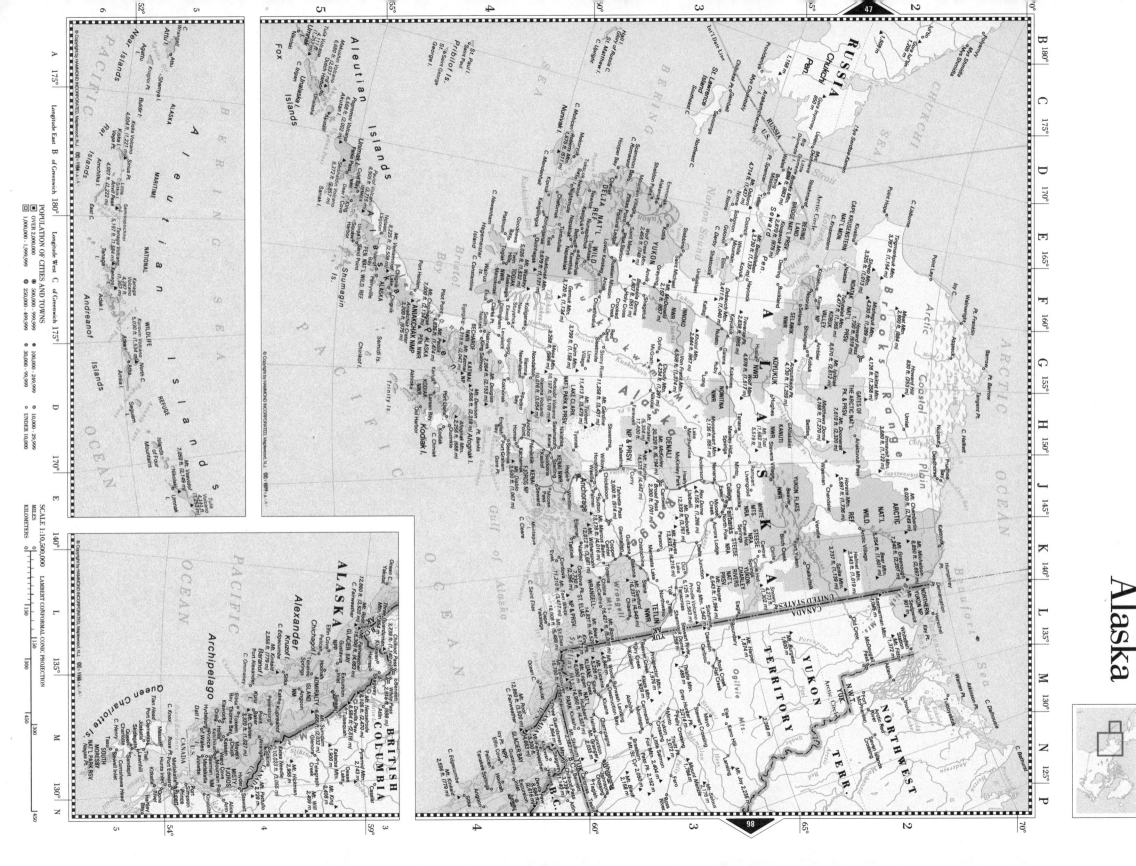

Alaska

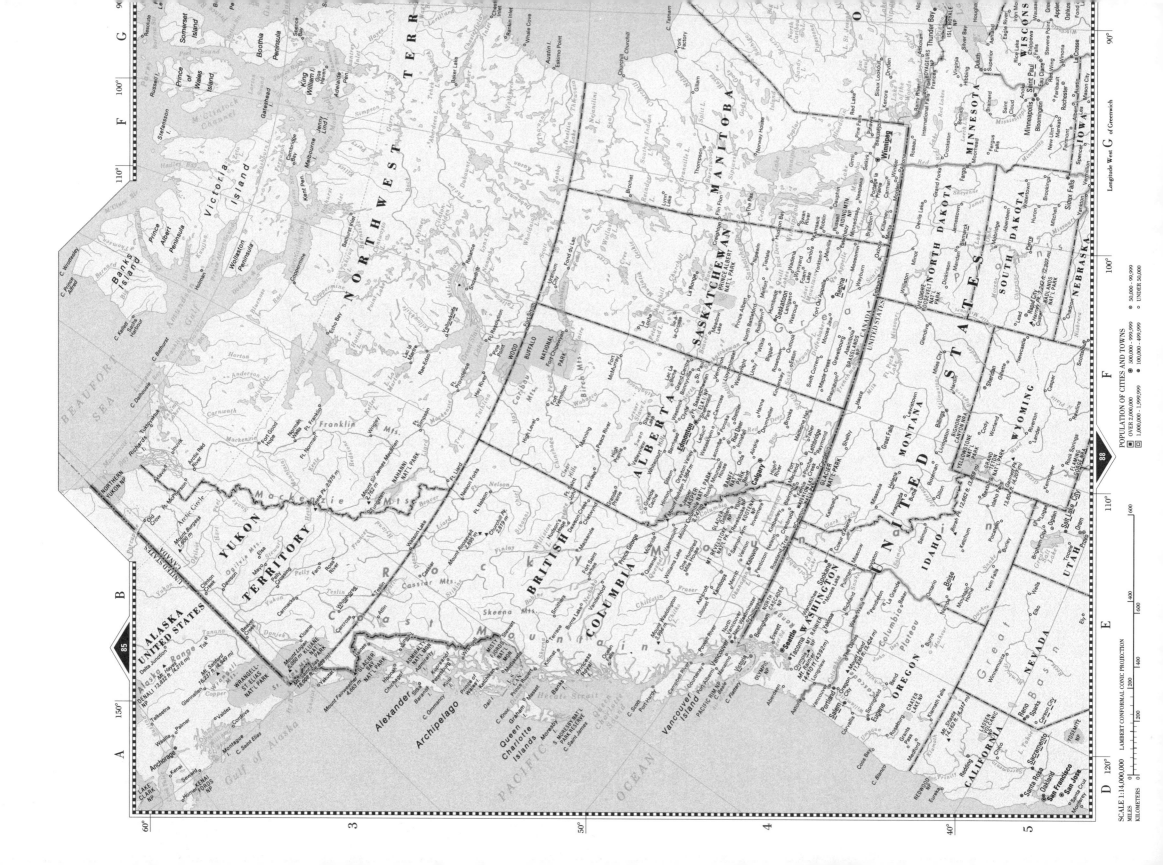

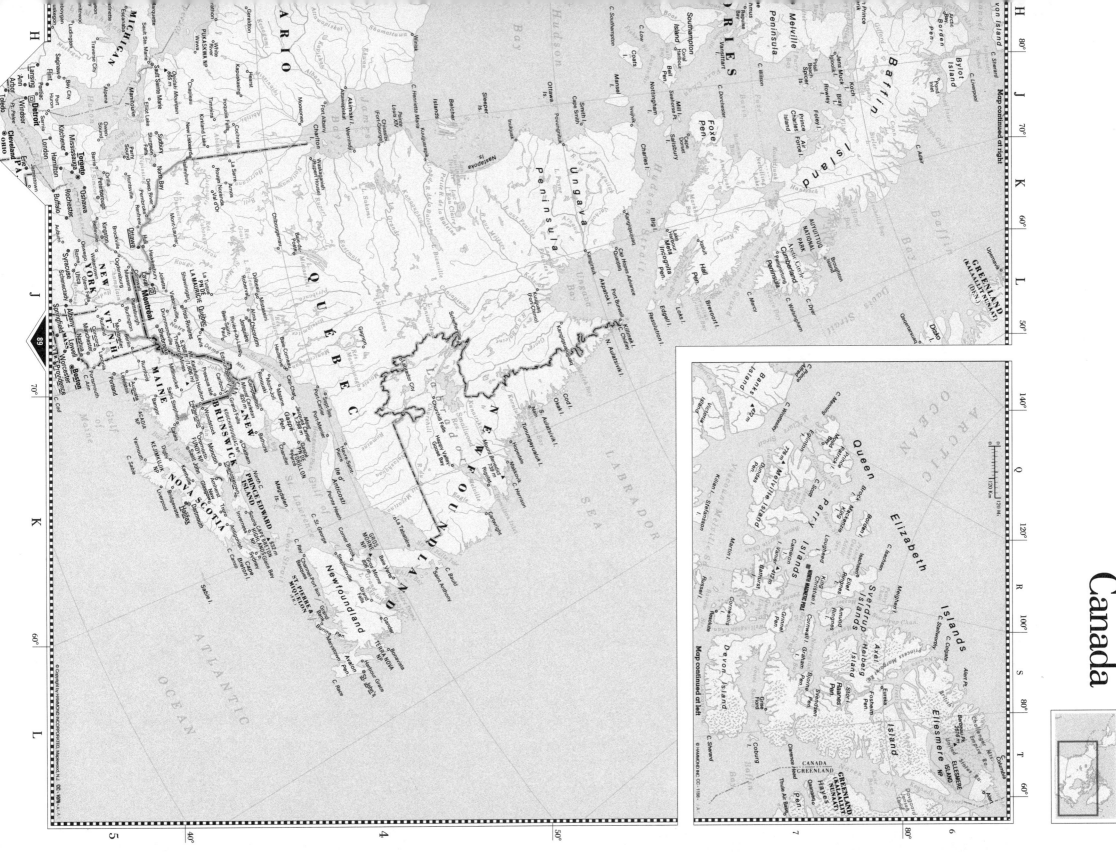

Canada

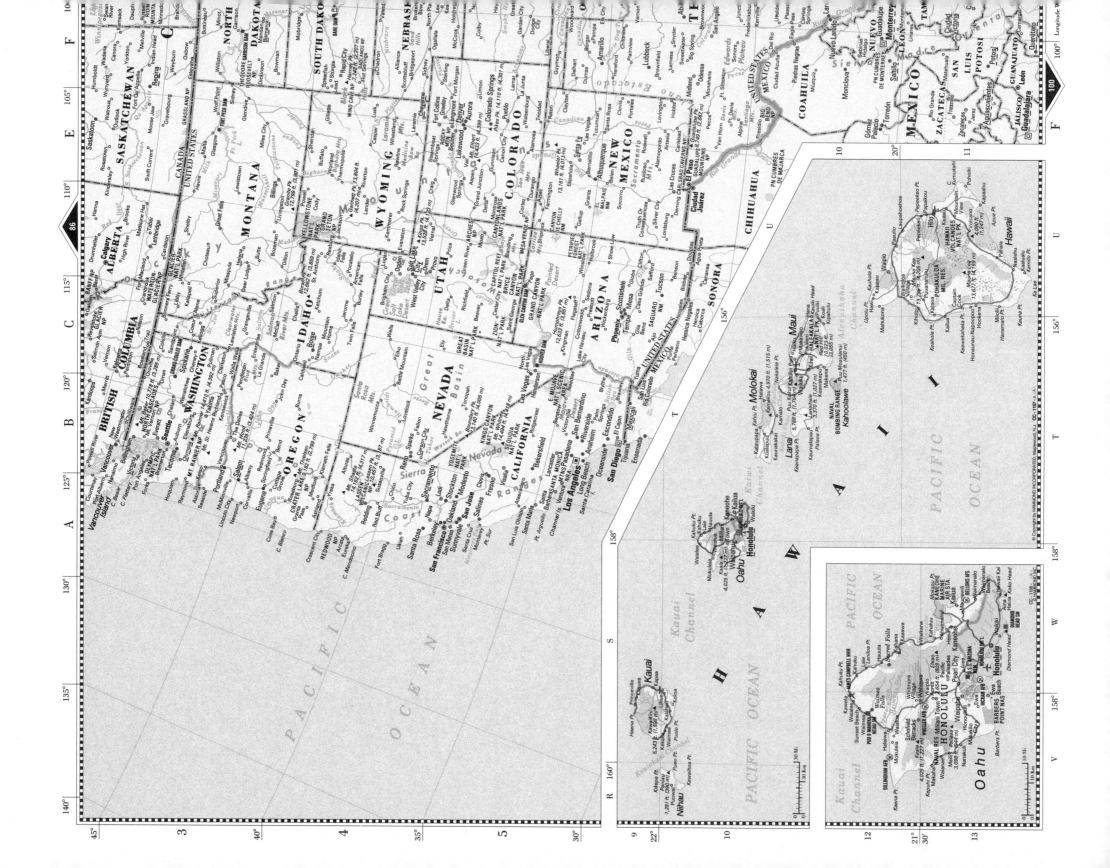

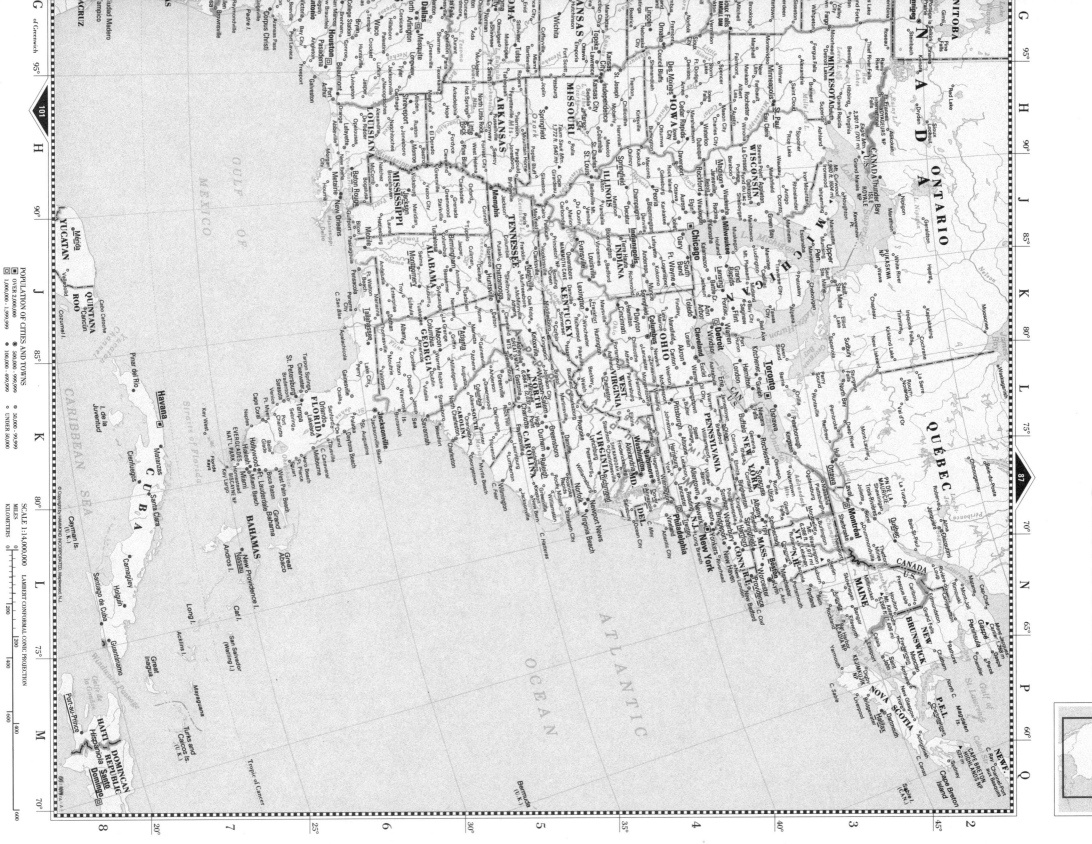

United States

SCALE 1:14,000,000

LAMBERT CONFORMAL CONIC PROJECTION

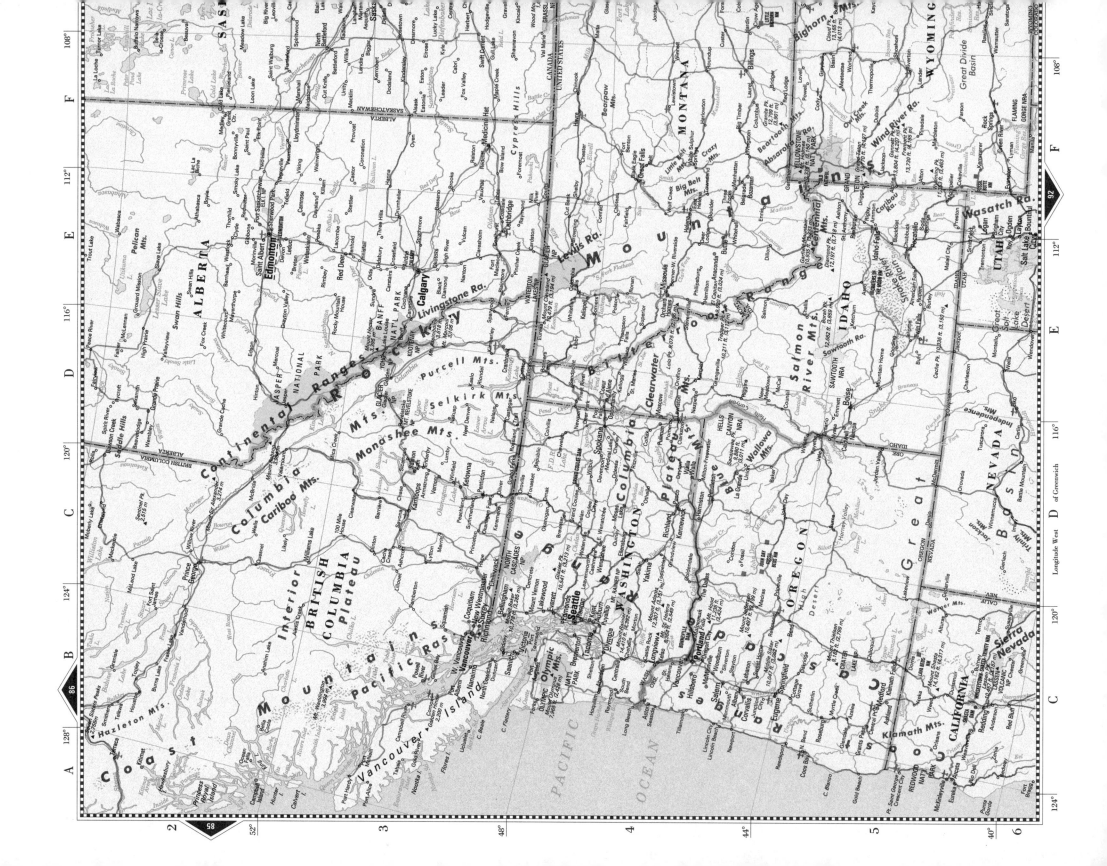

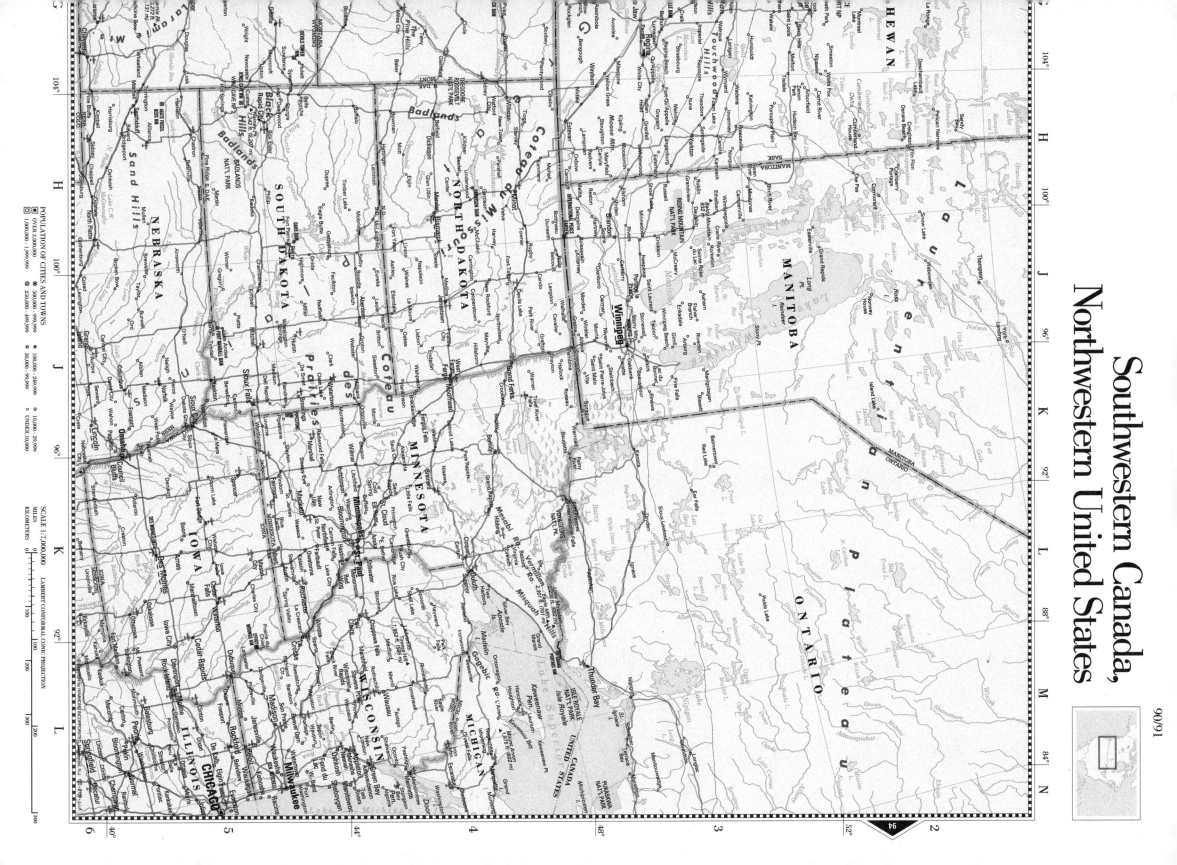

Southwestern Canada, Northwestern United States

90/91

POPULATION OF CITIES AND TOWNS
- OVER 2,000,000
- 1,000,000 - 1,999,999
- 500,000 - 999,999
- 250,000 - 499,999
- 100,000 - 249,999
- 30,000 - 99,999
- 10,000 - 29,999
- UNDER 10,000

SCALE 1:7,000,000
MILES
KILOMETERS
LAMBERT CONFORMAL CONIC PROJECTION

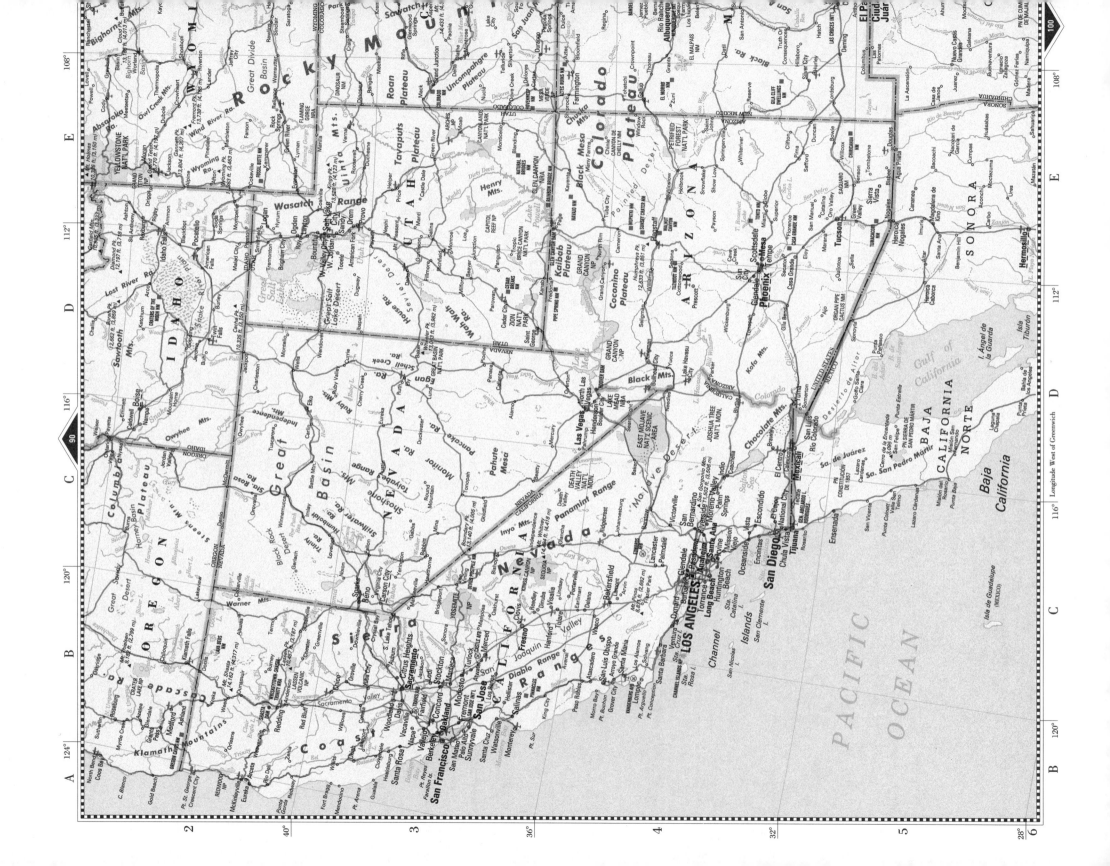

Southwestern United States

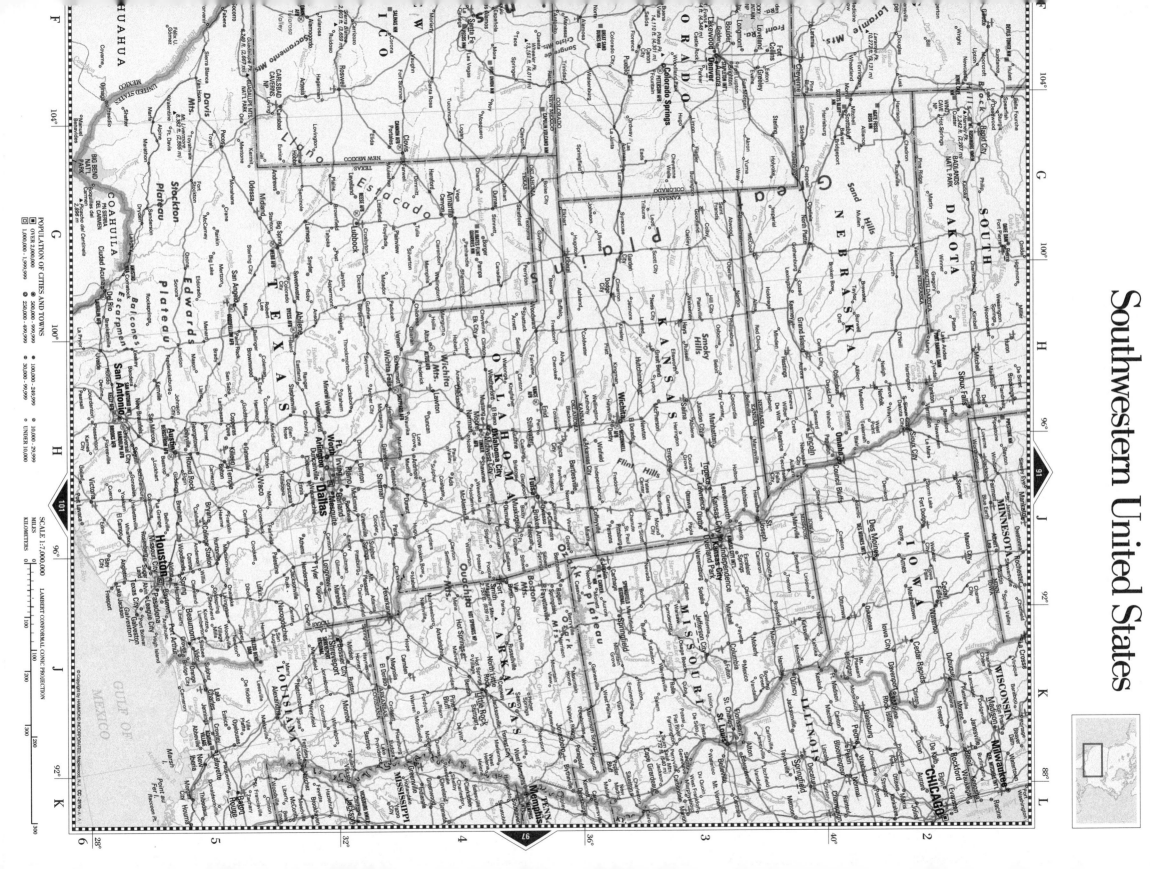

92/93

SCALE 1:7,000,000

LAMBERT CONFORMAL CONIC PROJECTION

POPULATION OF CITIES AND TOWNS

Southeastern Canada, Northeastern United States

94/95

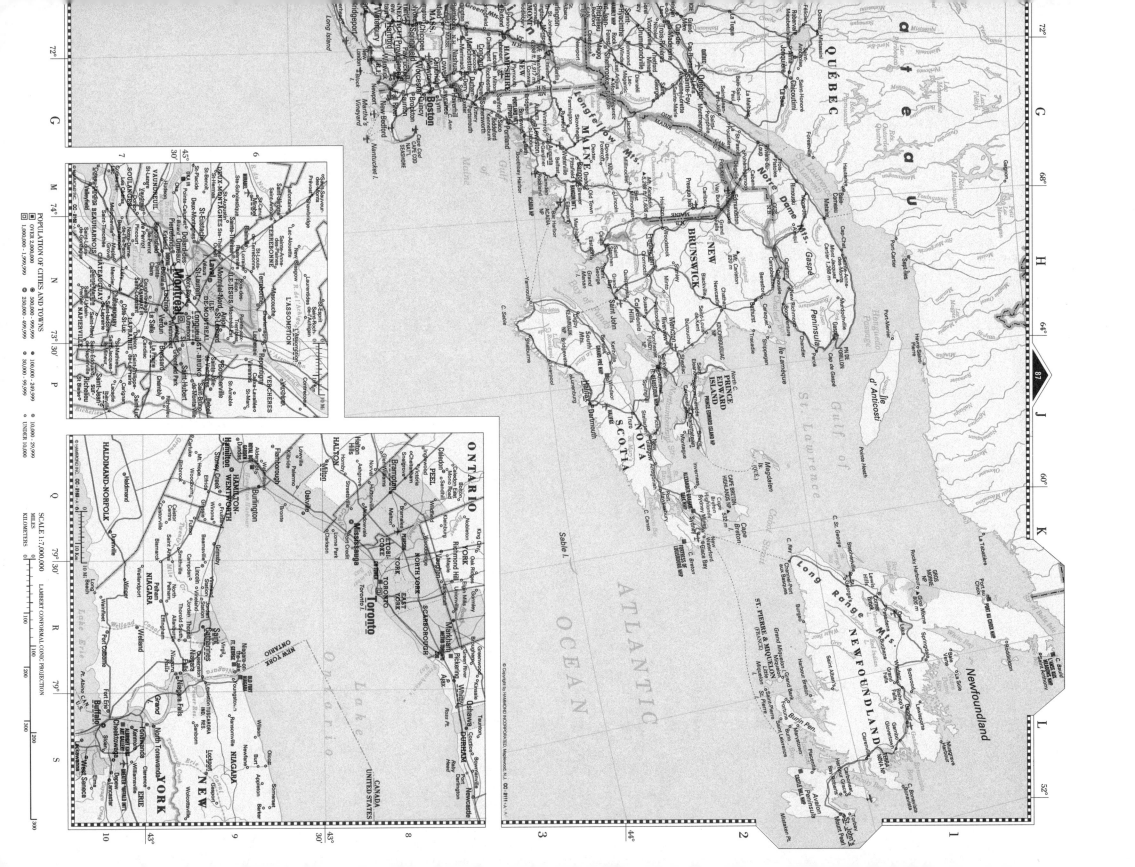

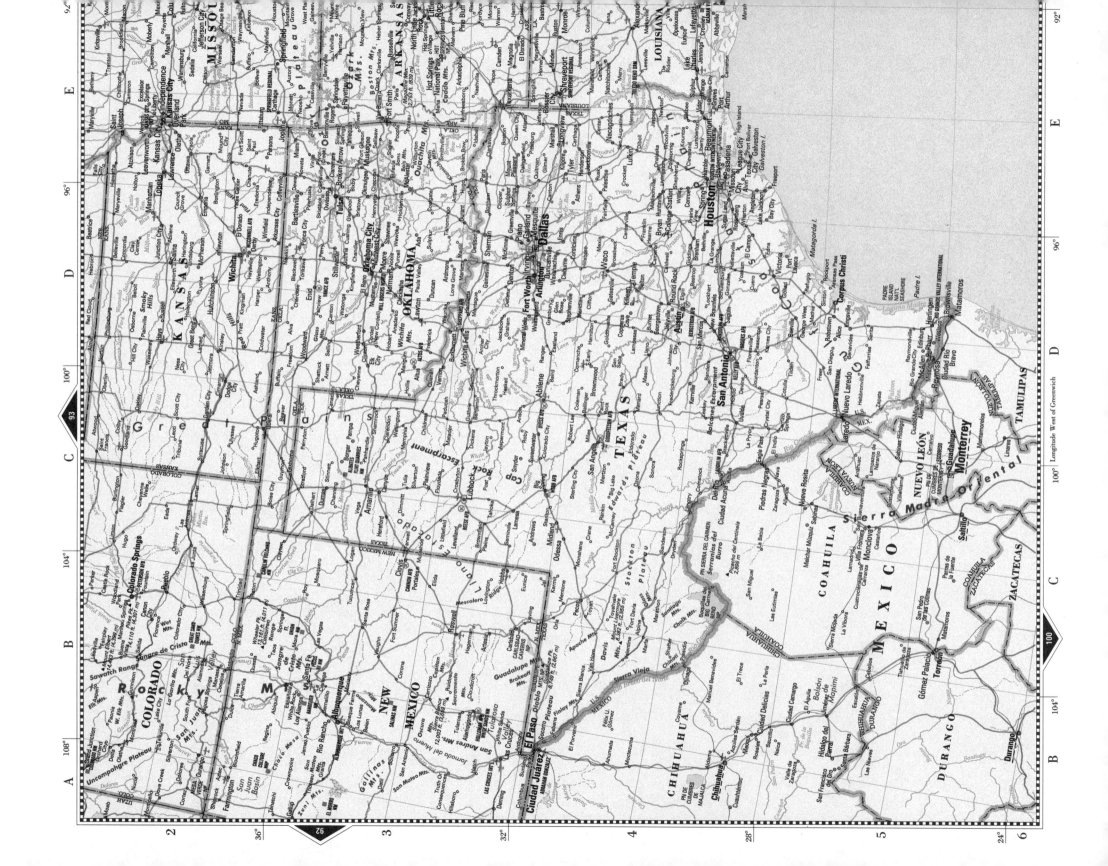

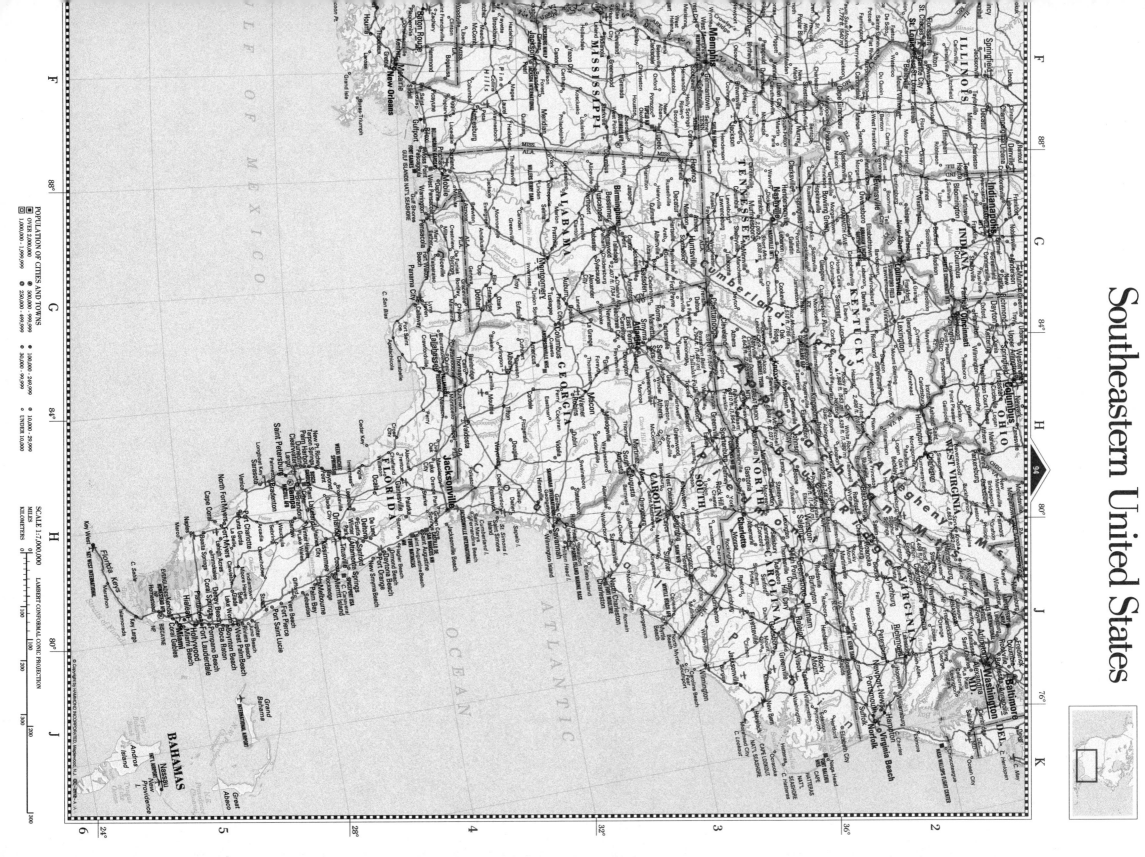

Southeastern United States

96/97

POPULATION OF CITIES AND TOWNS
■ OVER 2,000,000
● 1,000,000 - 1,999,999
● 500,000 - 999,999
● 250,000 - 499,999
● 100,000 - 249,999
● 50,000 - 99,999
● 30,000 - 99,999
• 10,000 - 29,999
• UNDER 10,000

SCALE 1:7,000,000
MILES
KILOMETERS

LAMBERT CONFORMAL CONIC PROJECTION

Los Angeles, New York, Philadelphia, Washington

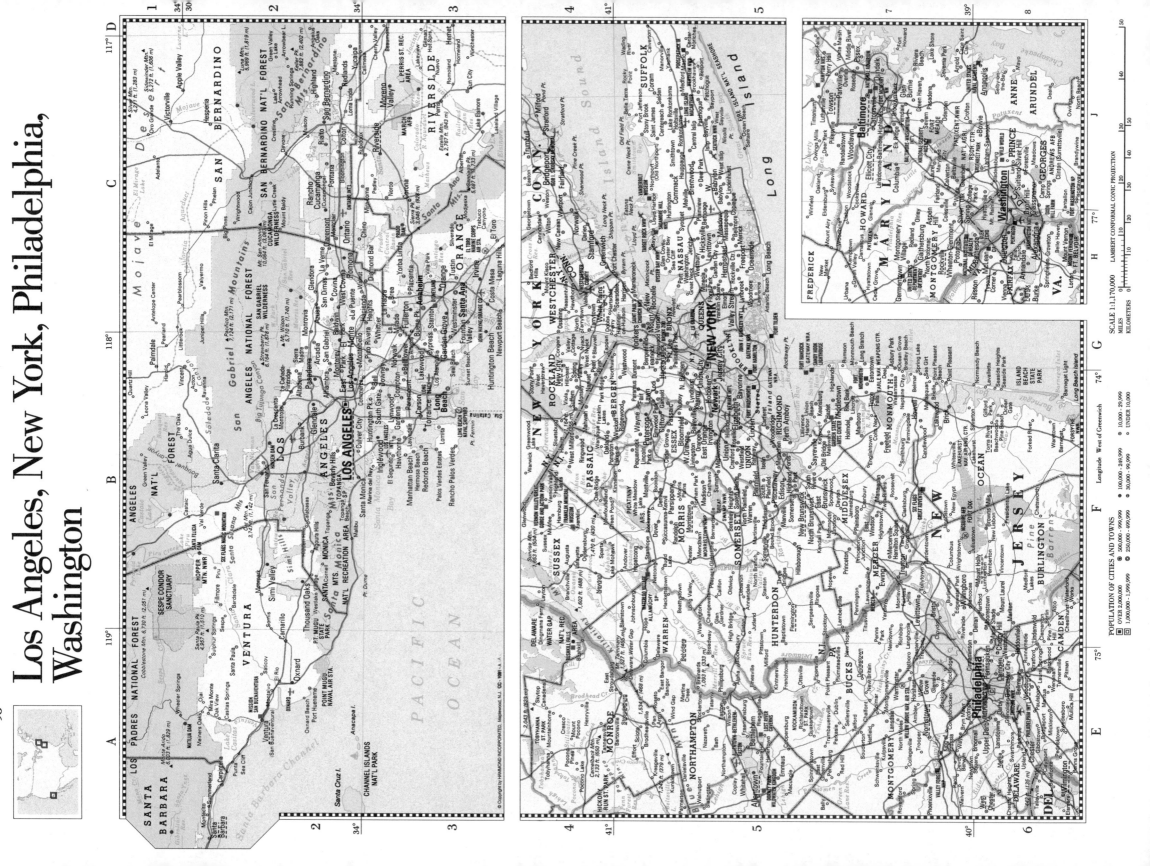

Seattle, San Francisco, Detroit, Chicago

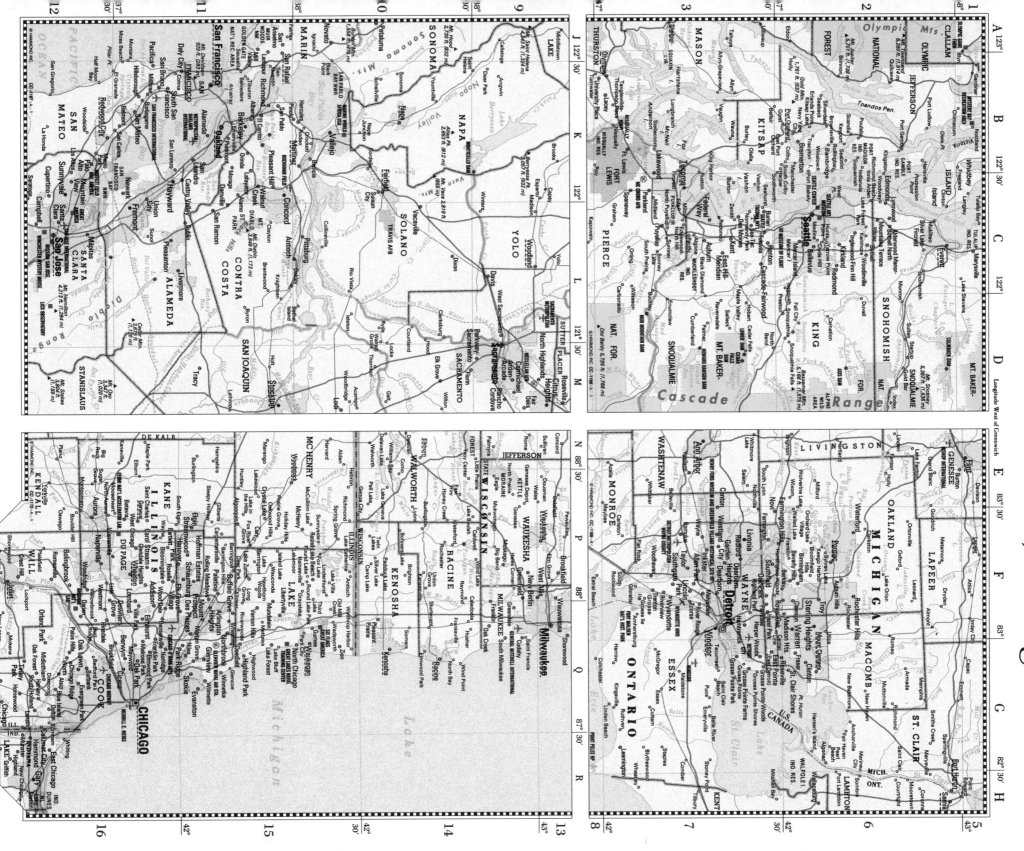

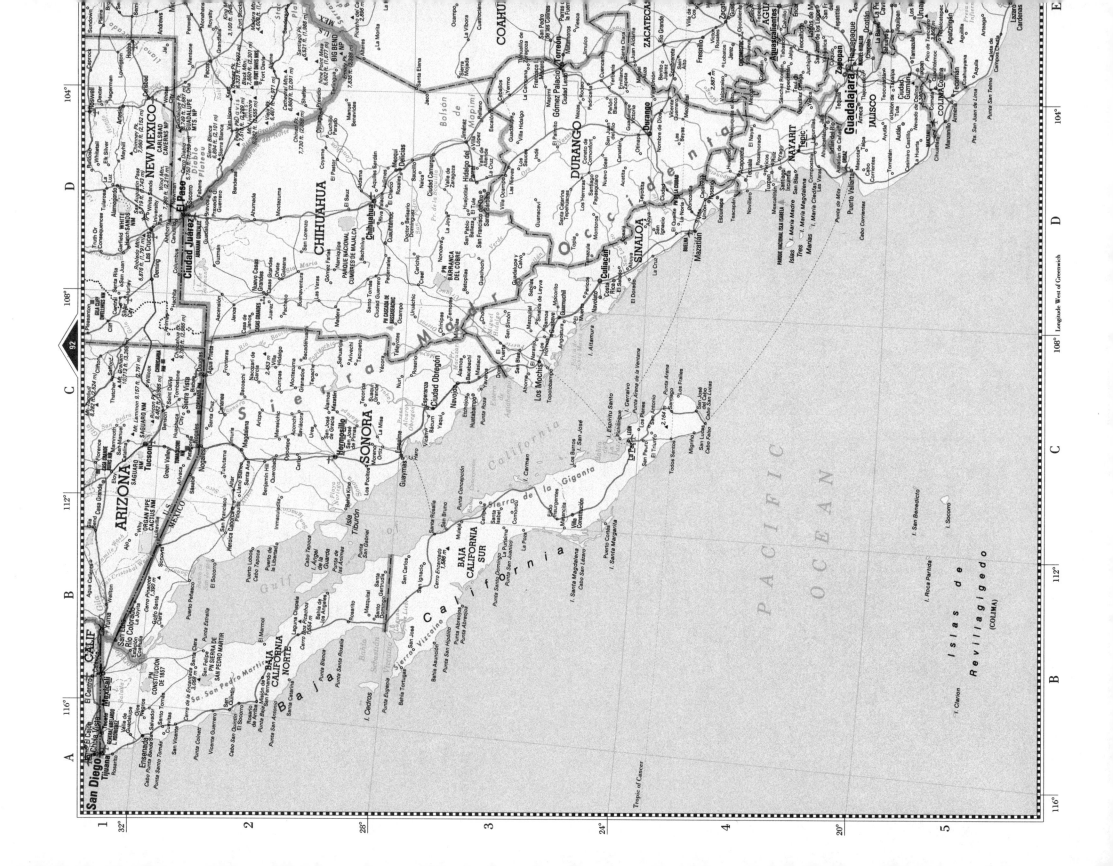

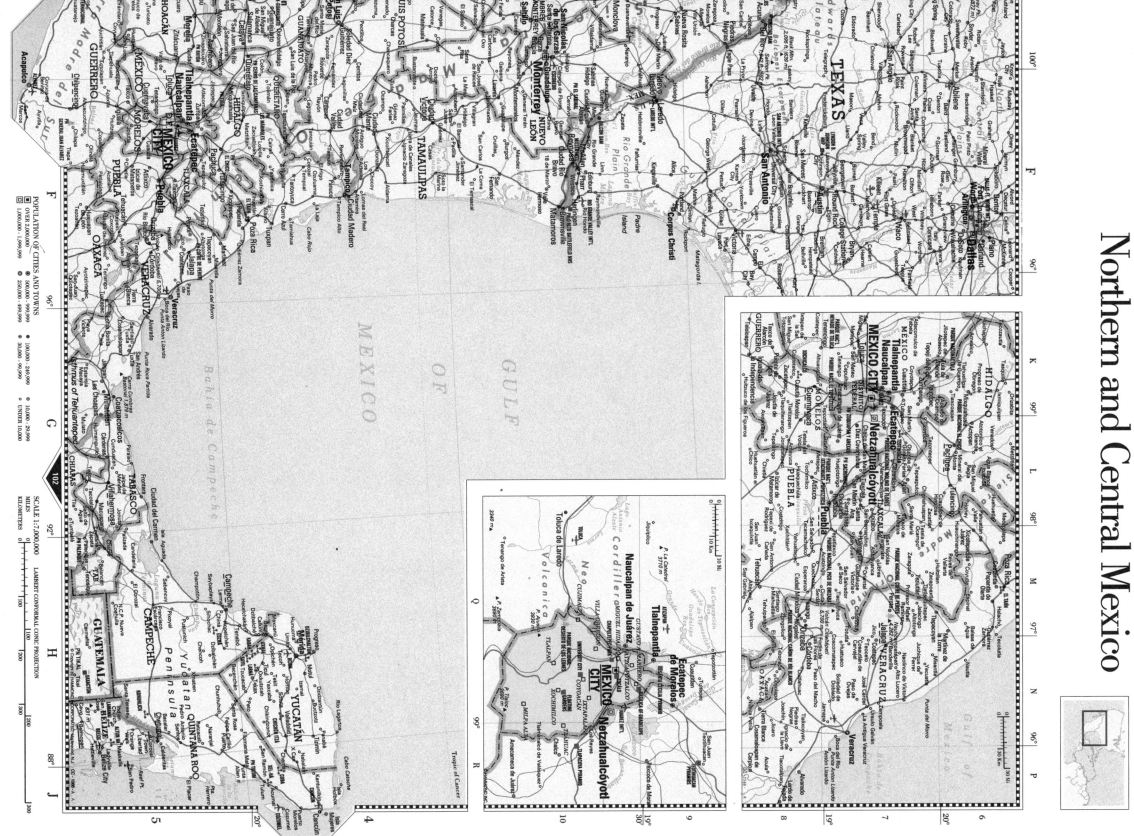

Northern and Central Mexico

POPULATION OF CITIES AND TOWNS

- ■ OVER 2,000,000
- ■ 1,000,000 - 1,999,999
- ■ 500,000 - 999,999
- ■ 250,000 - 499,999
- ● 100,000 - 249,999
- ● 30,000 - 99,999
- ○ 10,000 - 29,999
- ○ UNDER 10,000

SCALE 1:7,000,000

MILES
KILOMETERS

LAMBERT CONFORMAL CONIC PROJECTION

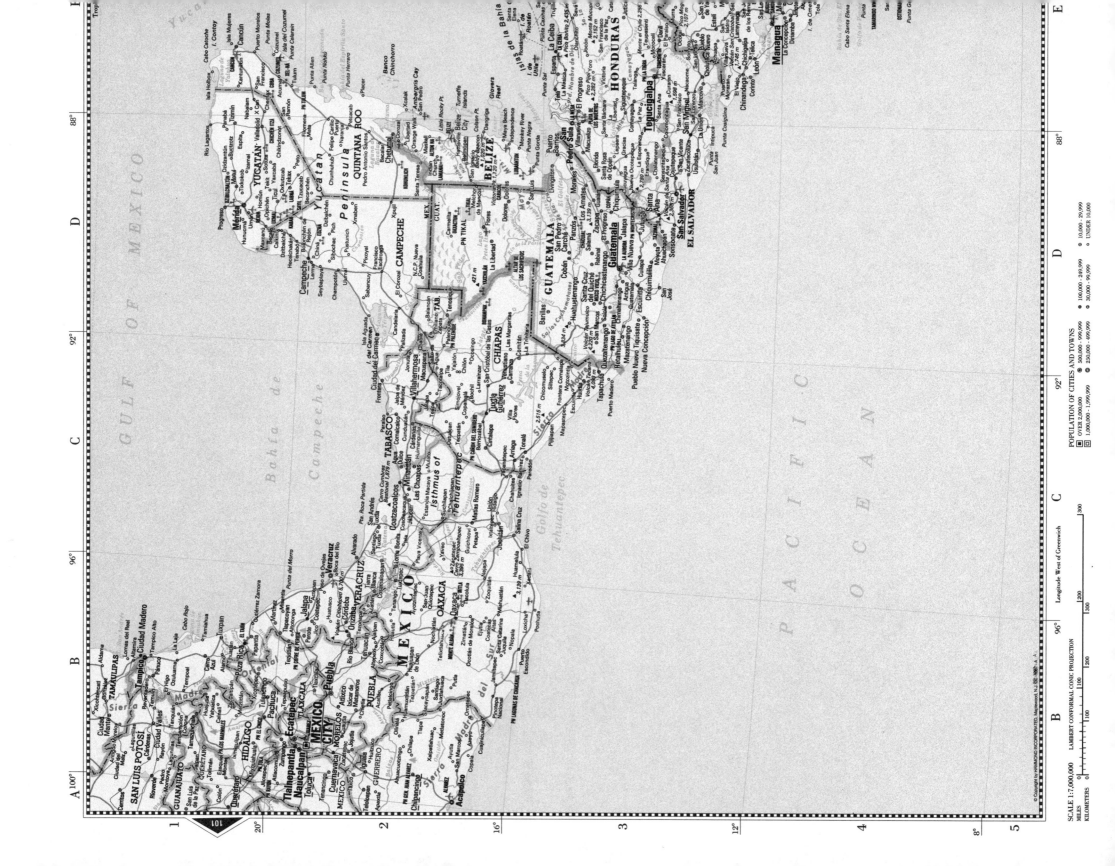

SCALE 1:7,000,000   LAMBERT CONFORMAL CONIC PROJECTION

POPULATION OF CITIES AND TOWNS

■ OVER 2,000,000   ● 500,000 - 999,999   ⊙ 100,000 - 249,999   ⊙ 10,000 - 29,999
▣ 1,000,000 - 1,999,999   ◉ 250,000 - 499,999   ⊙ 30,000 - 99,999   ○ UNDER 10,000

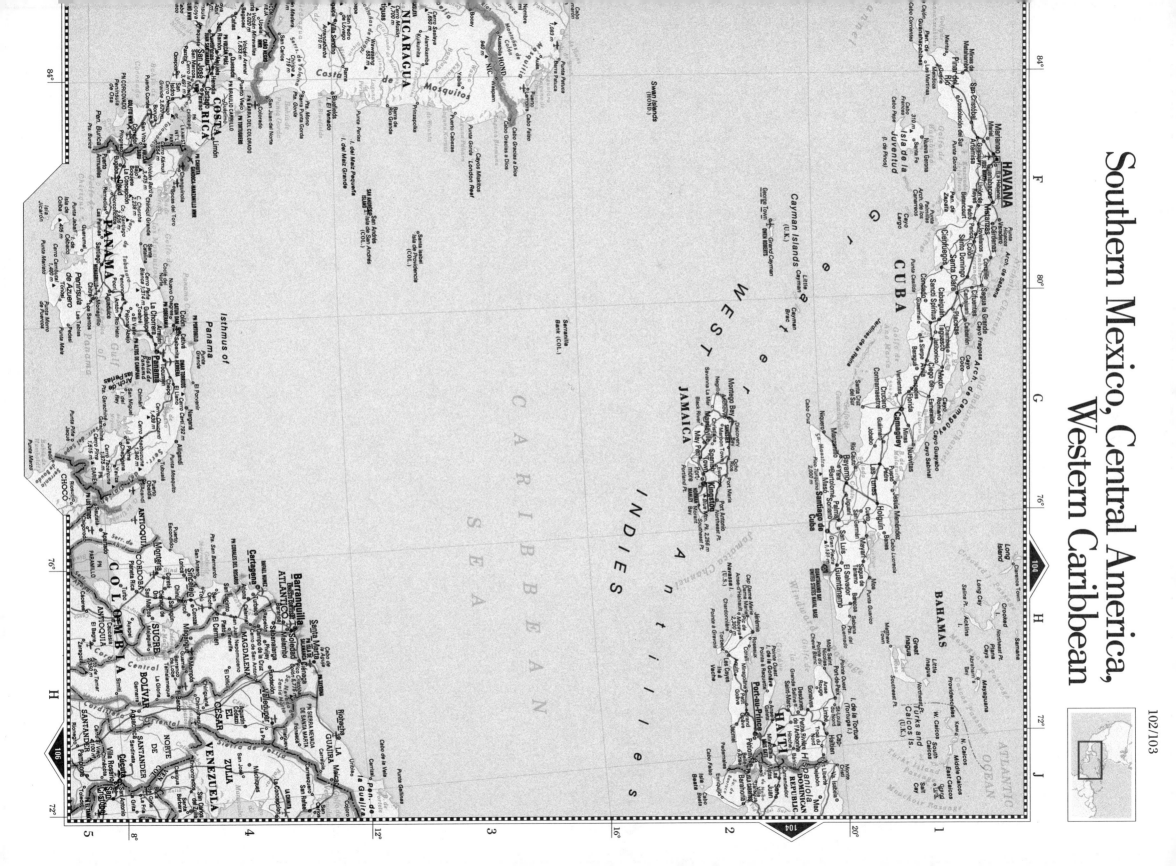

Eastern Caribbean, Bahamas

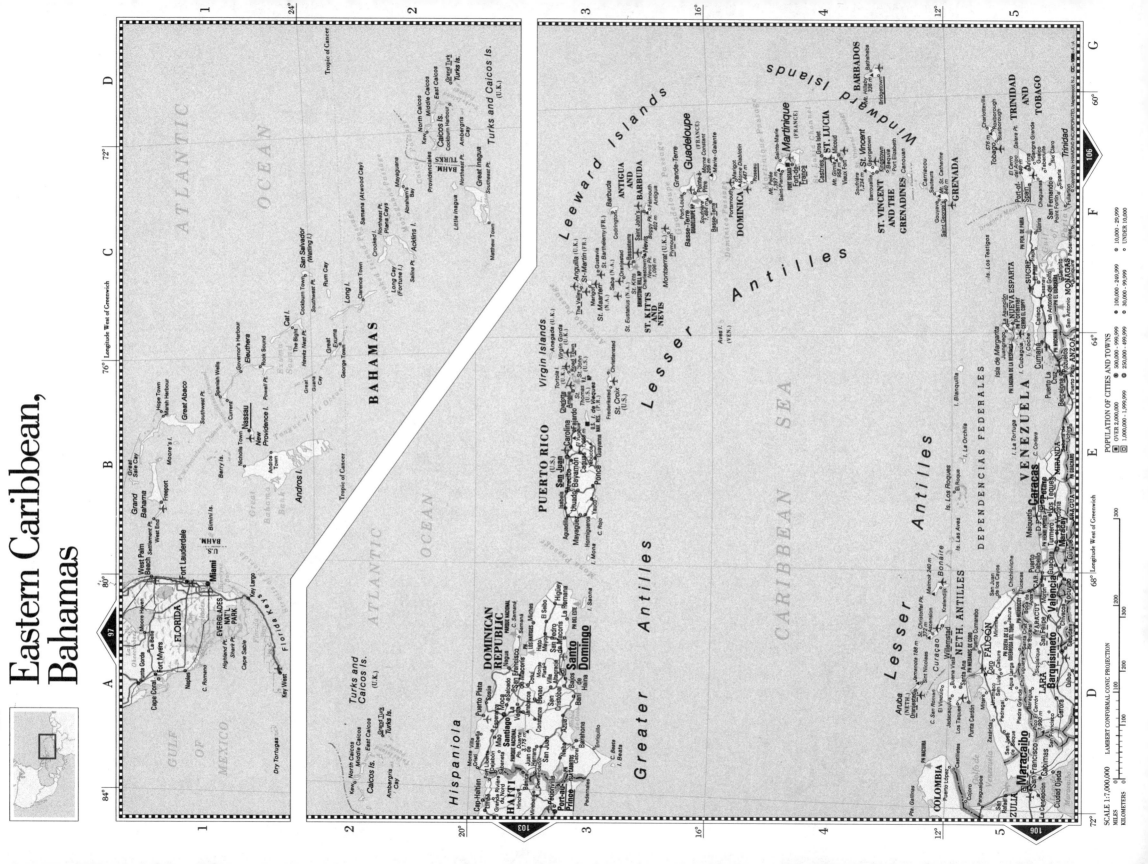

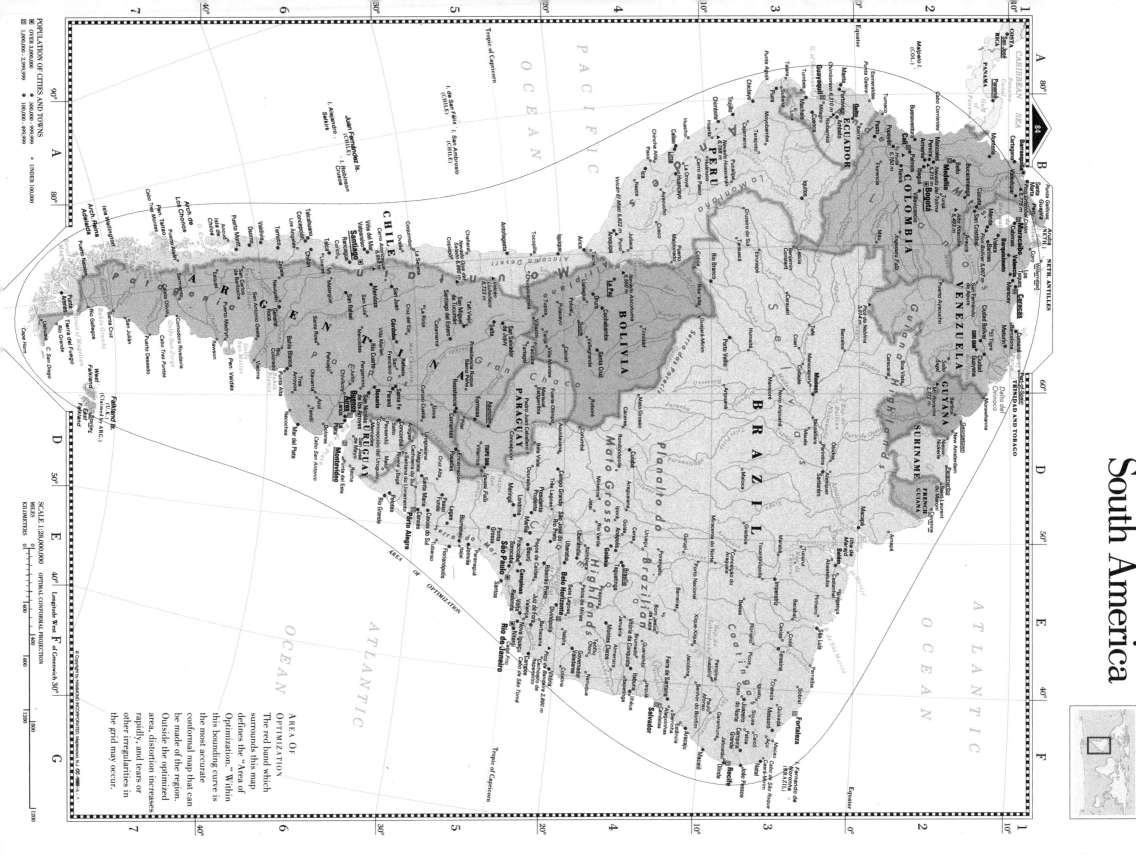

South America

105

SCALE 1:28,000,000
OPTIMAL CONFORMAL PROJECTION

MILES
KILOMETERS

Longitude West of Greenwich 30°

© Copyright by HAMMOND INCORPORATED, Maplewood, N.J.

AREA OF OPTIMIZATION

AREA OF OPTIMIZATION
The red band which surrounds this map defines the "Area of Optimization." Within this bounding curve is the most accurate conformal map that can be made of the region. Outside the optimized area, distortion increases rapidly, and tears or other irregularities in the grid may occur.

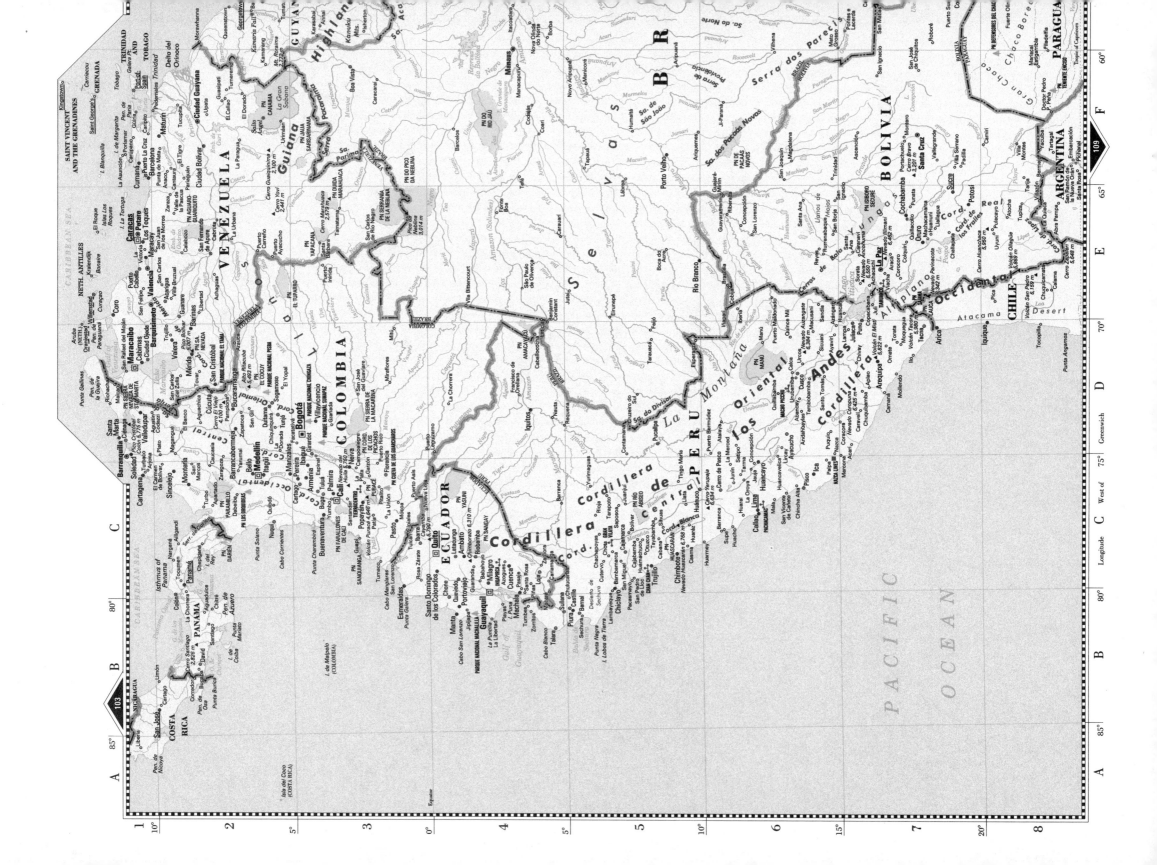

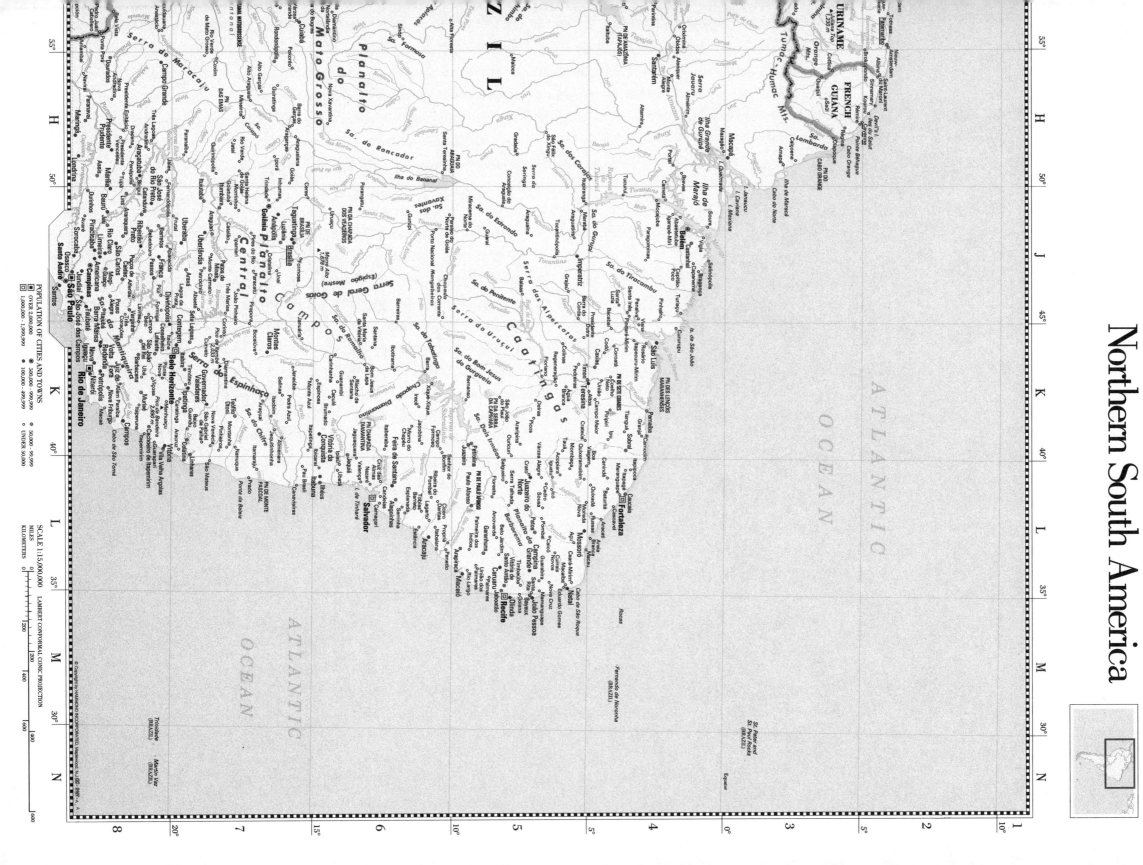

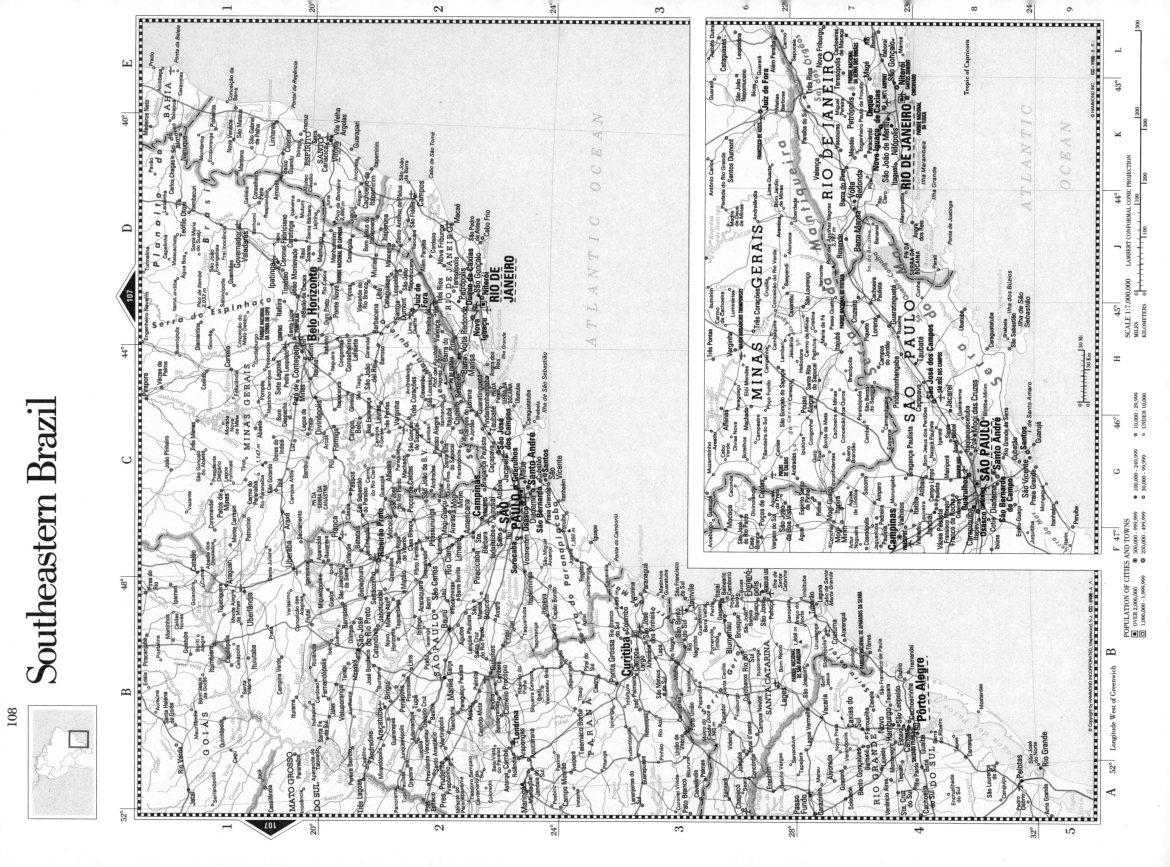

Southeastern Brazil

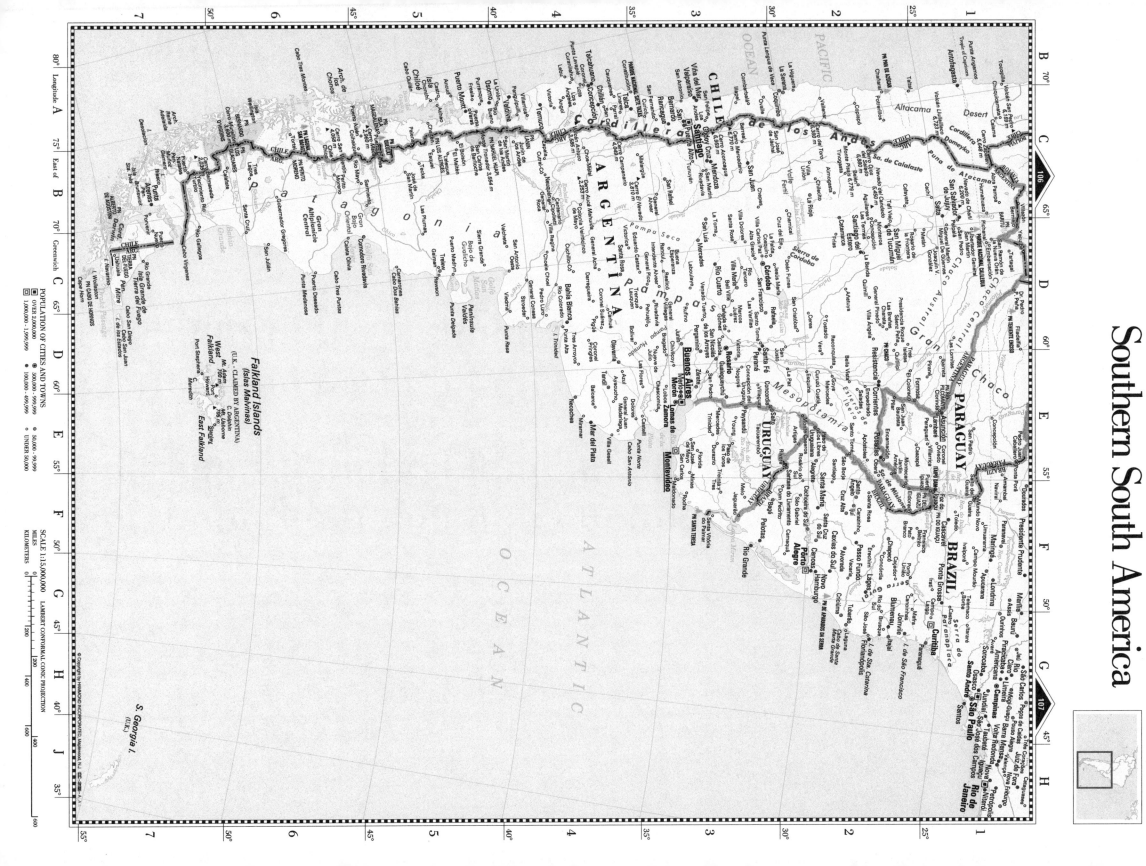

Southern South America

SCALE 1:13,500,000

LAMBERT CONFORMAL CONIC PROJECTION

POPULATION OF CITIES AND TOWNS
- ▣ OVER 2,000,000
- ◉ 1,000,000 - 1,999,999
- ⊡ 300,000 - 599,999
- ● 100,000 - 699,999
- ◦ 50,000 - 99,999
- ◦ UNDER 50,000

Falkland Islands
(Islas Malvinas)
(U.K.; CLAIMED BY ARGENTINA)

PACIFIC OCEAN

ATLANTIC OCEAN

CHILE

ARGENTINA

URUGUAY

PARAGUAY

BRAZIL

Buenos Aires

Montevideo

Santiago

São Paulo

Rio de Janeiro

109

Index of the World

This index lists places and geographic features found in the atlas. Every name is followed by the country or area to which it belongs. Except for cities, towns, countries and cultural areas, all entries include a reference to feature type, such as province, river, island, peak, and so on. The page number and alpha-numeric code appear in blue to the left of each listing. The page number directs you to the largest scale map on which the name can be found. The code refers to the grid squares formed by the horizontal and vertical lines of latitude and longitude on each map. Following the letters from left to right, and the numbers from top to bottom, helps you to locate quickly the square containing the place or feature. Inset maps have their own alpha-numeric codes. Names that are accompanied by a point symbol are indexed to the symbol's location on the map. Other names are indexed to the initial letter of the name. The primary abbreviations used in this index are listed below.

Index Abbreviations

A	**A.F.B.**	Air Force Base	
	Afghan.	Afghanistan	
	Ala.	Alabama	
	Alg.	Algeria	
	Alta.	Alberta	
	Ant. & Barb.	Antigua and Barbuda	
	Antarc.	Antarctica	
	arch.	archipelago	
	Arg.	Argentina	
	Ariz.	Arizona	
	Ark.	Arkansas	
	Austr.	Australia	
	aut.	autonomous	
B	**Bah.**	Bahamas	
	Bang.	Bangladesh	
	Belg.	Belgium	
	Bol.	Bolivia	
	Bosn.	Bosnia and Hercegovina	
	Bots.	Botswana	
	Braz.	Brazil	
	Br., Brit.	British	
	Br. Col.	British Columbia	
	Bulg.	Bulgaria	
	Burk. Faso	Burkina Faso	
C	**Calif.**	California	
	Camb.	Cambodia	
	Can.	Canada	
	cap.	capital	
	Cent. Afr. Rep.	Central African Republic	
	chan.	channel	
	Chan. Is.	Channel Islands	
	Col.	Colombia	
	Colo.	Colorado	
	Conn.	Connecticut	
	C. Rica	Costa Rica	
	Czech Rep.	Czech Republic	
D	**DC**	District of Columbia	
	Del.	Delaware	
	Dem.	Democratic	
	Den.	Denmark	
	depr.	depression	
	des.	desert	
	dist.	district	
	Dom. Rep.	Dominican Republic	
E	**E.**	East, Eastern	
	Ecua.	Ecuador	
	El Sal.	El Salvador	
	Eng.	England	
	Equat. Guin.	Equatorial Guinea	
	est.	estuary	
	Eth.	Ethiopia	
F	**Fed.**	Federal, Federated	
	Fin.	Finland	
	Fla.	Florida	
	for.	forest	
	Fr.	France, French	
	Fr. Pol.	French Polynesia	
	Ft.	Fort	
G	**Ga.**	Georgia	
	Ger.	Germany	
	Greenl.	Greenland	
	Gt.	Great	
	Guad.	Guadeloupe	
	Guat.	Guatemala	
	Guy.	Guyana	
H	**har., harb.**	harbor	
	Hon.	Honduras	
	Hun.	Hungary	
I	**Ill.**	Illinois	
	Ind.	Indiana	
	Indon.	Indonesia	
	Int'l	International	
	Ire.	Ireland	
	isl., isls.	isle, island, islands	
	Isr.	Israel	
	isth.	isthmus	
	Iv. Coast	Ivory Coast	
J	**Jam.**	Jamaica	
K	**Kans.**	Kansas	
	Ky.	Kentucky	
L	**La.**	Louisiana	
	Leb.	Lebanon	
	Lux.	Luxembourg	
M	**Madag.**	Madagascar	
	Man.	Manitoba	
	Mass.	Massachusetts	
	Maur.	Mauritania	
	Md.	Maryland	
	Mex.	Mexico	
	Mich.	Michigan	
	Minn.	Minnesota	
	Miss.	Mississippi	
	Mo.	Missouri	
	Mong.	Mongolia	
	Mont.	Montana	
	Mor.	Morocco	
	Moz.	Mozambique	
	mt.	mount	
	mtn., mts.	mountain, mountains	
N	**N., No.**	North, Northern	
	N. Amer.	North America	
	Nat'l Pk.	National Park	
	N. Br.	New Brunswick	
	N.C.	North Carolina	
	N. Dak.	North Dakota	
	Nebr.	Nebraska	
	Neth.	Netherlands	
	Neth. Ant.	Netherlands Antilles	
	Nev.	Nevada	
	Newf.	Newfoundland	
	N.H.	New Hampshire	
	Nic.	Nicaragua	
	N. Ire.	Northern Ireland	
	N.J.	New Jersey	
	N. Korea	North Korea	
	N. Mex.	New Mexico	
	Nor.	Norway	
	N.S.	Nova Scotia	
	N.W.T.	Northwest Territories	
	N.Y.	New York	
	N.Z.	New Zealand	
O	**Okla.**	Oklahoma	
	Ont.	Ontario	
	Oreg.	Oregon	
P	**Pa.**	Pennsylvania	
	Pak.	Pakistan	
	Pen.	Panama	
	Papua N.G.	Papua New Guinea	
	Par.	Paraguay	
	P.E.I.	Prince Edward Island	
	pen.	peninsula	
	Phil.	Philippines	
	pk.	park	
	plat.	plateau	
	Pol.	Poland	
	Port.	Portugal, Portuguese	
	P. Rico	Puerto Rico	
	prom.	promontory	
	prov.	province, provincial	
	pt., pte.	point, pointe	
Q	**Que.**	Québec	
R	**reg.**	region	
	Rep.	Republic	
	res.	reservoir	
	R.I.	Rhode Island	
	riv.	river	
	Rom.	Romania	
S	**S., So.**	South, Southern	
	sa.	serra, sierra	
	S. Africa	South Africa	
	S. Amer.	South America	
	São T. & Pr.	São Tomé and Príncipe	
	Sask.	Saskatchewan	
	S.C.	South Carolina	
	Scot.	Scotland	
	S. Dak.	South Dakota	
	Sen.	Senegal	
	Sing.	Singapore	
	S. Korea	South Korea	
	S. Leone	Sierra Leone	
	Sol. Is.	Solomon Islands	
	Sp.	Spain, Spanish	
	St., Ste.	Saint, Sainte	
	str.	strait	
	St. Vinc. & Grens.	Saint Vincent and the Grenadines	
	Switz.	Switzerland	
T	**Tanz.**	Tanzania	
	Tenn.	Tennessee	
	Terr.	Territory	
	Thai.	Thailand	
	Trin. & Tob.	Trinidad and Tobago	
	Tun.	Tunisia	
U	**U.A.E.**	United Arab Emirates	
	U.K.	United Kingdom	
	Ukr.	Ukraine	
	Urug.	Uruguay	
	U.S.	United States	
V	**Va.**	Virginia	
	Ven., Venez.	Venezuela	
	V.I. (Br.)	Virgin Islands (British)	
	V.I. (U.S.)	Virgin Islands (U.S.)	
	Viet.	Vietnam	
	vol.	volcano	
	Vt.	Vermont	
W	**W.**	West, Western	
	Wash.	Washington	
	W. Indies	West Indies	
	Wis.	Wisconsin	
	W. Samoa	Western Samoa	
	W. Va.	West Virginia	
	Wyo.	Wyoming	
Y	**Yugo.**	Yugoslavia	
Z	**Zim.**	Zimbabwe	

A

Aachen, Ger.
Aare (riv.), Switz.
Aba, Nigeria
Abadan, Iran
Abakan, Russia
Abbeville, France
Abeokuta, Nigeria
Aberdeen, S. Dak.
Aberdeen, Scot.
Aberdeen, Wash.
Abidjan, Iv. Coast
Abilene, Kans.
Abilene, Texas
Abitibi (lake), Ont.
Abraham Lincoln Birthplace Nat'l Hist. Site, Ky.
Abruzzi (reg.), Italy
Abu Dhabi (cap.), U.A.E.
Abuja (cap.), Nigeria
Acadia Nat'l Pk., Maine
Acapulco, Mex.
Accra (cap.), Ghana
Achinsk, Russia
Aconcagua (mt.), Arg.
Ada, Okla.
Adak (isl.), Alaska
Adamstown (cap.), Pitcairn
Adana, Turkey
Adelaide (cap.), Austr.
Aden (gulf), Afr., Asia
Aden, Yemen
Adige (riv.), Italy
Adirondack (mts.), N.Y.
Admiralty (isls.), Papua N.G.
Adrian, Mich.
Adriatic (sea), Europe
Aegean (sea)
Afghanistan
Africa
Agadir, Morocco
Agana (cap.), Guam
Agate Fossil Beds Nat'l Mon., Nebr.
Agra, India
Aguascalientes, Mex.
Ahaggar (mts.), Alg.
Ahmadabad, India
Ahvaz, Iran
Aiea, Hawaii
Aiken, S.C.
Aix-en-Provence, France
Ajaccio, France
Ajmer, India
Akashi, Japan
Akita, Japan
Akko, Isr.
Akola, India
Akron, Ohio
Aktyubinsk, Kazakhstan
Alabama (state), U.S.
Alabama (riv.), Ala.
Alameda, Calif.
Alamogordo, N. Mex.
Alamosa, Colo.
Åland (isls.), Fin.
Alaska (gulf), Alaska
Alaska (pen.), Alaska
Alaska (range), Alaska
Alaska (state), U.S.
Albacete, Spain
Albania
Albany, Ga.
Albany (cap.), N.Y.
Albany, Oreg.
Albany (riv.), Ont.
Albert (lake), Africa
Albert Lea, Minn.
Alberta (prov.), Can.
Ålborg, Den.
Albuquerque, N. Mex.
Alderney (isl.), Chan. Is.
Aleppo, Syria
Aleutian (isls.), Alaska
Alexander (arch.), Alaska
Alexandria, Egypt

Alexandria, La.
Alexandria, Va.
Al Fayyum, Egypt
Al Fujayrah, U.A.E.
Algeria
Algiers (cap.), Alg.
Alhambra, Calif.
Alicante, Spain
Al Jizah, Egypt
Al Khums, Libya
Al Kuwait (cap.), Kuwait
Allahabad, India
Allegheny (mts.), U.S.
Allegheny (riv.), U.S.
Allen Park, Mich.
Allentown, Pa.
Alliance, Ohio
Alma-Ata (cap.), Kazakhstan
Al Mahallah al Kubrá, Egypt
Al Mansûra, Egypt
Almería, Spain
Al Minyâ, Egypt
Alps (mts.), Europe
Alsace (reg.), Fr.
Altadena, Calif.
Altai (mts.), Asia
Altoona, Pa.
Altun (mts.), China
Altus, Okla.
Amarillo, Texas
Amazon (riv.), S. Amer.
Ambon, Indon.
American Fork, Utah
American Samoa
Americus, Ga.
Ames, Iowa
Amherst, N.S.
Amherst, Mass.
Amiens, France
Amistad Nat'l Rec. Area, Texas
Amman (cap.), Jordan
Amoy (Xiamen), China
Amravati, India
Amritsar, India
Amsterdam (cap.), Neth.
Amsterdam, N.Y.
Amu Darya (riv.), Asia
Amundsen (gulf), N.W.T.
Amundsen (sea), Antarc.
Amur (riv.), Asia
Anaconda, Mont.
Anadyr (gulf), Russia
Anaheim, Calif.
Anatolia (reg.), Turkey
Anchorage, Alaska
Andaman (isls.), India
Andaman (sea), Asia
Andalusia (reg.), Spain
Andalusia, Ala.
Anderson, Ind.
Anderson, S.C.
Andes (mts.), S. Amer.
Andizhan, Uzbekistan
Andorra
Andorra la Vella (cap.), Andorra
Andros (isl.), Bah.
Andros (isl.), Greece
Angara (riv.), Russia
Angel (falls), Ven.
Angers, France
Angkor (ruins), Camb.
Angola
Anguilla (isl.)
Ankara (cap.), Turkey
Annaba, Alg.
Annandale, Va.
Annapolis (cap.), Md.
Annapurna (mt.), Nepal
Ann Arbor, Mich.
Ann (cape), Mass.

Anniston, Ala.
Anqing, China
Anshan, China
Antakya (Antioch), Turkey
Antalya, Turkey
Antananarivo (cap.), Madag.
Antarctica
Anticosti (isl.), Que.
Antibes, France
Antigua and Barbuda
Antioch (Antakya), Turkey
Antioch, Calif.
Antofagasta, Chile
Antsiranana (Diego-Suarez), Madag.
Antwerp, Belg.
Anyang, China
Aomori, Japan
Apeldoorn, Neth.
Apennines (mts.), Italy
Apia (cap.), W. Samoa
Appalachian (mts.), U.S.
Appleton, Wis.
Aqaba (gulf), Asia
Aqaba, Jordan
Arabian (des.), Egypt
Arabian (pen.), Asia
Arabian (sea), Asia
Aracaju, Braz.
Arad, Rom.
Arafura (sea)
Aragón (reg.), Spain
Araguaia (riv.), Braz.
Arak, Iran
Aral (sea), Asia
Ararat (mt.), Turkey
Aran (isls.), Ire.
Arcadia, Calif.
Archangel, Russia
Arches Nat'l Pk., Utah
Arctic (ocean)
Ardabil, Iran
Ardennes (for.), Belg.
Ardmore, Okla.
Arecibo, P. Rico
Arequipa, Peru
Argenteuil, France
Argentina
Argonne Nat'l Lab., Ill.
Århus, Den.
Arica, Chile
Arizona (state), U.S.
Arkadelphia, Ark.
Arkansas (state), U.S.
Arkansas (riv.), U.S.
Arles, France
Arlington, Texas
Arlington Heights, Ill.
Arlington, Va.
Armagh, N. Ire.
Armavir, Russia
Armenia
Arnhem, Neth.
Arnhem Land (reg.), Austr.
Arno (riv.), Italy
Arran (isl.), Scot.
Aruba (isl.)
Asahikawa, Japan
Asansol, India
Ascension (isl.), St. Helena
Asheville, N.C.
Ashkhabad (cap.), Turkmenistan
Ashland, Ky.
Ashland, Oreg.
Ashtabula, Ohio
Asia
Asmara (cap.), Eritrea
As Salimiyah, Kuwait
Astoria, Oreg.
Astrakhan', Russia
Asturias (reg.), Spain
Asunción (cap.), Par.
Aswân, Egypt

Asyūt, Egypt
Atacama (des.), Chile
Atchison, Kans.
Athabasca (lake), Can.
Athabasca (riv.), Can.
Athens, Ga.
Athens (cap.), Greece
Athens, Ohio
Atka (isl.), Alaska
Atlanta (cap.), Ga.
Atlantic (ocean)
Atlantic City, N.J.
Atlas (mts.), Africa
Aţ Ţä'if, Saudi Arabia
Attu (isl.), Alaska
Auburn, Maine
Auburn, N.Y.
Auburn, Wash.
Auckland, N.Z.
Augsburg, Ger.
Augusta, Ga.
Augusta (cap.), Maine
Aurangabad, India
Aurora, Colo.
Aurora, Ill.
Auschwitz (Oswiecim), Poland
Austin (cap.), Texas
Australia
Australian Alps (mts.), Austr.
Australian Cap. Terr., Austr.
Austria
Avalon (pen.), Newf.
Avignon, France
Avon (riv.), Eng.
Ayers Rock (mt.), Austr.
Azerbaijan
Azores (isls.), Port.
Azov (sea), Europe
Aztec Ruins Nat'l Mon., N. Mex.
Azusa, Calif.
Az Zaqāziq, Egypt

B

Bāb el Mandeb (str.)
Bacău, Rom.
Bacolod, Phil.
Badajoz, Spain
Baden-Baden, Ger.
Badlands Nat'l Pk., S. Dak.
Baffin (bay), N. Amer.
Baffin (isl.), N.W.T.
Baghdad (cap.), Iraq
Bahamas
Bahawalpur, Pak.
Bahía Blanca, Arg.
Bahrain
Baicheng, China
Baikal (lake), Russia
Bairiki (cap.), Kiribati
Baja California (pen.), Mex.
Bakersfield, Calif.
Bakhtaran, Iran
Baku (cap.), Azerbaijan
Balakovo, Russia
Baldwin Park, Calif.
Balearic (isls.), Spain
Bali (isl.), Indon.
Balikpapan, Indon.
Balkan (mts.), Bulg.
Balkhash (lake), Kazakhstan
Baltic (sea), Europe
Baltimore, Md.
Baluchistan (reg.), Pak.
Bamako (cap.), Mali
Banaba (isl.), Kiribati
Bandar Seri Begawan (cap.), Brunei
Bandelier Nat'l Mon., N. Mex.
Bandung, Indon.
Banff Nat'l Pk., Alta.
Bangalore, India
Bangkok (cap.), Thai.
Bangladesh
Bangor, Maine
Bangui (cap.), Cent. Afr. Rep.
Banja Luka, Bosn.
Banjarmasin, Indon.
Banjul (cap.), Gambia
Banks (isl.), N.W.T.

Baoding, China
Baoji, China
Baotou, China
Baranovichi, Belarus
Barbados
Barcelona, Spain
Barcelona, Ven.
Bareilly, India
Barents (sea), Europe
Bar Harbor, Maine
Bari, Italy
Barkley (lake), Ky., Tenn.
Barnaul, Russia
Barquisimeto, Ven.
Barranquilla, Col.
Barrie, Ont.
Barrow (pt.), Alaska
Barstow, Calif.
Bartlesville, Okla.
Basel, Switz.
Bass (str.), Austr.
Basse-Terre (cap.), Guad.
Basseterre (cap.), St. Kitts & Nevis
Bastrop, La.
Bath, Eng.
Bathurst, N. Br.
Bathurst (isl.), N.W.T.
Batna, Alg.
Baton Rouge (cap.), La.
Battle Creek, Mich.
Batumi, Georgia
Bat Yam, Isr.
Bavaria (state), Ger.
Bavarian Alps (mts.), Austria, Ger.
Bay City, Mich.
Bayamon, P. Rico
Bayan Har (mts.), China
Bayeux, France
Baykal (lake), Russia
Bayonne, N.J.
Bayreuth, Ger.
Baytown, Texas
Bear (lake), U.S.
Beatrice, Nebr.
Beaufort (sea), N. Amer.
Beaufort, S.C.
Beaumont, Texas
Beckley, W. Va.
Beersheba, Isr.
Beijing (Peking) (cap.), China
Beirut (cap.), Leb.
Béja, Alg.
Belém, Braz.
Belfast, Maine
Belfast (cap.), N. Ire.
Belgaum, India
Belgium
Belgorod, Russia
Belgrade (cap.), Yugo.
Belize
Belize City, Belize
Bellary, India
Belleville, Ill.
Belleville, N.J.
Belleville, Ont.
Bellevue, Wash.
Bellflower, Calif.
Bellingham, Wash.
Bellingshausen (sea), Antarc.
Belmopan (cap.), Belize
Belo Horizonte, Braz.
Beloit, Wis.
Bemidji, Minn.
Benares (Varanasi), India
Bend, Oreg.

Bengal (bay), Asia
Benghazi, Libya
Benguela, Angola
Benin
Benin City, Nigeria
Benton Harbor, Mich.
Benton, Ark.
Bennington, Vt.
Berea, Ky.
Bergamo, Italy
Bergen, Nor.
Bering (sea)
Bering (str.)
Berkeley, Calif.
Berlin (cap.), Ger.
Berlin, N.H.
Bermuda
Bern (cap.), Switz.
Bernese Alps (range), Switz.
Berwyn, Ill.
Besançon, France
Bessemer, Ala.
Bethesda, Md.
Bethlehem, Pa.
Bethlehem, West Bank
Beverly Hills, Calif.
Bhagalpur, India
Bhavnagar, India
Bhopal, India
Bhutan
Bialystok, Pol.
Biarritz, France
Biddeford, Maine
Bielefeld, Ger.
Bielsko-Biała, Poland
Bien Hoa, Viet.
Big Bend Nat'l Pk., Texas
Bighorn (mts.), Wyo.
Bighorn (riv.), U.S.
Big Spring, Texas
Bikaner, India
Bikini (atoll), Marshall Is.
Bilbao, Spain
Billings, Mont.
Biloxi, Miss.
Binghamton, N.Y.
Bimini, The (isls.), Bah.
Birch (mts.), Alb.
Birkenhead, Eng.
Birmingham, Ala.
Birmingham, Eng.
Birmingham, Mich.
Biscay (bay), Europe
Bisbee, Ariz.
Bishkek (cap.), Kyrgyzstan
Bisho, S. Africa
Bismarck (arch.), Papua N.G.
Bismarck (cap.), N. Dak.
Bitterroot (range), U.S.
Biysk, Russia
Bizerte, Tun.
Black (sea)
Black (for.), Ger.
Black Hills (mts.), U.S.
Blackpool, Eng.
Blacksburg, Va.
Bladensburg, Md.
Blagoveshchensk, Russia
Blanc (mt.), Europe
Blantyre, Malawi
Block (isl.), R.I.
Bloemfontein, S. Africa
Bloomfield, N.J.
Bloomington, Ill.
Bloomington, Ind.
Bloomington, Minn.
Bluefield, W. Va.
Blue Nile (riv.), Africa

113

Da Lat – Glenda

65/E4 **Da Lat**, Viet.
95/H1 **Dalhousie**, N.Br.
58/A3 **Dalian**, China
96/D3 **Dallas**, Texas
97/G3 **Dalton**, Ga.
99/K11 **Daly City**, Calif.
49/B4 **Damanhur**, Egypt
49/E3 **Damascus** (cap.), Syria
51/H3 **Damavand** (mt.), Iran
51/E4 **Damietta**, Egypt
65/E2 **Da Nang**, Viet.
58/C2 **Dandong**, China
18/F4 **Danube** (riv.), Europe
95/C3 **Danville**, Ill.
94/E4 **Danville**, Va.
55/K2 **Daqing**, China
98/E6 **Darby**, Pa.
41/H5 **Dardanelles** (str.), Turkey
82/G2 **Dar es Salaam** (cap.), Tanz.
98/G4 **Darien**, Conn.
103/G4 **Darién** (mts.), Pan.
62/E2 **Darjiling**, India
70/B6 **Darling** (range), Austr.
73/C1 **Darling** (riv.), Austr.
72/C4 **Darling Downs** (ridge), Austr.
26/E4 **Darmstadt**, Ger.
95/J2 **Dartmouth**, N.S.
70/E2 **Darwin**, Austr.
59/C2 **Datong**, China
67/G2 **Davao**, Phil.
93/K2 **Davenport**, Iowa
83/F **Davis** (sea), Antarc.
99/L9 **Davis**, Calif.
84/M3 **Davis** (str.), N. Amer.
90/C2 **Dawson Creek**, Br. Col.
85/L3 **Dawson**, Yukon
97/H4 **Daytona Beach**, Fla.
94/C4 **Dayton**, Ohio
49/D4 **Dead** (sea), Asia
99/F7 **Dearborn**, Mich.
99/F7 **Dearborn Heights**, Mich.
92/C3 **Death Valley Nat'l Mon.**, U.S.
40/E2 **Debrecen**, Hung.
97/G3 **Decatur**, Ala.
97/G3 **Decatur**, Ga.
94/B4 **Decatur**, Ill.
62/C5 **Deccan** (plat.), India
99/Q15 **Deerfield**, Ill.
94/C3 **Defiance**, Ohio
53/L2 **Dehra Dun**, India
94/B3 **De Kalb**, Ill.
97/H4 **De Land**, Fla.
94/D3 **Delaware**, Ohio
94/F4 **Delaware** (bay), U.S.
98/E5 **Delaware** (riv.), U.S.
94/F4 **Delaware** (state), U.S.
98/F4 **Delaware Water Gap Nat'l Rec. Area**, U.S.
62/C2 **Delhi**, India
97/H5 **Delray Beach**, Fla.
96/C4 **Del Rio**, Texas
85/H3 **Denali Nat'l Pk.**, Alaska
20/C5 **Denmark**
18/A2 **Denmark** (str.)
96/D3 **Denton**, Texas
93/F3 **Denver** (cap.), Colo.
98/F5 **Denville**, N.J.
23/G6 **Derby**, Eng.
96/E4 **De Ridder**, La.
95/G3 **Derry**, N.H.
93/J2 **Des Moines** (cap.), Iowa
99/Q15 **Des Plaines**, Ill.
26/G3 **Dessau**, Ger.
99/F7 **Detroit**, Mich.
92/C3 **Devils Postpile Nat'l Mon.**, Calif.
91/G5 **Devils Tower Nat'l Mon.**, Wyo.
87/S7 **Devon** (isl.), N.W.T.
62/E3 **Dhaka** (Dacca) (cap.), Bang.
62/B3 **Dhulia**, India
88/W13 **Diamond** (head), Hawaii
91/H4 **Dickinson**, N. Dak.
48/G10 **Diego Garcia** (isls.), Br. Ind. Oc. Terr.
65/C1 **Dien Bien Phu**, Viet.
30/A4 **Dieppe**, France
36/A3 **Dijon**, France
40/C3 **Dinaric Alps** (mts.), Bosnia
92/E2 **Dinosaur Nat'l Mon.**, U.S.
77/P6 **Dire Dawa**, Eth.
98/K8 **District of Columbia**, U.S.
86/C3 **Dixon Entrance** (str.), N. Amer.
94/B3 **Dixon**, Ill.
50/E2 **Diyarbakir**, Turkey
76/H3 **Djado** (plat.), Niger
66/C5 **Djakarta** (Jakarta), Indon.
77/P5 **Djibouti**
77/P5 **Djibouti** (cap.), Djibouti
66/D5 **Djokjakarta** (Yogyakarta), Indon.
18/G3 **Dnepr** (Dnieper) (riv.), Europe
44/E2 **Dneprodzerzhinsk**, Ukraine
44/E2 **Dnepropetrovsk**, Ukraine
44/D3 **Dnestr** (Dniester) (riv.), Europe
98/G4 **Dobbs Ferry**, N.Y.
50/A2 **Dodecanese** (isls.), Greece
93/G3 **Dodge City**, Kans.
50/D1 **Dogukaradeniz** (mts.), Turkey
52/F3 **Doha** (cap.), Qatar
33/J3 **Dolomite Alps** (mts.), Italy
104/F4 **Dominica**
104/D3 **Dominican Republic**
62/D6 **Dondra** (head), Sri Lanka
21/A3 **Donegal**, Ire.
44/F3 **Donetsk**, Ukraine
45/G2 **Donets** (riv.), Ukraine
61/G4 **Dongguan**, China
45/G3 **Don** (riv.), Russia
32/D4 **Dordogne** (riv.), France
28/B5 **Dordrecht**, Neth.
37/F3 **Dornbirn**, Austria
75/W18 **Dorsale** (mts.), Tun.
29/E5 **Dortmund**, Ger.
97/G4 **Dothan**, Ala.
76/G7 **Douala**, Cameroon
92/E5 **Douglas**, Ariz.
22/D3 **Douglas** (cap.), I. of Man
94/F4 **Dover** (cap.), Del.
25/H4 **Dover**, Eng.
30/A2 **Dover** (str.), Europe
95/G3 **Dover**, N.H.
98/F5 **Dover**, N.J.
99/P16 **Downers Grove**, Ill.
98/B3 **Downey**, Calif.
109/C8 **Drake** (passage)
81/E2 **Drakensburg** (range), S. Africa
40/C3 **Dráva** (riv.), Europe
27/G3 **Dresden**, Ger.
72/B4 **Drummond** (range), Austr.
53/G3 **Dubayyi** (Dubai), U.A.E.
97/H3 **Dublin**, Ga.
22/B5 **Dublin** (cap.), Ire.
40/D4 **Dubrovnik**, Croatia
93/K2 **Dubuque**, Iowa
24/D2 **Dudley**, Eng.
36/D6 **Dufourspitze** (mt.), Eur.
28/D6 **Duisburg**, Ger.
91/L4 **Duluth**, Minn.
98/G5 **Dumont**, N.J.
93/H4 **Duncan**, Okla.
98/K7 **Dundalk**, Md.
21/D2 **Dundee**, Scot.
97/H4 **Dunedin**, Fla.
71/R12 **Dunedin**, N.Z.
30/B1 **Dunkirk** (Dunkerque), France
92/F3 **Durango**, Colo.
100/D3 **Durango**, Mex.
93/H4 **Durant**, Okla.
81/E3 **Durban**, S. Africa
62/E3 **Durgapur**, India
23/G2 **Durham**, Eng.
95/G3 **Durham**, N.H.
97/J3 **Durham**, N.C.
46/G6 **Dushanbe** (cap.), Tajikistan
28/D6 **Düsseldorf**, Ger.
43/J3 **Dvina, Northern** (Dvina, Severnaya) (riv.), Russia
42/E5 **Dvina, Western** (Dvina Zapadnaya) (riv.), Belarus
42/J4 **Dzerzhinsk**, Russia
46/H5 **Dzhambul**, Kazakhstan

E

96/C4 **Eagle Pass**, Texas
25/H2 **East Anglia** (reg.), Eng.
98/F5 **East Brunswick**, N.J.
99/R16 **East Chicago**, Ind.
48/M6 **East China** (sea), Asia
69/Q7 **Easter** (isl.), Chile
62/C5 **Eastern Ghats** (mts.), India
28/D1 **East Frisian** (isls.), Ger.
94/C3 **East Lansing**, Mich.
94/D3 **East Liverpool**, Ohio
80/D4 **East London**, S. Africa
98/B2 **East Los Angeles**, Calif.
98/G5 **East Meadow**, N.Y.
98/E5 **Easton**, Pa.
98/F5 **East Orange**, N.J.
99/G7 **East Pointe**, Mich.
97/G3 **East Point**, Ga.
47/S2 **East Siberian** (sea), Russia
94/B4 **East St. Louis**, Ill.
94/B2 **Eau Claire**, Wis.
35/F2 **Ebro** (riv.), Spain
100/F5 **Ecatepec**, Mex.
99/F7 **Ecorse**, Mich.
106/C4 **Ecuador**
97/J2 **Eden**, N.C.
97/J2 **Edenton**, N.C.
96/D5 **Edinburg**, Texas
21/D3 **Edinburgh** (cap.), Scot.
98/F5 **Edison**, N.J.
99/C2 **Edmonds**, Wash.
90/E2 **Edmonton** (cap.), Alta.
95/G2 **Edmundston**, N.Br.
96/C4 **Edwards** (plat.), Texas
92/C4 **Edwards A.F.B.**, Calif.
94/B4 **Edwardsville**, Ill.
92/B3 **Eel** (riv.), Calif.
91/L5 **Effigy Mounds Nat'l Mon.**, Iowa
94/B4 **Effingham**, Ill.
71/R10 **Egmont** (mt.), N.Z.
77/L2 **Egypt**
28/C6 **Eindhoven**, Neth.
49/D5 **Elat** (Elath), Isr.
50/D2 **Elazig**, Turkey
38/B1 **Elba** (isl.), Italy
26/E2 **Elbe** (riv.), Ger.
92/F3 **Elbert** (mt.), Colo.
45/G4 **El'brus** (mt.), Russia
51/G2 **Elburz** (mts.), Iran
92/C4 **El Cajon**, Calif.
92/D4 **El Centro**, Calif.
76/D3 **El Djouf** (des.), Maur.
93/J4 **El Dorado**, Ark.
42/H5 **Elektrostal'**, Russia
104/B1 **Eleuthera** (isl.), Bah.
99/P15 **Elgin**, Ill.
97/J2 **Elizabeth City**, N.C.
98/F5 **Elizabeth**, N.J.
99/Q15 **Elk Grove Village**, Ill.
94/C3 **Elkhart**, Ind.
90/C4 **Ellensburg**, Wash.
87/T6 **Ellesmere** (isl.), N.W.T.
83/U **Ellsworth Land** (reg.), Antarc.
99/Q16 **Elmhurst**, Ill.
94/E3 **Elmira**, N.Y.
98/B2 **El Monte**, Calif.
99/Q16 **Elmwood Park**, Ill.
96/A4 **El Paso**, Texas
92/H4 **El Reno**, Okla.
102/D3 **El Salvador**
94/D3 **Elyria**, Ohio
98/E5 **Emmaus**, Pa.
93/H3 **Emporia**, Kans.
83/D **Enderby Land** (reg.), Antarc.
94/E3 **Endicott**, N.Y.
68/F3 **Enewetak** (atoll), Marshall Is.
21/D4 **England**, U.K.
98/G5 **Englewood**, N.J.
32/B2 **English** (chan.), Europe
93/H3 **Enid**, Okla.
28/D4 **Enschede**, Neth.
77/M8 **Entebbe**, Uganda
79/G5 **Enugu**, Nigeria
51/G2 **Enzeli** (Bandar-e Anzali), Iran
76/G7 **Equatorial Guinea**
26/F3 **Erfurt**, Ger.
94/D3 **Erie** (lake), N. Amer.
94/D3 **Erie**, Pa.
52/C5 **Eritrea**
26/G3 **Erzgebirge** (mts.), Europe
50/E2 **Erzurum**, Turkey
20/H3 **Esbo** (Espoo), Fin.
94/C2 **Escanaba**, Mich.
92/C4 **Escondido**, Calif.
51/G3 **Esfahān**, Iran
50/B2 **Eskişehir**, Turkey
68/F6 **Espiritu Santo** (isl.), Vanuatu
20/H3 **Espoo** (Esbo), Fin.
28/E6 **Essen**, Ger.
98/K7 **Essex**, Md.
42/E4 **Estonia**
77/N5 **Ethiopia**
38/D4 **Etna** (vol.), Italy
39/H3 **Euboea** (Évvoia) (isl.), Greece
94/D3 **Euclid**, Ohio
90/C4 **Eugene**, Oreg.
96/E4 **Eunice**, La.
50/F4 **Euphrates** (riv.), Asia
92/A2 **Eureka**, Calif.
18/* **Europe**
93/F3 **Evans** (mt.), Colo.
99/Q15 **Evanston**, Ill.
94/C4 **Evansville**, Ind.
62/E2 **Everest** (mt.), Asia
99/C2 **Everett**, Wash.
97/H5 **Everglades Nat'l Pk.**, Fla.
39/H3 **Évvoia** (isl.), Greece
24/C5 **Exeter**, Eng.
95/G3 **Exeter**, N.H.
70/F5 **Eyre** (lake), Austr.
70/F6 **Eyre** (pen.), Austr.

F

85/J3 **Fairbanks**, Alaska
98/J8 **Fairfax**, Va.
99/K10 **Fairfield**, Calif.
98/G4 **Fairfield**, Conn.
94/C4 **Fairfield**, Ohio
98/F5 **Fair Lawn**, N.J.
90/D4 **Fairmont**, W. Va.
85/L4 **Fairweather** (mt.), N. Amer.
64/B2 **Faisalabad**, Pak.
96/D5 **Falcon** (res.), N. Amer.
109/D7 **Falkland Islands**
95/G3 **Fall River**, Mass.
49/C2 **Famagusta**, Cyprus
69/K4 **Fanning** (Tabuaeran) (isl.), Kiribati
92/B3 **Farallon** (isls.), Calif.
91/J4 **Fargo**, N. Dak.
91/K5 **Faribault**, Minn.
92/E3 **Farmington**, N. Mex.
99/F7 **Farmington Hills**, Mich.
34/B4 **Faro**, Port.
18/C2 **Faroe** (isls.), Den.
93/J3 **Fayetteville**, Ark.
97/J3 **Fayetteville**, N.C.
99/C3 **Federal Way**, Wash.
59/F2 **Fengcheng**, China
46/H5 **Fergana**, Uzbekistan
91/K4 **Fergus Falls**, Minn.
33/J4 **Ferrara**, Italy
75/M13 **Fès**, Mor.
76/H2 **Fezzan** (reg.), Libya
81/H8 **Fianarantsoa**, Madag.
107/L6 **Fiera de Santana**, Braz.
68/G6 **Fiji**
94/D3 **Findlay**, Ohio
34/A1 **Finisterre** (cape), Spain
20/H2 **Finland**
42/E4 **Finland** (gulf), Europe
86/D3 **Finlay** (riv.), Br. Col.
98/G5 **Fire Isl. Nat'l Seashore**, N.Y.
33/J5 **Firenze** (Florence), Italy
40/B3 **Fiume** (Rijeka), Croatia
38/C2 **Fiumicino**, Italy
92/E4 **Flagstaff**, Ariz.
92/E2 **Flaming Gorge** (res.), U.S.
30/B2 **Flanders** (reg.), Eur.
90/B3 **Flattery** (cape), Wash.
26/E1 **Flensburg**, Ger.
73/D3 **Flinders** (isl.), Austr.
70/F6 **Flinders** (ranges), Austr.
99/E5 **Flint**, Mich.
98/G5 **Floral Park**, N.Y.
97/G3 **Florence**, Ala.
33/J5 **Florence** (Firenze), Italy
97/J3 **Florence**, S.C.
67/F5 **Flores** (isl.), Indon.
67/E5 **Flores** (sea), Indon.
108/B3 **Florianópolis**, Braz.
97/H5 **Florida** (bay), Fla.
97/H4 **Florida** (state), U.S.
93/K3 **Florissant**, Mo.
38/D2 **Foggia**, Italy
25/H4 **Folkestone**, Eng.
94/B3 **Fond du Lac**, Wis.
68/G5 **Fongafale** (cap.), Tuvalu
102/E3 **Fonseca** (gulf), Cent. Amer.
32/E2 **Fontainebleau**, France
98/C2 **Fontana**, Calif.
61/H3 **Foochow** (Fuzhou), China
33/K4 **Forlì**, Italy
109/L4 **Fortaleza**, Braz.
98/J8 **Ft. Belvoir**, Va.
92/F2 **Ft. Collins**, Colo.
104/F4 **Ft.-de-France** (cap.), Martinique
93/J2 **Ft. Dodge**, Iowa
21/D2 **Forth** (firth), Scot.
97/H5 **Ft. Lauderdale**, Fla.
98/G5 **Ft. Lee**, N.J.
90/E3 **Ft. Macleod**, Alta.
93/K2 **Ft. Madison**, Iowa
98/K7 **Ft. McHenry Nat'l Mon.**, Md.
86/E3 **Ft. McMurray**, Alta.
98/K7 **Ft. Meade**, Md.
97/H5 **Ft. Myers**, Fla.
90/G4 **Ft. Peck Lake** (res.), Mont.
97/H5 **Ft. Pierce**, Fla.
93/J4 **Ft. Smith**, Ark.
86/E2 **Ft. Smith**, N.W.T.
97/G4 **Ft. Walton Beach**, Fla.
94/C3 **Ft. Wayne**, Ind.
96/D3 **Ft. Worth**, Texas
94/D3 **Fostoria**, Ohio
98/C3 **Fountain Valley**, Calif.
76/C5 **Fouta Djallon** (reg.), Guinea
87/J2 **Foxe** (basin), N.W.T.
85/E5 **Fox** (isls.), Alaska
32/D3 **France**
91/J5 **Francis Case** (lake), S. Dak.
82/E5 **Francistown**, Botswana
94/C3 **Frankfort**, Ind.
94/C4 **Frankfort** (cap.), Ky.
26/E3 **Frankfurt am Main**, Ger.
27/H2 **Frankfurt an der Oder**, Ger.
86/D2 **Franklin** (mts.), N.W.T.
90/D3 **Franklin D. Roosevelt** (lake), Wash.
46/F2 **Franz Josef Land** (isls.), Russia
90/C3 **Fraser** (riv.), Br. Col.
99/G6 **Fraser**, Mich.
20/D5 **Fredericia**, Den.
94/E4 **Frederick**, Md.
94/E4 **Fredericksburg**, Va.
95/H2 **Fredericton** (cap.), N.Br.
20/D4 **Frederikshavn**, Den.
94/B3 **Freeport**, Ill.
98/G5 **Freeport**, N.Y.
78/D4 **Freetown** (cap.), S. Leone
36/D2 **Freiburg**, Ger.
90/B3 **Fremont**, Calif.
93/H2 **Fremont**, Nebr.
107/H3 **French Guiana**
69/M6 **French Polynesia**
92/C3 **Fresno**, Calif.
36/D4 **Fribourg**, Switz.
37/F2 **Friedrichshafen**, Ger.
73/B1 **Frome** (lake), Austr.
93/F2 **Front** (range), Colo., Wyo.
97/J2 **Front Royal**, Va.
46/H5 **Frunze** (Bishkek) (cap.), Kyrgyzstan
61/H3 **Fujian** (Fukien) (prov.), China
57/F3 **Fujisawa**, Japan
57/F3 **Fujiyama** (mt.), Japan
56/E2 **Fukui**, Japan
56/B4 **Fukuoka**, Japan
57/G2 **Fukushima**, Japan
56/C3 **Fukuyama**, Japan
98/C3 **Fullerton**, Calif.
93/K3 **Fulton**, Mo.
57/H7 **Funabashi**, Japan
35/V15 **Funchal**, Port.
95/H2 **Fundy** (bay), N. Amer.
95/H2 **Fundy Nat'l Pk.**, N.Br.
26/F4 **Fürth**, Ger.
58/B2 **Fushun**, China
37/G2 **Füssen**, Ger.
58/A1 **Fuxin**, China
61/H3 **Fuzhou**, China

G

76/H7 **Gabon**
80/D2 **Gaborone** (cap.), Bots.
97/G3 **Gadsden**, Ala.
97/H3 **Gaffney**, S.C.
97/H4 **Gainesville**, Fla.
97/H3 **Gainesville**, Ga.
70/F6 **Gairdner** (lake), Austr.
98/J7 **Gaithersburg**, Md.
16/E6 **Galápagos** (isls.), Ecua.
41/J3 **Galați**, Rom.
94/B3 **Galesburg**, Ill.
34/A1 **Galicia** (reg.), Spain
97/G2 **Gallatin**, Tenn.
62/D6 **Galle**, Sri Lanka
41/H5 **Gallipoli**, Turkey
92/E4 **Gallup**, N. Mex.
92/E4 **Galveston**, Texas
21/H7 **Galway**, Ire.
78/B3 **Gambia**
95/L1 **Gander**, Newf.
48/H7 **Ganges** (riv.), Asia
62/E2 **Gangtok**, India
33/J4 **Garda** (lake), Italy
93/G3 **Garden City**, Kans.
98/J5 **Garden City**, N.Y.
98/C3 **Garden Grove**, Calif.
98/F5 **Garfield**, N.J.
92/D3 **Garland**, Texas
37/H3 **Garmisch-Partenkirchen**, Ger.
32/D4 **Garonne** (riv.), France
99/R16 **Gary**, Ind.
95/H1 **Gaspé** (pen.), Que.
97/H3 **Gastonia**, N.C.
85/H2 **Gates of the Arctic Nat'l Pk.**, Alaska
98/F5 **Gateway Nat'l Rec. Area**, U.S.
63/F2 **Gauhati**, India
70/E6 **Gawler** (range), Austr.
62/E3 **Gaya**, India
49/D4 **Gaza Strip**
49/E1 **Gaziantep**, Turkey
27/K1 **Gdańsk**, Pol.
27/K1 **Gdańsk** (gulf), Pol.
27/K1 **Gdynia**, Pol.
73/C3 **Geelong**, Austr.
60/D4 **Gejiu**, China
28/E5 **Gelsenkirchen**, Ger.
36/C5 **Geneva** (Léman) (lake), Europe
94/E3 **Geneva**, N.Y.
36/C5 **Geneva**, Switz.
33/H4 **Genoa** (Genova), Italy
33/H5 **Genova** (gulf), It.
30/C1 **Gent**, Belg.
104/F2 **George Town** (cap.), Cayman Is.
106/G2 **Georgetown** (cap.), Guyana
66/B2 **George Town** (Pinang), Malaysia
45/G4 **Georgia**
90/C3 **Georgia** (str.), Br. Col.
97/G3 **Georgia** (state), U.S.
94/D2 **Georgian** (bay), Ont.
70/A5 **Geraldton**, Austr.
26/E3 **Germany**
94/E4 **Gettysburg**, Pa.
78/E4 **Ghana**
53/J2 **Ghazni**, Afghan.
34/C4 **Gibraltar**
34/C5 **Gibraltar** (str.)
70/D4 **Gibson** (des.), Austr.
57/E3 **Gifu**, Japan
34/C1 **Gijón**, Spain
92/D4 **Gila** (riv.), U.S.
92/E4 **Gila Cliff Dwellings Nat'l Mon.**, N. Mex.
68/G5 **Gilbert Is.** (Kiribati)
90/G4 **Gillette**, Wyo.
32/C4 **Gironde** (riv.), France
95/K2 **Glace Bay**, N.S.
86/G3 **Glacier Bay Nat'l Pk.**, Alaska
90/D2 **Glacier Nat'l Pk.**, Br. Col.
90/E3 **Glacier Nat'l Pk.**, Mont.
21/C3 **Glasgow**, Scot.
98/E6 **Glassboro**, N.J.
98/K7 **Glen Burnie**, Md.
92/E3 **Glen Canyon Nat'l Rec. Area**, U.S.
98/J5 **Glen Cove**, N.Y.
92/D4 **Glendale**, Ariz.
98/B2 **Glendale**, Calif.

114

Glens F – Juncti

95/F3 **Glens Falls**, N.Y.
99/Q15 **Glenview**, Ill.
27/K3 **Gliwice**, Pol.
24/D3 **Gloucester**, Eng.
62/B4 **Goa** (dist.), India
108/J7 **Goânia**, Braz.
54/E3 **Gobi** (des.), Asia
62/D4 **Godavari** (riv.), India
84/M3 **Godthåb** (Nuuk) (cap.), Greenl.
53/L1 **Godwin Austen** (K2) (mt.), Asia
49/D3 **Golan Heights**, Syria
72/D4 **Gold Coast**, Austr.
93/F3 **Golden**, Colo.
99/J11 **Golden Gate Nat'l Rec. Area**, Calif.
97/J3 **Goldsboro**, N.C.
44/D1 **Gomel'**, Belarus
103/H2 **Gonâve** (isl.), Haiti
77/N5 **Gonder**, Eth.
80/B4 **Good Hope** (cape), S. Africa
92/B2 **Goose** (lake), U.S.
87/K3 **Goose Bay-Happy Valley**, Newf.
43/K4 **Gor'kiy** (Nizhniy Novgorod), Russia
62/D2 **Gorakhpur**, India
44/F2 **Gorlovka**, Ukraine
20/D4 **Göteborg**, Sweden
20/F4 **Gotland** (isl.), Sweden
29/G5 **Göttingen**, Ger.
28/B4 **Gouda**, Neth.
54/D3 **Govi Altayn** (mts.), Mong.
21/C2 **Grampian** (mts.), Scot.
34/D4 **Granada**, Spain
35/X17 **Gran Canaria** (isl.), Spain
105/C5 **Gran Chaco** (reg.), S. Amer.
59/D4 **Grand** (canal), China
104/B1 **Grand Bahama** (isl.), Bah.
92/D3 **Grand Canyon Nat'l Pk.**, Ariz.
103/F2 **Grand Cayman** (isl.), Cayman Is.
90/D2 **Grande Prairie**, Alta.
76/E1 **Grand Erg Occidental** (des.), Alg.
76/G1 **Grand Erg Oriental** (des.), Alg.
96/C4 **Grande, Rio** (riv.), N. Amer.
91/J4 **Grand Forks**, N. Dak.
93/H2 **Grand Island**, Nebr.
92/E3 **Grand Junction**, Colo.
95/H2 **Grand Manan** (isl.), N.Br.
94/B2 **Grand Portage Nat'l Mon.**, Minn.
94/C3 **Grand Rapids**, Mich.
90/F5 **Grand Teton Nat'l Pk.**, Wyo.
97/F2 **Granite City**, Ill.
92/F4 **Grants**, N. Mex.
90/C5 **Grants Pass**, Oreg.
33/G5 **Grasse**, France
25/G4 **Gravesend**, Eng.
33/L3 **Graz**, Austria
104/B1 **Great Abaco** (isl.), Bah.
70/D6 **Great Australian** (bight), Austr.
72/B1 **Great Barrier** (reef), Austr.
90/C2 **Great Basin** (basin), U.S.
92/D3 **Great Basin Nat'l Park**, Nev.
86/D2 **Great Bear** (lake), N.W.T.
93/H3 **Great Bend**, Kans.
21/E3 **Great Britain** (isl.), U.K.
71/H7 **Great Dividing** (range), Austr.
103/F1 **Greater Antilles** (isls.), N. Amer.
66/C4 **Greater Sunda** (isls.), Indon.
104/C2 **Great Exuma** (isl.), Bah.
90/F4 **Great Falls**, Mont.
104/C2 **Great Inagua** (isl.), Bah.
62/B2 **Great Indian** (Thar) (des.), India
93/G2 **Great Plains** (plains), U.S.
92/D2 **Great Salt** (lake), Utah
93/F3 **Great Sand Dunes Nat'l Mon.**, Colo.
77/K2 **Great Sand Sea** (des.), Egypt, Libya
70/C4 **Great Sandy** (des.), Austr.
86/E2 **Great Slave** (lake), N.W.T.
97/H3 **Great Smoky Mts. Nat'l Pk.**, Tenn.
70/D5 **Great Victoria** (des.), Austr.
59/B3 **Great Wall**, China
39/G3 **Greece**
93/F2 **Greeley**, Colo.
92/E3 **Green** (riv.), U.S.
94/B2 **Green Bay**, Wis.
97/H2 **Greeneville**, Tenn.
95/F3 **Greenfield**, Mass.
99/P14 **Greenfield**, Wis.
84/N2 **Greenland**
84/R2 **Greenland** (sea)
95/F3 **Green** (mts.), Vt.
21/C3 **Greenock**, Scot.
97/J2 **Greensboro**, N.C.
94/E3 **Greensburg**, Pa.
97/F3 **Greenville**, Miss.
97/J3 **Greenville**, N.C.
97/H3 **Greenville**, S.C.
98/G4 **Greenwich**, Conn.
97/F3 **Greenwood**, Miss.
97/H3 **Greenwood**, S.C.
72/A2 **Gregory** (range), Austr.
104/F5 **Grenada**
32/F4 **Grenoble**, France
97/F4 **Gretna**, La.
72/A5 **Grey** (range), Austr.
97/G3 **Griffin**, Ga.
42/E5 **Grodno**, Belarus
28/D2 **Groningen**, Neth.
99/G7 **Grosse Pointe Woods**, Mich.
33/K3 **Grossglockner** (mt.), Austria
45/H4 **Groznyy**, Russia
100/E4 **Guadalajara**, Mex.
34/D2 **Guadalajara**, Spain
68/E6 **Guadalcanal** (isl.), Sol. Is.
34/D4 **Guadalquivir** (riv.), Spain
96/B3 **Guadalupe** (mts.), U.S.
96/B4 **Guadalupe Mts. Nat'l Pk.**, Texas
104/F3 **Guadeloupe**
103/H4 **Guajira** (pen.), S. Amer.
68/D3 **Guam**
103/F1 **Guanabacoa**, Cuba
61/G3 **Guangdong** (prov.), China
61/G4 **Guangzhou** (Canton), China
103/H1 **Guantánamo**, Cuba
102/D3 **Guatemala**
102/D3 **Guatemala** (cap.), Guat.
106/B4 **Guayaquil**, Ecua.
106/B4 **Guayaquil** (gulf), Ecua.
94/D3 **Guelph**, Ont.
32/B2 **Guernsey** (isl.), Chan. Is.
106/F2 **Guiana Highlands** (range), S. Amer.
61/F3 **Guilin**, China
78/C4 **Guinea**
78/B3 **Guinea-Bissau**
76/F7 **Guinea** (gulf), Africa
60/E3 **Guiyang**, China
64/C1 **Gujranwala**, Pak.
62/C4 **Gulbarga**, India
96/D5 **Gulf Coastal** (plain), Texas
97/F4 **Gulf Isls. Nat'l Seashore**, Fla.
97/F4 **Gulfport**, Miss.
62/D4 **Guntur**, India
45/J3 **Gur'yev**, Kazakhstan
93/H4 **Guthrie**, Okla.
106/G3 **Guyana**
62/C2 **Gwalior**, India
82/E4 **Gweru**, Zim.
45/H4 **Gyandzhe**, Azerbaijān
40/C2 **Gyor**, Hung.

H

28/B4 **Haarlem**, Neth.
57/L10 **Habikino**, Japan
57/F3 **Hachioji**, Japan
98/F5 **Hackensack**, N.J.
98/E6 **Haddonfield**, N.J.
52/E5 **Hadhramaut** (reg.), Yemen
58/C3 **Haeju**, N. Korea
29/E6 **Hagen**, Ger.
94/E4 **Hagerstown**, Md.
28/B4 **Hague, The** (cap.), Neth.
49/D3 **Haifa**, Isr.
61/F4 **Haikou**, China
61/F5 **Hainan** (isl.), China
59/L9 **Haining**, China
65/D1 **Haiphong**, Viet.
103/H2 **Haiti**
55/N3 **Hakodate**, Japan
49/E1 **Halab** (Aleppo), Syria
88/T10 **Haleakala Nat'l Pk.**, Hawaii
95/J2 **Halifax** (cap.), N.S.
26/F3 **Halle**, Ger.
67/G3 **Halmahera** (isl.), Indon.
20/E4 **Hälsingborg**, Sweden
53/G3 **Hamadan**, Iran
49/E2 **Hamāh**, Syria
57/E3 **Hamamatsu**, Japan
28/G1 **Hamburg**, Ger.
70/B4 **Hamersley** (range), Austr.
58/E2 **Hamgyong** (mts.), N. Korea
58/D3 **Hamhung**, N. Korea
71/S10 **Hamilton**, N.Z.
94/C4 **Hamilton**, Ohio
94/E3 **Hamilton**, Ont.
20/G1 **Hammerfest**, Nor.
29/E5 **Hamm**, Ger.
98/R16 **Hammond**, Ind.
97/F4 **Hammond**, La.
94/E4 **Hampton**, Va.
99/F7 **Hamtramck**, Mich.
58/D4 **Han** (riv.), S. Korea
57/F3 **Hanchiōji**, Japan
59/C3 **Handan**, China
92/C3 **Hanford**, Calif.
54/D2 **Hangayn** (mts.), Mong.
59/L9 **Hangzhou** (Hangchow), China
93/K3 **Hannibal**, Mo.
29/G4 **Hannover**, Ger.
65/D1 **Hanoi** (cap.), Viet.
95/F3 **Hanover**, N.H.
54/F5 **Hanzhong**, China
82/F4 **Harare** (cap.), Zim.
55/K2 **Harbin**, China
77/P6 **Hargeysa**, Somalia
96/D5 **Harlingen**, Texas
95/E4 **Harpers Ferry Nat'l Hist. Site**, W. Va.
99/G7 **Harper Woods**, Mich.
94/E3 **Harrisburg** (cap.), Pa.
94/E4 **Harrisonburg**, Va.
98/G5 **Harrison**, N.Y.
94/C4 **Harrodsburg**, Ky.
95/F3 **Hartford** (cap.), Conn.
99/Q16 **Harvey**, Ill.
29/H5 **Harz** (mts.), Ger.
93/H2 **Hastings**, Nebr.
97/F4 **Hattiesburg**, Miss.
103/F1 **Havana** (cap.), Cuba
92/D4 **Havasu** (lake), U.S.
95/G3 **Haverhill**, Mass.
90/F3 **Havre**, Mont.
88/U11 **Hawaii** (isl.), Hawaii
88/S10 **Hawaii** (state), U.S.
69/H2 **Hawaiian** (isls.), U.S.
88/U11 **Hawaii Volcanoes Nat'l Pk.**, Hawaii
52/E3 **Ḩawalli**, Kuwait
98/B3 **Hawthorne**, Calif.
86/E2 **Hay River**, N.W.T.
93/H3 **Hays**, Kans.
99/K11 **Hayward**, Calif.
99/F7 **Hazel Park**, Mich.
90/A2 **Hazleton** (mts.), Br. Col.
94/F3 **Hazleton**, Pa.
59/G6 **Hebei** (Hopei) (prov.), China
21/B2 **Hebrides, Inner** (isls.), Scot.
21/B2 **Hebrides, Outer** (isls.), Scot.
49/D4 **Hebron**, West Bank
59/D5 **Hefei**, China
57/L2 **Hegang**, China
26/E4 **Heidelberg**, Ger.
20/N7 **Hekla** (mt.), Iceland
90/F4 **Helena** (cap.), Mont.
53/H2 **Helmand** (riv.), Afghan.
20/H3 **Helsinki** (cap.), Fin.
98/G5 **Hempstead**, N.Y.
59/B4 **Henan** (Honan) (prov.) China
97/G2 **Henderson**, Ky.
92/D3 **Henderson**, Nev.
97/J2 **Henderson**, N.C.
61/G3 **Hengyang**, China
53/H2 **Herat**, Afghan.
49/D3 **Hermon** (mt.), Asia
100/C2 **Hermosillo**, Mex.
29/E5 **Herne**, Ger.
26/E3 **Hesse** (state), Ger.
97/H5 **Hialeah**, Fla.
91/K4 **Hibbing**, Minn.
97/H3 **Hickory**, N.C.
98/G5 **Hicksville**, N.Y.
57/L10 **Higashi-Osaka**, Japan
99/Q15 **Highland Park**, Ill.
99/F7 **Highland Park**, Mich.
97/H3 **High Point**, N.C.
52/C3 **Hijāz, Jabal al** (mts.), Saudi Arabia
90/C4 **Hillsboro**, Oreg.
98/F5 **Hillside**, N.J.
88/U11 **Hilo**, Hawaii
48/G6 **Himalaya** (mts.), Asia
56/D3 **Himeji**, Japan
49/E2 **Ḩimş**, Syria
53/J1 **Hindu Kush** (mts.), Asia
99/Q16 **Hinsdale**, Ill.
56/D3 **Hirakata**, Japan
55/N3 **Hirosaki**, Japan
56/C3 **Hiroshima**, Japan
104/C2 **Hispaniola** (isl.), W. Indies
57/G2 **Hitachi**, Japan
73/C4 **Hobart**, Austr.
93/G4 **Hobbs**, N. Mex.
98/F5 **Hoboken**, N.J.
65/D4 **Ho Chi Minh City** (Saigon), Viet.
99/P15 **Hoffman Estates**, Ill.
59/B2 **Hohhot**, China
55/N3 **Hokkaidō** (isl.), Japan
103/G1 **Holguín**, Cuba
94/C3 **Holland**, Mich.
97/H5 **Hollywood**, Fla.
49/D3 **Holon**, Isr.
95/F3 **Holyoke**, Mass.
97/H5 **Homestead**, Fla.
102/E3 **Honduras**
102/D2 **Honduras** (gulf), Cent. Amer.
61/G4 **Hong Kong**
68/E5 **Honiara** (cap.), Sol. Is.
88/T10 **Honolulu** (cap.), Hawaii
55/M5 **Honshu** (isl.), Japan
90/C4 **Hood** (mt.), Oreg.
92/D3 **Hoover** (dam), U.S.
96/E3 **Hope**, Ark.
94/E4 **Hopewell**, Va.
94/B4 **Hopkinsville**, Ky.
109/C8 **Horn** (cape), Chile
94/E3 **Hornell**, N.Y.
96/E3 **Hot Springs Nat'l Park**, Ark.
97/F4 **Houma**, La.
96/E4 **Houston**, Texas
92/E3 **Hovenweep Nat'l Mon.**, U.S.
62/E3 **Howrah**, India
27/H3 **Hradec Králové**, Czech Rep.
61/J3 **Hsinchu**, Taiwan
59/D4 **Huainan**, China
106/C6 **Huancayo**, Peru
55/H4 **Huang He** (Yellow) (riv.), China
105/B3 **Huascarán** (mt.), Peru
62/C4 **Hubli-Dharwar**, India
23/G4 **Huddersfield**, Eng.
87/H2 **Hudson** (bay), Can.
87/J2 **Hudson** (str.), Can.
94/F3 **Hudson** (riv.), U.S.
34/B4 **Huelva**, Spain
65/D2 **Hue**, Viet.
82/B4 **Huila** (plat.), Angola
23/H4 **Hull**, Eng.
94/F2 **Hull**, Que.
23/H4 **Humber** (riv.), Eng.
92/E4 **Humphreys** (peak), Ariz.
61/F2 **Hunan** (prov.), China
40/D2 **Hungary**
58/D3 **Hŭngnam**, N. Korea
55/K3 **Hunjiang**, China
94/C3 **Huntington**, Ind.
98/G5 **Huntington**, N.Y.
94/D4 **Huntington**, W. Va.
98/C3 **Huntington Beach**, Calif.
98/B3 **Huntington Park**, Calif.
97/G3 **Huntsville**, Ala.
96/E4 **Huntsville**, Texas
94/D2 **Huron** (lake), N. Amer.
91/J4 **Huron**, S. Dak.
93/H3 **Hutchinson**, Kans.
59/E5 **Huzhou**, China
98/K8 **Hyattsville**, Md.
62/C4 **Hyderabad**, India
53/J3 **Hyderabad**, Pak.

I

41/H2 **Iaşi**, Rom.
79/F5 **Ibadan**, Nigeria
106/C3 **Ibagué**, Col.
35/F3 **Ibiza** (isl.), Spain
20/N7 **Iceland**
59/B5 **Ichang** (Yichang), China
57/H7 **Ichikawa**, Japan
56/E3 **Ichinomiya**, Japan
90/E5 **Idaho** (state), U.S.
90/E5 **Idaho Falls**, Idaho
30/B2 **Ieper**, Belg.
79/G5 **Ife**, Nigeria
105/D5 **Iguazú** (falls), S. Amer.
76/D2 **Iguidi, Èrg** (des.), Alg.
28/C3 **IJsselmeer** (lake), Neth.
76/F6 **Ilesha**, Nigeria
85/G4 **Iliamna** (lake), Alaska
94/B3 **Illinois** (riv.), Ill.
94/B4 **Illinois** (state), U.S.
67/F1 **Iloilo**, Phil.
79/G4 **Ilorin**, Nigeria
60/B3 **Imphal**, India
58/D4 **Inch'ŏn**, S. Korea
93/J3 **Independence**, Kans.
93/J3 **Independence**, Mo.
48/G7 **India**
94/E3 **Indiana**, Pa.
94/C3 **Indiana** (state), U.S.
99/R16 **Indiana Dunes Nat'l Lakeshore**, Ind.
94/C4 **Indianapolis** (cap.), Ind.
17/N6 **Indian Ocean**
47/Q3 **Indigirka** (riv.), Russia
92/C4 **Indio**, Calif.
65/C1 **Indochina** (reg.), Asia
66/E4 **Indonesia**
62/C3 **Indore**, India
48/F7 **Indus** (riv.), Asia
98/B3 **Inglewood**, Calif.
99/F7 **Inkster**, Mich.
33/K2 **Inn** (riv.), Europe
21/B2 **Inner Hebrides** (isls.), Scot.
54/G3 **Inner Mongolia** (reg.), China
37/H3 **Innsbruck**, Austria
60/C5 **Insein**, Burma
90/B2 **Interior** (plat.), Br. Col.
91/H3 **International Peace Garden**, N. Amer.
85/M2 **Inuvik**, N.W.T.
71/Q12 **Invercargill**, N.Z.
21/C2 **Inverness**, Scot.
21/B2 **Iona** (isl.), Scot.
39/F3 **Ionian** (sea), Eur.
39/F3 **Ionian** (isls.), Greece
93/K2 **Iowa City**, Iowa
93/J2 **Iowa** (state), U.S.
66/B3 **Ipoh**, Malaysia
25/H2 **Ipswich**, Eng.
87/K2 **Iqaluit**, N.W.T.
106/D4 **Iquitos**, Peru
39/J5 **Iráklion**, Greece
48/E6 **Iran**
101/E4 **Irapuato**, Mex.
50/E3 **Iraq**
60/B5 **Irawaddy** (riv.), Burma
49/D3 **Irbid**, Jordan
51/F2 **Irbil**, Iraq
21/A4 **Ireland**
21/B3 **Ireland, Northern**, U.K.
67/J4 **Irian Jaya** (reg.), Indon.
22/C4 **Irish** (sea), Europe
54/E1 **Irkutsk**, Russia
94/D4 **Ironton**, Ohio
60/B5 **Irrawaddy** (riv.), Burma
46/G4 **Irtysh** (riv.), Russia
98/C3 **Irvine**, Calif.
92/D3 **Irving**, Texas
98/F5 **Irvington**, N.J.
38/C2 **Ischia** (isl.), Italy
57/E3 **Ise**, Japan
32/F4 **Isère** (riv.), France
49/E1 **Iskenderun**, Turkey
64/B1 **Islamabad** (cap.), Pak.
22/D3 **Isle of Man**, U.K.
94/B1 **Isle Royale** (isl.), Mich.
94/B2 **Isle Royale Nat'l Pk.**, Mich.
98/G5 **Islip**, N.Y.
49/C4 **Ismailia**, Egypt
49/D3 **Israel**
50/B1 **Istanbul**, Turkey
18/E4 **Italy**
94/E3 **Ithaca**, N.Y.
42/J4 **Ivanovo**, Russia
78/D5 **Ivory Coast**
57/G2 **Iwaki**, Japan
68/D2 **Iwo Jima** (isl.), Japan
43/M4 **Izhevsk**, Russia
50/A2 **Izmir**, Turkey
41/J5 **Izmit**, Turkey

J

62/C3 **Jabalpur**, India
94/C3 **Jackson**, Mich.
97/F3 **Jackson** (cap.), Miss.
97/F3 **Jackson**, Tenn.
96/E3 **Jacksonville**, Ark.
97/H4 **Jacksonville**, Fla.
94/B4 **Jacksonville**, Ill.
97/J3 **Jacksonville**, N.C.
64/G4 **Jaffna**, Sri Lanka
62/C2 **Jaipur**, India
66/C5 **Jakarta** (cap.), Indon.
101/N7 **Jalapa Enriquez**, Mex.
103/G2 **Jamaica**
66/B4 **Jambi**, Indon.
87/H3 **James** (bay), Can.
94/E4 **James** (riv.), Va.
91/J4 **Jamestown**, N. Dak.
94/E3 **Jamestown**, N.Y.
64/C1 **Jammu**, India
53/K2 **Jammu & Kashmir** (state), India
62/B3 **Jamnagar**, India
62/E3 **Jamshedpur**, India
94/B3 **Janesville**, Wis.
18/C1 **Jan Mayen** (isl.), Nor.
55/M4 **Japan**
55/L4 **Japan** (sea), Asia
57/E3 **Japanese Alps** (mts.), Japan
60/D5 **Jars** (plain), Laos
69/J5 **Jarvis** (isl.), Pacific
66/C5 **Java** (isl.), Indon.
66/D5 **Java** (sea), Indon.
93/J3 **Jefferson City** (cap.), Mo.
94/C4 **Jeffersonville**, Ind.
34/B4 **Jerez de la Frontera**, Spain
49/D4 **Jericho**, West Bank
32/B2 **Jersey** (isl.), Chan. Is.
98/F5 **Jersey City**, N.J.
49/D4 **Jerusalem** (cap.), Isr.
95/N6 **Jésus** (isl.), Que.
91/H5 **Jewel Cave Nat'l Mon.**, S. Dak.
64/B2 **Jhang Sadar**, Pak.
62/C2 **Jhansi**, India
55/L2 **Jiamusi**, China
59/E5 **Jiaxing**, China
52/C4 **Jiddah**, Saudi Arabia
55/K3 **Jilin**, China
59/D3 **Jinan** (Tsinan), China
61/H2 **Jingdezhen**, China
61/H2 **Jinhua**, China
59/E2 **Jinzhou**, China
55/L2 **Jixi**, China
107/M5 **João Pessoa**, Braz.
62/B2 **Jodhpur**, India
80/D2 **Johannesburg**, S. Africa
90/C4 **John Day** (riv.), Oreg.
97/H2 **Johnson City**, Tenn.
94/E3 **Johnstown**, Pa.
66/B3 **Johor Baharu**, Malaysia
99/P16 **Joliet**, Ill.
97/F3 **Jonesboro**, Ark.
20/E4 **Jönköping**, Sweden
95/G1 **Jonquière**, Que.
93/J3 **Joplin**, Mo.
50/D4 **Jordan**
49/D4 **Jordan** (riv.), Asia
92/D4 **Joshua Tree Nat'l Mon.**, Calif.
90/B3 **Juan de Fuca** (str.), N. Amer.
105/A6 **Juan Fernández** (isls.), Chile
31/G8 **Judaea** (reg.), Asia
108/D2 **Juiz de Fora**, Braz.
64/C2 **Jullundur**, India
93/H3 **Junction City**, Kans.

108/C2 **Jundiaí**, Braz.
85/M4 **Juneau** (cap.), Alaska
36/D4 **Jungfrau** (mt.), Switz.
36/B4 **Jura** (mts.), Europe
103/K7 **Juventud** (isl.), Cuba

K

53/L1 **K2** (mt.), Asia
53/J2 **Kabul** (cap.), Afghan.
82/E3 **Kabwe, Zambia**
79/G4 **Kaduna**, Nigeria
58/D3 **Kaesŏng**, N. Korea
56/B5 **Kagoshima**, Japan
88/T10 **Kahoolawe** (isl.), Hawaii
50/D2 **Kahramanmaras**, Turkey
54/G5 **Kaifeng**, China
88/T10 **Kailua**, Hawaii
31/G5 **Kaiserslautern**, Ger.
88/T10 **Kaiwi** (chan.), Hawaii
62/D4 **Kakinada**, India
84/N2 **Kalaallit Nunaat** (Greenland)
82/D5 **Kalahari** (des.), Africa
94/C3 **Kalamazoo**, Mich.
59/C2 **Kalgan** (Zhangjiakou), China
66/D4 **Kalimantan** (reg.), Indon.
42/D5 **Kaliningrad** (Königsberg), Russia
42/H5 **Kaliningrad**, Moscow Oblast, Russia
42/H5 **Kaluga**, Russia
57/H7 **Kamakura**, Japan
47/R4 **Kamchatka** (pen.), Russia
90/C3 **Kamloops**, Br. Col.
77/M7 **Kampala** (cap.), Uganda
65/D3 **Kampuchea** (Cambodia)
82/D2 **Kananga**, Zaire
57/E2 **Kanazawa**, Japan
62/E2 **Kanchenjunga** (mt.), Asia
62/D6 **Kandy**, Sri Lanka
88/T10 **Kaneohe**, Hawaii
58/C2 **Kangnam** (mts.), N. Korea
43/K2 **Kanin** (pen.), Russia
94/C3 **Kankakee**, Ill.
97/H3 **Kannapolis**, N.C.
79/H3 **Kano**, Nigeria
62/D2 **Kānpur**, India
93/H3 **Kansas** (riv.), Kans.
92/D2 **Kansas** (state), U.S.
93/J3 **Kansas City**, Kans.
93/J3 **Kansas City**, Mo.
61/J4 **Kaohsiung**, Taiwan
82/B4 **Kaokoveld** (mts.), Namibia
78/A3 **Kaolack**, Sen.
46/G2 **Kara** (sea), Russia
45/K4 **Kara-Bogaz-Gol** (gulf), Turkmenistan
53/J4 **Karachi**, Pak.
46/H5 **Karaganda**, Kazakhstan
51/G3 **Karaj**, Iran
53/K1 **Karakoram** (mts.), Asia
54/E2 **Karakorum** (ruins), Mong.
45/L5 **Karakumy** (des.), Turkmenistan
82/E4 **Kariba** (lake), Africa
26/E4 **Karlsruhe**, Ger.
50/A3 **Kárpathos** (isl.), Greece
82/D2 **Kasai** (riv.), Zaire
51/G3 **Kashan**, Iran
47/H6 **Kashi** (Kashgar), China
29/G6 **Kassel**, Ger.
95/G2 **Katahdin** (mt.), Maine
82/D2 **Katanga** (reg.), Zaire
62/E2 **Kathmandu** (cap.), Nepal
85/G4 **Katmai Nat'l Pk.**, Alaska
27/K3 **Katowice**, Pol.
20/D4 **Kattegat** (str.), Europe
88/S10 **Kauai** (chan.), Hawaii
88/S9 **Kauai** (isl.), Hawaii
42/D5 **Kaunas**, Lithuania
57/F3 **Kawagoe**, Japan
57/F3 **Kawaguchi**, Japan
57/F3 **Kawasaki**, Japan
50/C2 **Kayseri**, Turkey
46/G5 **Kazakhstan**
43/L5 **Kazan'**, Russia
93/H2 **Kearney**, Nebr.
98/F5 **Kearny**, N.J.
40/D2 **Kecskemét**, Hun.
66/D5 **Kediri**, Indon.
61/J3 **Keelung**, Taiwan
95/F3 **Keene**, N.H.
66/B3 **Kelang**, Malaysia
90/D3 **Kelowna**, Br. Col.
90/C4 **Kelso**, Wash.
46/J4 **Kemerovo**, Russia
85/J3 **Kenai Fjords Nat'l Pk.**, Alaska
97/H5 **Kendall**, Fla.
75/L13 **Kenitra**, Mor.
95/S10 **Kenmore**, N.Y.
97/F4 **Kenner**, La.
90/D4 **Kennewick**, Wash.
99/Q14 **Kenosha**, Wis.
94/D3 **Kent**, Ohio
94/B4 **Kentucky** (lake), U.S.
94/C4 **Kentucky** (state), U.S.
74/F4 **Kenya**
77/M8 **Kenya** (Batian) (mt.), Kenya
93/K2 **Keokuk**, Iowa
64/F3 **Kerala** (state), India
44/F3 **Kerch**, Ukraine
39/F3 **Kérkira** (Corfu) (isl.), Greece
68/G7 **Kermadec** (isls.), N.Z.
51/J4 **Kerman**, Iran
92/D4 **Kerrville**, Texas
85/M4 **Ketchikan**, Alaska
94/C4 **Kettering**, Ohio
94/B2 **Keweenaw** (pen.), Mich.
94/C2 **Keweenaw** (pt.), Mich.
97/H5 **Key West**, Fla.
55/M2 **Khabarovsk**, Russia
44/F2 **Khar'kov**, Ukraine
62/E3 **Kharagpur**, India
52/B5 **Khartoum** (cap.), Sudan
44/E3 **Kherson**, Ukraine
91/K3 **Khíos** (isl.), Greece
44/C2 **Khmel'nitskiy**, Ukraine
51/G3 **Khorramabad**, Iran
51/G4 **Khorramshahr**, Iran
62/E3 **Khulna**, Bang.
53/K2 **Khyber** (pass), Asia
27/L3 **Kielce**, Pol.
26/F1 **Kiel**, Ger.
44/D2 **Kiev** (cap.), Ukraine
82/F1 **Kigali** (cap.), Rwanda
82/C2 **Kikwit**, Zaire
96/E3 **Kilgore**, Texas
82/G1 **Kilimanjaro** (mt.), Tanz.
21/B4 **Kilkenny**, Ire.
21/H7 **Killarney**, Ire.
96/D4 **Killeen**, Texas
70/D3 **Kimberley** (plat.), Austr.
80/D3 **Kimberley**, S. Africa
73/C3 **King** (isl.), Austr.
92/D4 **Kingman**, Ariz.
92/C3 **Kings Canyon Nat'l Pk.**, Calif.
97/H2 **Kingsport**, Tenn.
103/G2 **Kingston** (cap.), Jam.
94/F3 **Kingston**, N.Y.
104/F4 **Kingstown** (cap.), St. Vinc. & Grens.
96/D5 **Kingsville**, Texas
82/C1 **Kinshasa** (cap.), Zaire
97/J3 **Kinston**, N.C.
68/H5 **Kiribati**
50/C2 **Kirikkale**, Turkey
69/K4 **Kiritimati** (isl.), Kiribati
99/C2 **Kirkland**, Wash.
93/J2 **Kirksville**, Mo.
51/F3 **Kirkuk**, Iraq
45/H4 **Kirovakan**, Armenia
44/E2 **Kirovograd**, Ukraine
57/F2 **Kiryu**, Japan
77/L7 **Kisangani**, Zaire
41/J2 **Kishinev** (cap.), Moldova
56/D3 **Kishiwada**, Japan
77/M8 **Kisumu**, Kenya
56/B4 **Kitakyushu**, Japan
94/D3 **Kitchener**, Ont.
82/E3 **Kitwe**, Zambia
82/E1 **Kivu** (lake), Africa
20/E2 **Kjølen** (Kölen) (mts.), Europe
42/D5 **Klaipeda**, Lithuania
92/B2 **Klamath** (mts.), Calif., Oreg.
90/C5 **Klamath Falls**, Oreg.
85/K3 **Kluane Nat'l Pk.**, Yukon
97/H3 **Knoxville**, Tenn.
56/D3 **Kobe**, Japan
31/G3 **Koblenz**, Ger.
85/G2 **Kobuk** (riv.), Alaska
85/G2 **Kobuk Valley Nat'l Pk.**, Alaska
56/C4 **Kochi**, Japan
85/H4 **Kodiak** (isl.), Alaska
41/H2 **Kodry** (hills), Moldova
57/F3 **Kofu**, Japan
94/C3 **Kokomo**, Ind.
42/H1 **Kola** (pen.), Russia
31/F2 **Köln** (Cologne), Ger.
42/H5 **Kolomna**, Russia
68/E4 **Kolonia** (cap.), Micronesia
82/E3 **Kolwezi**, Zaire
47/R3 **Kolyma** (range), Russia
55/M1 **Komsomol'sk**, Russia
53/J1 **Kondūz**, Afghan.
50/C2 **Konya**, Turkey
90/D3 **Kootenai** (riv.), U.S.
43/P5 **Kopeysk**, Russia
58/D2 **Korea, North**
58/D4 **Korea, South**
56/A4 **Korea** (str.), Japan, S. Korea
57/G2 **Koriyama**, Japan
68/C4 **Koror** (cap.), Palau
48/R3 **Koryak** (range), Russia
73/D3 **Kosciusko** (mt.), Austr.
27/L4 **Košice**, Slovakia
50/A2 **Kos** (isl.), Greece
76/D6 **Kossou** (lake), Iv. Coast
42/J4 **Kostroma**, Russia
66/B2 **Kota Baharu**, Malaysia
62/C2 **Kota**, India
67/E2 **Kota Kinabalu**, Malaysia
62/C6 **Kotte**, Sri Lanka
85/E2 **Kotzebue** (sound), Alaska
42/J4 **Kovrov**, Russia
61/G4 **Kowloon**, Hong Kong
65/B4 **Kra** (isth.), Thai.
66/C5 **Krakatau** (isl.) Indon.
27/K3 **Kraków**, Pol.
44/F2 **Kramatorsk**, Ukraine
44/F3 **Krasnodar**, Russia
46/K4 **Krasnoyarsk**, Russia
28/D6 **Krefeld**, Ger.
44/E2 **Kremenchug**, Ukraine
20/C4 **Kristiansand**, Nor.
44/E3 **Krivoy Rog**, Ukraine
65/C3 **Krung Thep** (Bangkok), Thai.
66/B3 **Kuala Lumpur** (cap.), Malaysia
66/B2 **Kuala Terengganu**, Malaysia
66/D3 **Kuching**, Malaysia
77/K3 **Kufrah** (oasis), Libya
56/B4 **Kumamoto**, Japan
79/E5 **Kumasi**, Ghana
45/G4 **Kumayri**, Armenia
46/H6 **Kunlun** (mts.), Asia
60/D3 **Kunming**, China
58/D5 **Kunsan**, S. Korea
56/C3 **Kurashiki**, Japan
51/E2 **Kurdistan** (reg.), Asia
56/C3 **Kure**, Japan
43/Q5 **Kurgan**, Russia
47/P5 **Kuril** (isls.), Russia
62/C4 **Kurnool**, India
44/F2 **Kursk**, Russia
56/B4 **Kurume**, Japan
55/N3 **Kushiro**, Japan
85/G3 **Kuskokwim** (mts.), Alaska
85/F3 **Kuskokwim** (riv.), Alaska
43/P5 **Kustanay**, Kazakhstan
45/G4 **Kutaisi**, Georgia
62/A3 **Kutch, Rann of** (salt marsh), India
51/F4 **Kuwait**
45/J1 **Kuybyshev** (Samara), Russia
68/F4 **Kwajalein** (atoll), Marshall Is.
58/D5 **Kwangju**, S. Korea
82/C1 **Kwango** (riv.), Ang., Zaire
82/N7 **Kyoga** (lake), Uganda
58/C4 **Kyŏnggi** (bay), S. Korea
58/E5 **Kyŏngju**, S. Korea
56/D3 **Kyoto**, Japan
46/H5 **Kyrgyzstan**
56/B5 **Kyushu** (isl.), Japan
54/C1 **Kyzyl**, Russia
46/G5 **Kyzyl-Kum** (des.), Uzbekistan
46/G5 **Kzyl-Orda**, Kazakhstan

L

76/C2 **Laayoune**, W. Sahara
87/K3 **Labrador** (dist.), Newf.
87/L3 **Labrador** (sea), Can.
62/B5 **Laccadive** (Cannanore) (isls.), India
73/A3 **Lacepede** (bay), Austr.
95/S10 **Lackawanna**, N.Y.
95/G3 **Laconia**, N.H.
34/A1 **La Coruña**, Spain
94/B3 **La Crosse**, Wis.
53/L2 **Ladakh** (mts.), Asia
42/F3 **Ladoga** (lake), Russia
68/D5 **Lae**, Papua N.G.
94/C3 **Lafayette**, Ind.
96/E4 **Lafayette**, La.
79/F5 **Lagos**, Nigeria
90/D4 **La Grande**, Oreg.
97/G3 **La Grange**, Ga.
98/C3 **La Habra**, Calif.
64/C2 **Lahore**, Pak.
96/E4 **Lake Charles**, La.
86/A2 **Lake Clark Nat'l Pk.**, Alaska
99/Q15 **Lake Forest**, Ill.
92/D4 **Lake Havasu City**, Ariz.
97/H4 **Lakeland**, Fla.
90/D3 **Lake Louise**, Alta.
92/D4 **Lake Mead Nat'l Rec. Area**, U.S.
98/B3 **Lakewood**, Calif.
98/F5 **Lakewood**, N.J.
97/H5 **Lake Worth**, Fla.
34/D3 **La Mancha** (reg.), Spain
76/H8 **Lambaréné**, Gabon
98/B3 **La Mirada**, Calif.
88/T10 **Lanai** (isl.), Hawaii
92/C4 **Lancaster**, Calif.
23/F3 **Lancaster**, Eng.
94/D4 **Lancaster**, Ohio
94/E3 **Lancaster**, Pa.
24/A6 **Land's End** (prom.), Eng.
99/Q16 **Lansing**, Ill.
94/C3 **Lansing** (cap.), Mich.
61/H2 **Lanxi**, China
54/E4 **Lanzhou** (Lanchow), China
65/C2 **Laos**
106/E7 **La Paz** (cap.), Bol.
55/N2 **La Pérouse** (str.), Asia
20/F1 **Lapland** (reg.), Europe
105/D6 **La Plata**, Arg.
94/C3 **La Porte**, Ind.
47/M2 **Laptev** (sea), Russia
98/C2 **La Puente**, Calif.
90/G5 **Laramie** (mts.), U.S.
90/G5 **Laramie**, Wyo.
96/D5 **Laredo**, Texas
97/H5 **Largo**, Fla.
39/H3 **Lárisa**, Greece
92/F4 **Las Cruces**, N. Mex.
35/X16 **Las Palmas de Gran Canaria**, Spain
92/B2 **Lassen Volcanic Nat'l Pk.**, Calif.
92/C3 **Las Vegas**, Nev.
93/F4 **Las Vegas**, N. Mex.
49/D2 **Latakia**, Syria
42/E4 **Latvia**
73/C4 **Launceston**, Austr.
98/K7 **Laurel**, Md.
97/F4 **Laurel**, Miss.
94/C1 **Laurentian** (plat.), Can.
36/C5 **Lausanne**, Switz.
92/B2 **Lava Beds Nat'l Mon.**, Calif.
95/F2 **Laval**, Que.
98/C2 **La Verne**, Calif.
98/B3 **Lawndale**, Calif.
93/J3 **Lawrence**, Kans.
95/G3 **Lawrence**, Mass.
93/H4 **Lawton**, Okla.
93/J3 **Leavenworth**, Kans.
49/D3 **Lebanon**
94/E3 **Lebanon**, Pa.
23/G4 **Leeds**, Eng.
104/F3 **Leeward** (isls.), W. Indies
32/D2 **Le Havre**, France
25/E1 **Leicester**, Eng.
28/B4 **Leiden**, Neth.
22/B5 **Leinster** (reg.), Ire.
26/G3 **Leipzig**, Ger.
61/F4 **Leizhou** (pen.), China
32/D2 **Le Mans**, France
47/N3 **Lena** (riv.), Russia
42/F4 **Leningrad** (St. Petersburg), Russia
46/J4 **Leninsk-Kuznetskiy**, Russia
101/E4 **León**, Mex.
102/E3 **León**, Nic.
34/C1 **León**, Spain
37/E5 **Lepontine Alps** (mts.), Italy, Switz.
35/F2 **Lérida**, Spain
60/D2 **Leshan**, China
80/D3 **Lesotho**
104/E3 **Lesser Antilles** (isls.), W. Indies
90/E2 **Lesser Slave** (lake), Alta.
39/J3 **Lésvos** (isl.), Greece
98/G5 **Levittown**, N.Y.
90/E3 **Lewis** (range), Mont.
21/B1 **Lewis** (isl.), Scot.
21/B1 **Lewis, Butt of** (prom.), Scot.
90/D4 **Lewiston**, Idaho
95/G2 **Lewiston**, Maine
94/C4 **Lexington**, Ky.
97/H3 **Lexington**, N.C.
60/A2 **Lhasa**, China
35/G2 **L'Hospitalet**, Spain
59/D4 **Lianyungang**, China
59/E2 **Liaodong** (gulf), China
59/E3 **Liaodong** (pen.), China
59/F2 **Liaoyuan**, China
93/G3 **Liberal**, Kans.
78/C5 **Liberia**
76/G7 **Libreville** (cap.), Gabon
77/J2 **Libya**
77/K2 **Libyan** (des.), Africa
77/K1 **Libyan** (plat.), Egypt, Libya
37/F3 **Liechtenstein**
31/E2 **Liège**, Belg.
33/H5 **Ligurian** (sea), Italy
88/S10 **Lihue**, Hawaii
30/C2 **Lille**, France
82/F3 **Lilongwe** (cap.), Malawi
106/C6 **Lima** (cap.), Peru
94/C3 **Lima**, Ohio
49/C2 **Limassol**, Cyprus
21/A4 **Limerick**, Ire.
32/D4 **Limoges**, France
82/F5 **Limpopo** (riv.), Africa
61/H3 **Linchuan**, China
94/B3 **Lincoln**, Ill.
93/H2 **Lincoln** (cap.), Nebr.
99/F7 **Lincoln Park**, Mich.
98/G5 **Lindenhurst**, N.Y.
98/F5 **Linden**, N.J.
69/K4 **Line** (isls.), Kiribati
20/E4 **Linköping**, Sweden
33/L2 **Linz**, Austria
35/H1 **Lions** (gulf), France
38/D3 **Lipari** (isls.), Italy
44/F1 **Lipetsk**, Russia
28/D5 **Lippe** (riv.), Ger.
34/A3 **Lisbon** (cap.), Port.
42/D5 **Lithuania**
90/G4 **Little Big Horn Nat'l Mon.**, Mont.
103/F2 **Little Cayman** (isl.), Cayman Is.
92/E4 **Little Colorado** (riv.), U.S.
85/E2 **Little Diomede** (isl.), Alaska
93/J4 **Little Rock** (cap.), Ark.
61/F3 **Liuzhou**, China
99/L11 **Livermore**, Calif.
23/F5 **Liverpool**, Eng.
23/E5 **Liverpool** (bay), Eng.
98/F5 **Livingston**, N.J.
90/E3 **Livingstone** (range), Alb.
82/E4 **Livingstone**, Zambia
99/F7 **Livonia**, Mich.
33/J5 **Livorno** (Leghorn), Italy
40/B2 **Ljubljana** (cap.), Slovenia
96/C3 **Llano Estacado** (plain), U.S.
109/C1 **Llullaillaco** (vol.), Chile
94/E3 **Lockport**, N.Y.
99/M10 **Lodi**, Calif.
49/F8 **Lod** (Lydda), Isr.
27/K3 **Łódź**, Pol.
20/D2 **Lofoten** (isls.), Nor.
85/K3 **Logan** (mt.), Yukon
94/C3 **Logansport**, Ind.
92/E2 **Logan**, Utah
32/C3 **Loire** (riv.), France
76/C6 **Loma** (mts.), S. Leone
109/E3 **Lomas de Zamora**, Arg.
99/P16 **Lombard**, Ill.
33/J4 **Lombardy** (reg.), Italy
79/F5 **Lomé** (cap.), Togo
21/C2 **Lomond** (lake), Scot.
92/B4 **Lompoc**, Calif.
22/A2 **Londonderry**, N. Ire.
25/F3 **London** (cap.), U.K.
94/D3 **London**, Ont.
108/B2 **Londrina**, Braz.
104/C2 **Long** (isl.), Bah.
98/G5 **Long** (isl.), N.Y.
98/B3 **Long Beach**, Calif.
98/G5 **Long Beach**, N.Y.
98/G5 **Long Branch**, N.J.
95/G2 **Longfellow** (mts.), Maine
98/G5 **Long Island** (sound), U.S.
93/F2 **Longmont**, Colo.
95/K2 **Long Range** (mts.), Newf.
96/E3 **Longview**, Texas
90/C4 **Longview**, Wash.
47/R4 **Lopatka** (cape), Russia
54/C3 **Lop Nur** (Lop Nor) (dry lake), China
94/D3 **Lorain**, Ohio
71/K6 **Lord Howe** (isl.), Austr.
31/E5 **Lorraine** (reg.), Fr.
93/F4 **Los Alamos**, N. Mex.
99/K12 **Los Altos**, Calif.
98/B2 **Los Angeles**, Calif.
65/C2 **Louangphrabang**, Laos
96/E4 **Louisiana** (state), U.S.
94/C4 **Louisville**, Ky.
32/C5 **Lourdes**, France
93/F2 **Loveland**, Colo.
95/G3 **Lowell**, Mass.
46/K3 **Lower Tunguska** (riv.), Russia
69/V12 **Loyalty** (isls.), New Caledonia
82/E1 **Lualaba** (riv.), Zaire
82/B2 **Luanda** (cap.), Angola
82/F3 **Luangwa** (riv.), Moz., Zambia
82/E3 **Luanshya**, Zambia
96/C3 **Lubbock**, Texas
26/F2 **Lübeck**, Ger.
27/M3 **Lublin**, Pol.
82/E3 **Lubumbashi**, Zaire
37/E3 **Lucerne** (lake), Switz.
37/E3 **Lucerne** (Luzern), Switz.
62/D2 **Lucknow**, India
58/A3 **Lüda** (Dalian), China
64/C2 **Ludhiana**, India
26/E4 **Ludwigshafen**, Ger.
96/E4 **Lufkin**, Texas
44/F2 **Lugansk**, Ukraine
82/G3 **Lugenda** (riv.), Moz.
97/J3 **Lumberton**, N.C.
61/F3 **Luoyang**, China
82/G3 **Lúrio** (riv.), Moz.
82/E4 **Lusaka** (cap.), Zambia
25/F3 **Luton**, Eng.
44/C2 **Lutsk**, Ukraine
31/E4 **Luxembourg**
31/F4 **Luxembourg** (cap.), Lux.
52/B3 **Luxor**, Egypt
61/H5 **Luzon** (isl.), Phil.
44/C2 **Lviv** (L'vov), Ukraine
24/C5 **Lyme** (bay), Eng.
98/G5 **Lynbrook**, N.Y.
97/J2 **Lynchburg**, Va.
95/G3 **Lynn**, Mass.
98/B3 **Lynwood**, Calif.
36/A6 **Lyon**, France
44/F1 **Lyubertsy**, Russia

M

20/H1 **Maanselkä** (mts.), Fin.
26/D3 **Maas** (riv.), Neth.
31/E2 **Maastricht**, Neth.
107/H3 **Macapa**, Braz.
61/G4 **Macau**
70/E4 **Macdonnell** (ranges), Austr.
39/G2 **Macedonia**
107/L5 **Maceió**, Braz.
57/H7 **Machida**, Japan
85/N2 **Mackenzie** (riv.), N.W.T.
94/B3 **Macomb**, Ill.
97/H3 **Macon**, Ga.
73/C1 **Macquarie** (riv.), Austr.
49/D4 **Ma'daba**, Jordan
81/H8 **Madagascar**
106/F5 **Madeira** (riv.), Braz.
35/U14 **Madeira** (isl.), Port.
94/B3 **Madison** (cap.), Wis.
99/F6 **Madison Heights**, Mich.
66/D5 **Madiun**, Indon.
62/D5 **Madras**, India

116

Madre – North A

100/D3 Madre Occidental, Sierra (range), Mex.
101/F4 Madre Oriental, Sierra (range), Mex.
34/D2 Madrid (cap.), Spain
64/G4 Madurai, India
57/F2 Maebashi, Japan
47/R4 Magadan, Russia
95/J2 Magdalen (isls.), Que.
106/D3 Magdalena (riv.), Col.
26/F2 Magdeburg, Ger.
109/B7 Magellan (str.), S. Amer.
37/E6 Maggiore (lake), Europe
43/N5 Magnitogorsk, Russia
76/H5 Maiduguri, Nigeria
26/E4 Main (riv.), Ger.
95/G3 Maine (gulf), U.S.
95/G2 Maine (state), U.S.
31/H3 Mainz, Ger.
35/G3 Majorca (isl.), Spain
68/G4 Majuro (atoll), Marshall Is.
67/E4 Makassar (str.), Indon.
44/F3 Makeyevka, Ukraine
45/H4 Makhachkala, Russia
62/B5 Malabar (coast), India
76/G7 Malabo (cap.), Equat. Guin.
65/B5 Malacca (str.), Asia
34/C4 Málaga, Spain
66/D5 Malang, Indon.
82/C2 Malange, Angola
50/D2 Malatya, Turkey
82/F3 Malawi
47/B2 Malay (pen.), Asia
66/B3 Malaya (reg.), Malaysia
47/C2 Malaysia
48/G9 Maldives
48/G9 Male (cap.), Maldives
62/B3 Malegaon, India
76/E4 Mali
31/F3 Malmédy, Belg.
20/E5 Malmö, Sweden
38/D5 Malta
98/G5 Mamaroneck, N.Y.
94/C4 Mammoth Cave Nat'l Pk., Ky.
67/F3 Manado, Indon.
102/E3 Managua (cap.), Nic.
52/F3 Manama (cap.), Bahrain
94/E4 Manassas, Va.
106/F4 Manaus, Braz.
23/F5 Manchester, Eng.
95/G3 Manchester, N.H.
55/J3 Manchuria (reg.), China
60/C4 Mandalay, Burma
91/H4 Mandan, N. Dak.
77/P5 Mandeb, Bab el (str.)
62/B5 Mangalore, India
93/H3 Manhattan, Kans.
98/B3 Manhattan Beach, Calif.
48/M8 Manila (cap.), Phil.
50/A2 Manisa, Turkey
22/D3 Man, Isle of (isl.)
86/F3 Manitoba (prov.), Can.
94/D2 Manitoulin (isl.), Ont.
94/C2 Manitowoc, Wis.
106/C2 Manizales, Col.
91/K5 Mankato, Minn.
62/C6 Mannar (gulf), India, Sri Lanka
26/E4 Mannheim, Ger.
94/D3 Mansfield, Ohio
33/J4 Mantova, Italy
71/R10 Manukau, N.Z.
98/F5 Maplewood, N.J.
81/F2 Maputo (cap.), Moz.
106/D1 Maracaibo, Ven.
106/E1 Maracay, Ven.
109/E4 Mar del Plata, Arg.
104/E5 Margarita (isl.), Ven.
103/F1 Marianao, Cuba
40/B2 Maribor, Slovenia
83/T Marie Byrd Land (reg.), Antarc.
97/G3 Marietta, Ga.
94/C3 Marion, Ind.
94/D3 Marion, Ohio
33/G4 Maritime Alps (mts.), Europe
44/F3 Mariupol', Ukraine
94/E3 Markham, Ont.
50/B1 Marmara (sea), Turkey
32/E2 Marne (riv.), France
69/M5 Marquesas (isls.), Fr. Poly.
94/C2 Marquette, Mich.
76/D1 Marrakech, Mor.
32/F5 Marseille, France
96/E3 Marshall, Texas
68/G3 Marshall Islands
93/J2 Marshalltown, Iowa
95/G3 Martha's Vineyard (isl.), Mass.
104/F4 Martinique
94/E4 Maryland (state), U.S.
95/L2 Marystown, Newf.
82/G1 Masai Steppe (grsld.), Tanz.
58/E5 Masan, S. Korea
67/F1 Masbate (isl.), Phil.
80/D3 Maseru (cap.), Lesotho
53/G1 Mashhad, Iran
93/J2 Mason City, Iowa
95/F3 Massachusetts (state), U.S.
98/G5 Massapequa, N.Y.
32/E4 Massif Central (plat.), Fr.
94/D3 Massillon, Ohio
82/B2 Matadi, Zaire
96/D4 Matagorda (isl.), Texas
101/F3 Matamoros, Mex.
95/H1 Matane, Que.
68/H6 Mata Utu (cap.), Wallis & Futuna
107/G6 Mato Grosso (plat.), Braz.
57/H7 Matsudo, Japan
57/E2 Matsumoto, Japan
56/C4 Matsuyama, Japan
94/B4 Mattoon, Ill.
106/F2 Maturin, Ven.
88/T10 Maui (isl.), Hawaii
88/U11 Mauna Kea (mt.), Hawaii
88/U11 Mauna Loa (mt.), Hawaii
76/C4 Mauritania
81/S15 Mauritius
95/F4 May (cape), N.J.
85/L3 Mayo, Yukon
81/H6 Mayotte
99/Q16 Maywood, Ill.
53/J1 Mazar-i-Sharif, Afghan.
100/D4 Mazatlán, Mex.
27/L2 Mazury (reg.), Pol.
81/E2 Mbabane (cap.), Swaziland
77/J7 Mbandaka, Zaire
82/F2 Mbeya, Tanz.
82/D2 Mbuji-Mayi, Zaire
93/J4 McAlester, Okla.
96/D5 McAllen, Texas
17/N8 McDonald (isls.), Austr.
94/E3 McKeesport, Pa.
85/H3 McKinley (mt.), Alaska
86/F1 M'Clintock (chan.), N.W.T.
87/R7 M'Clure (str.), N.W.T.
92/D3 Mead (lake), U.S.
52/C4 Mecca, Saudi Arabia
26/F2 Mecklenburg-Western Pomerania (state), Ger.
66/A3 Medan, Indon.
106/C2 Medellín, Col.
90/C5 Medford, Oreg.
92/F2 Medicine Bow (range), Wyo.
90/F3 Medicine Hat, Alta.
52/C4 Medina, Saudi Arabia
17/K4 Mediterranean (sea)
62/C2 Meerut, India
49/G6 Megiddo, Isr.
75/M14 Meknès, Mor.
65/D4 Mekong (riv.), Asia
66/B3 Melaka (Malacca), Malaysia
68/E5 Melanesia (reg.), Pacific
73/C3 Melbourne, Austr.
97/H4 Melbourne, Fla.
44/E3 Melitopol, Ukraine
70/E2 Melville (isl.), Austr.
87/R7 Melville (isl.), N.W.T.
87/H2 Melville (pen.), N.W.T.
97/F3 Memphis, Tenn.
88/B3 Mendocino (cape), Calif.
109/C3 Mendoza, Arg.
99/K12 Menlo Park, Calif.
94/B3 Menominee Falls, Wis.
94/D3 Mentor, Ohio
92/B3 Merced, Calif.
99/C2 Mercer Island, Wash.
65/B4 Mergui (arch.), Burma
101/H4 Mérida, Mex.
97/F3 Meridian, Miss.
109/E3 Merlo, Arg.
52/B5 Meroe (ruins), Sudan
98/G5 Merrick, N.Y.
23/F5 Mersey (riv.), Eng.
49/D1 Mersin, Turkey
92/E4 Mesa, Ariz.
92/E3 Mesa Verde Nat'l Pk., Colo.
51/E3 Mesopotamia (reg.), Iraq
96/D3 Mesquite, Texas
38/D3 Messina, Italy
33/K4 Mestre, Italy
97/F4 Metairie, La.
31/F5 Metz, France
32/F1 Meuse (riv.), Europe
84/G7 Mexico
84/H7 Mexico (gulf), N. Amer.
101/K7 Mexico City (cap.), Mex.
97/H5 Miami, Fla.
97/H5 Miami Beach, Fla.
60/E2 Mianyang, China
61/E2 Mianyang, China
43/P5 Miass, Russia
94/C2 Michigan (lake), U.S.
94/C2 Michigan (state), U.S.
94/C3 Michigan City, Ind.
94/C2 Michipicoten (isl.), Ont.
68/E3 Micronesia (reg.), Pacific
95/F3 Middlebury, Vt.
23/G2 Middlesbrough, Eng.
98/F5 Middletown, N.J.
94/C3 Midland, Mich.
94/E2 Midland, Ont.
96/C4 Midland, Texas
68/H2 Midway Islands
93/H4 Midwest City, Okla.
39/J4 Mikonos (isl.), Greece
33/H4 Milan, Italy
98/G4 Milford, Conn.
88/U13 Mililani Town, Hawaii
98/F5 Millburn, N.J.
91/K4 Mille Lacs (lake), Minn.
99/L12 Milpitas, Calif.
99/Q13 Milwaukee, Wis.
21/C1 Minch, The (sound), Scot.
67/F2 Mindanao (isl.), Phil.
67/F1 Mindoro (isl.), Phil.
98/G5 Mineola, N.Y.
91/K4 Minneapolis, Minn.
89/K4 Minnesota (state), U.S.
35/H2 Minorca (Menorca) (isl.), Sp.
34/A1 Miño (riv.), Spain
91/H3 Minot, N. Dak.
44/C1 Minsk (cap.), Belarus
39/H4 Mirtóön (sea), Greece
94/C3 Mishawaka, Ind.
40/E1 Miskolc, Hung.
76/J1 Mişrātah, Libya
96/D5 Mission, Texas
92/C4 Mission Viejo, Calif.
97/F4 Mississippi (riv.), U.S.
97/F3 Mississippi (state), U.S.
90/E4 Missoula, Mont.
93/J3 Missouri (riv.), U.S.
93/J3 Missouri (state), U.S.
106/D7 Misti, El (mt.), Peru
102/B2 Mitla (ruin), Mex.
57/G2 Mito, Japan
82/E2 Mitumba (mts.), Zaire
56/B5 Miyazaki, Japan
97/F4 Mobile, Ala.
33/J4 Modena, Italy
92/B3 Modesto, Calif.
77/Q7 Mogadishu (cap.), Somalia
44/D1 Mogilev, Belarus
92/C4 Mojave (des.), Calif.
58/D5 Mokp'o, S. Korea
94/B3 Moline, Ill.
88/T10 Molokai (isl.), Hawaii
67/G3 Moluccas (isls.), Indon.
82/G1 Mombasa, Kenya
104/D3 Mona (passage), W. Indies
33/G5 Monaco
90/D3 Monashee (mts.), Br. Col.
31/F1 Monchengladbach, Ger.
95/H2 Moncton, N. Br.
54/D2 Mongolia
96/E3 Monroe, La.
94/D3 Monroe, Mich.
98/C2 Monrovia, Calif.
78/C5 Monrovia (cap.), Liberia
30/C3 Mons, Belg.
90/F4 Montana (state), U.S.
98/F5 Montclair, N.J.
98/B2 Montebello, Calif.
38/B1 Montecristo (isl.), Italy
40/D4 Montenegro (rep.), Yugo.
92/B3 Monterey, Calif.
101/E3 Monterrey, Mex.
98/B2 Monterey Park, Calif.
109/E3 Montevideo (cap.), Urug.
97/G3 Montgomery (cap.), Ala.
94/F2 Mont-Laurier, Que.
95/G2 Montmagny, Que.
32/E5 Montpellier, France
95/F2 Montpelier (cap.), Vt.
94/F2 Montréal, Que.
95/N6 Mont-Royal, Que.
104/F3 Montserrat
33/H4 Monza, Italy
69/K6 Moorea (isl.), Fr. Poly.
93/H4 Moore, Okla.
91/J4 Moorhead, Minn.
95/G2 Moosehead (lake), Maine
90/G3 Moose Jaw, Sask.
62/C1 Moradabad, India
27/J4 Morava (riv.), Europe
39/G1 Morava (riv.), Yugo.
27/J4 Moravia (reg.), Czech Rep.
21/D2 Moray (firth), Scot.
101/E5 Morelia, Mex.
92/C4 Moreno Valley, Calif.
97/F4 Morgan City, La.
94/E4 Morgantown, W. Va.
55/N4 Morioka, Japan
76/C1 Morocco
67/F2 Moro (gulf), Phil.
109/E3 Morón, Arg.
81/G5 Moroni (cap.), Comoros
98/F5 Morristown, N.J.
97/H2 Morristown, Tenn.
90/D4 Moscow, Idaho
42/H5 Moscow (cap.), Russia
31/G3 Mosel (riv.), Ger.
33/G2 Moselle (riv.), France
90/D4 Moses Lake, Wash.
103/E4 Mosquito Coast (reg.), Nic.
103/F4 Mosquitos (gulf), Pan.
97/F4 Moss Point, Miss.
51/E2 Mosul, Iraq
60/C5 Moulmein, Burma
99/K12 Mountain View, Calif.
99/C2 Mountlake Terrace, Wash.
95/L2 Mount Pearl, Newf.
99/Q15 Mount Prospect, Ill.
90/C4 Mount Rainier Nat'l Pk., Wash.
93/G2 Mount Rushmore Nat'l Mem., S. Dak.
94/B4 Mount Vernon, Ill.
98/G5 Mount Vernon, N.Y.
94/D3 Mount Vernon, Ohio
90/C3 Mount Vernon, Wash.
82/G4 Mozambique
74/G6 Mozambique (chan.), Africa
82/F3 Muchinga (mts.), Zambia
55/K3 Mudanjiang, China
82/E3 Mufulira, Zambia
99/J11 Muir Woods Nat'l Mon., Calif.
34/D4 Mulhacén (mt.), Spain
36/D2 Mülheim, Ger.
36/D2 Mulhouse, France
64/A2 Multan, Pak.
94/C3 Muncie, Ind.
55/K3 Mundanjiang, China
99/P15 Mundelein, Ill.
37/H1 Munich (München), Ger.
29/E5 Münster, Ger.
99/Q16 Munster, Ind.
35/E4 Murcia, Spain
41/G2 Mureş (riv.), Rom.
97/G3 Murfreesboro, Tenn.
42/G1 Murmansk, Russia
33/L3 Mur (Mura) (riv.), Europe
73/A2 Murray (riv.), Austr.
73/C2 Murrumbidgee (riv.), Austr.
51/H5 Musandam, Ras (cape), Oman
53/G4 Muscat (cap.), Oman
70/E5 Musgrave (ranges), Austr.
94/C3 Muskegon, Mich.
93/J4 Muskogee, Okla.
82/F4 Mutare, Zim.
82/F1 Mwanza, Tanz.
82/E2 Mweru (lake), Africa
97/J3 Myrtle Beach, S.C.
62/C5 Mysore, India

N

43/M5 Naberezhnye Chelny, Russia
49/D3 Nabulus, West Bank
96/E4 Nacogdoches, Texas
63/F2 Nagaland (state), India
57/F2 Nagano, Japan
57/F2 Nagaoka, Japan
56/A4 Nagasaki, Japan
64/F4 Nagercoil, India
57/E3 Nagoya, Japan
62/C3 Nagpur, India
68/B2 Naha, Japan
77/M8 Nairobi (cap.), Kenya
52/D3 Najd (reg.), Saudi Arabia
45/G4 Nalchik, Russia
46/H5 Namangan, Uzbekistan
63/J3 Nam Dinh, Viet.
82/B5 Namib (des.), Namibia
82/C5 Namibia
90/D5 Nampa, Idaho
58/C3 Namp'o, N. Korea
90/C3 Nanaimo, Br. Col.
61/G2 Nanchang, China
60/E2 Nanchong, China
31/F6 Nancy, France
53/K1 Nanga Parbat (mt.), Pak.
59/D4 Nanjing (Nanking), China
61/F4 Nanning, China
32/C3 Nantes, France
59/E4 Nantong, China
95/G3 Nantucket (isl.), Mass.
99/K10 Napa, Calif.
99/P16 Naperville, Ill.
97/H5 Naples, Fla.
38/D2 Naples, Italy
56/D3 Nara, Japan
62/C3 Narmada (riv.), India
95/G3 Nashua, N.H.
97/G2 Nashville (cap.), Tenn.
62/B4 Nasik, India
104/B1 Nassau (cap.), Bah.
106/L5 Natal, Braz.
97/F4 Natchez, Miss.
96/E4 Natchitoches, La.
92/C4 National City, Calif.
92/E3 Natural Bridges Nat'l Mon., Utah
100/F5 Naucalpan, Mex.
68/F5 Nauru
92/E3 Navajo Nat'l Mon., Ariz.
47/T3 Navarin (cape), Russia
34/D1 Navarre (reg.), Spain
39/J4 Náxos (isl.), Greece
49/D3 Nazareth, Isr.
76/J5 N'Djamena (cap.), Chad
82/E3 Ndola, Zambia
22/B2 Neagh (lake), N. Ire.
93/G2 Nebraska (state), U.S.
26/E4 Neckar (riv.), Ger.
94/B2 Neenah, Wis.
50/D4 Negev (reg.), Isr.
109/D5 Negro (riv.), Arg.
67/F2 Negros (isl.), Phil.
54/G3 Nei Monggol (plat.), China
106/C3 Neiva, Col.
90/D3 Nelson, Br. Col.
86/G3 Nelson (riv.), Man.
62/D2 Nepal
98/F5 Neptune City, N.J.
21/C2 Ness (lake), Scot.
26/C3 Netherlands
104/D5 Netherlands Antilles
101/N10 Netzahualcóycotl, Mex.
34/D4 Nevada, Sierra (mts.), Spain
92/C3 Nevada, Sierra (mts.), U.S.
92/C3 Nevada (state), U.S.
104/F3 Nevis (isl.), St. Kitts & Nevis
94/C4 New Albany, Ind.
99/K11 Newark, Calif.
98/F5 Newark, N.J.
94/D3 Newark, Ohio
95/G3 New Bedford, Mass.
99/P14 New Berlin, Wis.
97/J3 New Bern, N.C.
96/D4 New Braunfels, Texas
95/F3 New Britain, Conn.
68/D5 New Britain (isl.), Papua N.G.
95/H2 New Brunswick (prov.), Can.
98/F5 New Brunswick, N.J.
68/F6 New Caledonia
98/G4 New Canaan, Conn.
73/D2 Newcastle, Austr.
94/C4 New Castle, Ind.
95/H2 Newcastle, N. Br.
94/D3 New Castle, Pa.
23/G2 Newcastle upon Tyne, Eng.
98/G4 New City, N.Y.
62/C2 New Delhi (cap.), India
87/K3 Newfoundland (prov.), Can.
95/L1 Newfoundland (isl.), Newf.
68/E5 New Georgia (isl.), Sol. Is.
95/J2 New Glasgow, N.S.
67/J4 New Guinea (isl.), Pacific
95/G3 New Hampshire (state), U.S.
68/D5 New Hanover (isl.), Papua N.G.
95/F3 New Haven, Conn.
96/F4 New Iberia, La.
68/E5 New Ireland (isl.), Papua N.G.
94/F3 New Jersey (state), U.S.
95/F3 New London, Conn.
94/E2 Newmarket, Ont.
92/F4 New Mexico (state), U.S.
97/F4 New Orleans, La.
94/C4 Newport, Ky.
95/G3 Newport, R.I.
98/C3 Newport Beach, Calif.
94/E4 Newport News, Va.
104/B1 New Providence (isl.), Bah.
98/G5 New Rochelle, N.Y.
47/P2 New Siberian (isls.), Russia
73/C1 New South Wales (state), Austr.
93/H3 Newton, Kans.
95/G3 Newton, Mass.
91/K4 New Ulm, Minn.
90/C3 New Westminster, Br. Col.
98/G5 New York, N.Y.
94/F3 New York (state), U.S.
71/Q10 New Zealand
57/L10 Neyagawa, Japan
65/E3 Nha Trang, Viet.
94/E3 Niagara Falls, N.Y.
94/E3 Niagara Falls, Ont.
95/R9 Niagara (riv.), N. Amer.
79/F3 Niamey (cap.), Niger
66/A3 Nias (isl.), Indon.
103/E3 Nicaragua
35/G5 Nice, France
63/F6 Nicobar (isls.), India
49/C2 Nicosia (cap.), Cyprus
76/G4 Niger
76/G6 Nigeria
79/G5 Niger (riv.), Africa
57/F2 Niigata, Japan
88/R10 Niihau (isl.), Hawaii
28/C5 Nijmegen, Neth.
44/D3 Nikolayev, Ukraine
77/M2 Nile (riv.), Africa
99/Q15 Niles, Ill.
94/D3 Niles, Ohio
32/F5 Nimes, France
61/J2 Ningbo (Ningpo), China
86/F3 Nipawin, Sask.
94/B1 Nipigon (lake), Ont.
94/E2 Nipissing (lake), Ont.
57/L10 Nishinomiya, Japan
40/E4 Niš, Yugo.
108/D2 Niteroi, Braz.
69/J7 Niue
43/K4 Nizhniy Novgorod, Russia
43/N4 Nizhniy Tagil, Russia
76/G7 N'Kongsamba, Cameroon
92/E5 Nogales, Ariz.
85/E3 Nome, Alaska
20/H1 Nordkapp (cape), Nor.
71/M5 Norfolk I. (terr.), Austr.
93/H2 Norfolk, Nebr.
94/E4 Norfolk, Va.
46/J3 Noril'sk, Russia
94/B3 Normal, Ill.
93/H4 Norman, Okla.
86/D2 Norman Wells, N.W.T.
98/E5 Norristown, Pa.
20/F4 Norrköping, Sweden
18/D3 North (sea), Europe
71/R10 North (isl.), N.Z.
84/* North America

33/K4 Venice (Venezia), Italy
98/A2 Ventura, Calif.
101/F5 Veracruz, Mex.
76/B5 Verde (cape), Sen.
31/E5 Verdun-sur-Meuse, France
47/P3 Verkhoyansk, Russia
47/N3 Verkhoyansk (range), Russia
91/J5 Vermillion, S. Dak.
95/F2 Vermont (state), U.S.
97/H5 Vero Beach, Fla.
33/J4 Verona, Italy
30/B6 Versailles, France
38/D2 Vesuvius (vol.), Italy
33/J4 Vicenza, Italy
32/E3 Vichy, France
97/F3 Vicksburg, Miss.
74/F5 Victoria (lake), Africa
73/C3 Victoria (state), Austr.
90/C4 Victoria (cap.), Br. Col.
61/G4 Victoria (cap.), Hong Kong
82/E4 Victoria (Mosi-Oa-Tunya) (falls), Africa
86/E1 Victoria (isl.), N.W.T.
96/D4 Victoria, Tex.
33/M2 Vienna, Austria
98/J8 Vienna, Va.
65/C2 Vientiane (cap.), Laos
65/D2 Vietnam
34/A1 Vigo, Spain
62/D4 Vijayawada, India
68/F6 Vila (cap.), Vanuatu
101/G5 Villahermosa, Mex.
99/Q16 Villa Park, Ill.
42/E5 Vilnius (cap.), Lithuania
109/B3 Viña del Mar, Chile
94/C4 Vincennes, Ind.
94/F4 Vineland, N.J.
63/J4 Vinh, Viet.
44/D2 Vinnitsa, Ukraine
83/U Vinson Massif (mt.), Antarc.
91/K4 Virginia, Minn.
94/E4 Virginia (state), U.S.
94/F4 Virginia Beach, Va.
104/E3 Virgin Is. (Br.)
104/E3 Virgin Is. Nat'l Pk., V.I. (U.S.)
104/E3 Virgin Is. (U.S.)
62/D4 Visakhapatnam, India
92/C3 Visalia, Calif.
92/C4 Vista, Calif.
42/F5 Vitebsk, Belarus
108/D2 Vitória, Braz.
34/D1 Vitoria, Spain
45/H4 Vladikavkaz, Russia
42/J4 Vladimir, Russia
55/L3 Vladivostok, Russia
28/A6 Vlissingen, Neth.
27/H4 Vltava (riv.), Czech Rep.
81/H9 Vohimena (cape), Madag.

46/E5 Volga (riv.), Russia
45/H2 Volgograd, Russia
42/H4 Vologda, Russia
78/E5 Volta (lake), Ghana
108/C2 Volta Redonda, Braz.
45/H2 Volzhskiy, Russia
46/G3 Vorkuta, Russia
44/F2 Voronezh, Russia
44/F2 Voroshilovgrad (Lugansk), Ukraine
36/C2 Vosges (mts.), France
91/K3 Voyageurs Nat'l Pk., Minn.
43/L4 Vyatka, Russia

W

94/C4 Wabash (riv.), U.S.
96/D4 Waco, Tex.
88/V13 Wahiawa, Hawaii
88/V10 Wailuku, Hawaii
88/S10 Waipahu, Hawaii
88/D3 Wakayama, Japan
68/F3 Wake (isl.), Pacific
27/J3 Walbrzych, Pol.
21/C4 Wales, U.K.
24/D1 Walsall, Eng.
90/D4 Walla Walla, Wash.
68/G6 Wallis & Futuna
92/E4 Walnut Canyon Nat'l Mon., Ariz.
99/K11 Walnut Creek, Calif.
82/B5 Walvis Bay, Namibia
61/F2 Wanxian, China
62/C4 Warangal, India
97/H3 Warner Robins, Ga.
72/B4 Warrego (range), Austr.
99/F6 Warren, Mich.
94/D4 Warren, Ohio
93/J3 Warrensburg, Mo.
23/F5 Warrington, Eng.
27/L2 Warsaw (cap.), Pol.
95/G3 Warwick, R.I.
92/E2 Wasatch (range), U.S.
95/G2 Washington (mt.), N.H.
94/D3 Washington, Pa.
90/C4 Washington (state), U.S.
98/J8 Washington, D.C. (cap.), U.S.
21/H4 Wash, The (bay), Eng.
95/F3 Waterbury, Conn.
21/B4 Waterford, Ire.
93/J2 Waterloo, Iowa
94/H3 Watertown, N.Y.
91/J4 Watertown, S. Dak.
94/B3 Watertown, Wis.
95/G2 Waterville, Maine
104/C1 Watling (San Salvador) (isl.), Bah.
92/B3 Watsonville, Calif.
99/Q15 Waukegan, Ill.

99/P13 Waukesha, Wis.
94/B2 Wausau, Wis.
99/P13 Wauwatosa, Wis.
97/H4 Waycross, Ga.
99/F7 Wayne, Mich.
98/F5 Wayne, N.J.
83/W Weddell (sea), Antarc.
94/D3 Weirton, W. Va.
95/R10 Welland, Ont.
71/R11 Wellington (cap.), N.Z.
90/C4 Wenatchee, Wash.
61/J3 Wenzhou, China
29/F1 Weser (riv.), Ger.
80/D2 Wes-Rand, S. Africa
99/P13 West Allis, Wis.
49/G7 West Bank
94/B3 West Bend, Wis.
98/E6 West Chester, Pa.
98/C2 West Covina, Calif.
70/C4 Western Australia (state), Austr.
64/F3 Western Ghats (mts.), India
76/B3 Western Sahara
69/H6 Western Samoa
94/D3 Westerville, Ohio
91/J4 West Fargo, N. Dak.
98/F5 Westfield, N.J.
84/L7 West Indies
98/F7 Westland, Mich.
93/K4 West Memphis, Ark.
98/B3 Westminster, Calif.
23/F3 Westmorland (reg.), Eng.
98/F5 West Orange, N.J.
97/H5 West Palm Beach, Fla.
98/G4 Westport, Conn.
95/S10 West Seneca, N.Y.
92/E2 West Valley City, Utah
94/D4 West Virginia (state), U.S.
99/P16 Wheaton, Ill.
99/Q15 Wheeling, Ill.
94/D3 Wheeling, W. Va.
94/E3 Whitby, Ont.
94/C4 White (riv.), Ind.
42/H2 White (sea), Russia
85/L3 Whitehorse (cap.), Yukon
77/M5 White Nile (riv.), Africa
98/G4 White Plains, N.Y.
92/E4 White Sands Nat'l Mon., N. Mex.
92/C3 Whitney (mt.), Calif.
98/B3 Whittier, Calif.
93/H3 Wichita, Kans.
93/H4 Wichita (mts.), Okla.
96/D3 Wichita Falls, Tex.
33/M2 Wien (Vienna), Austria
31/H3 Wiesbaden, Ger.
25/E5 Wight (isl.), Eng.
29/F2 Wilhelmshaven, Ger.
94/F3 Wilkes-Barre, Pa.
83/J Wilkes Land (reg.), Antarc.

90/B4 Willamette (riv.), Oreg.
104/D4 Willemstad (cap.), Neth. Ant.
94/E4 Williamsburg, Va.
94/E3 Williamsport, Pa.
98/F5 Willingboro, N.J.
91/H3 Williston, N. Dak.
91/K4 Willmar, Minn.
99/Q15 Wilmette, Ill.
98/E6 Wilmington, Del.
97/J3 Wilmington, N.C.
97/J3 Wilson, N.C.
98/G4 Wilton, Conn.
25/E4 Winchester, Eng.
94/E4 Winchester, Va.
91/H5 Wind Cave Nat'l Pk., S. Dak.
82/C5 Windhoek (cap.), Namibia
99/F7 Windsor, Ont.
104/F4 Windward (isls.), W. Indies
93/H3 Winfield, Kans.
94/B3 Winnebago (lake), Wis.
99/Q15 Winnetka, Ill.
91/J3 Winnipeg (cap.), Man.
91/J3 Winnipeg (lake), Man.
91/H2 Winnipegosis (lake), Man.
91/L4 Winona, Minn.
92/E4 Winslow, Ariz.
97/H2 Winston-Salem, N.C.
97/H4 Winter Haven, Fla.
97/H4 Winter Park, Fla.
37/E3 Winterthur, Switz.
94/B2 Wisconsin (state), U.S.
94/B2 Wisconsin (riv.), Wis.
94/B2 Wisconsin Rapids, Wis.
26/G3 Wittenberg, Ger.
73/D2 Wollongong, Austr.
24/D2 Wolverhampton, Eng.
58/D4 Wŏnju, S. Korea
58/D3 Wŏnsan, N. Korea
98/F5 Woodbridge, N.J.
86/E2 Wood Buffalo Nat'l Pk., Can.
99/L9 Woodland, Calif.
99/P16 Woodridge, Ill.
99/L3 Woods, Lake of the (lake), N. Amer.
94/D3 Wooster, Ohio
24/D2 Worcester, Eng.
95/G3 Worcester, Mass.
16* World
26/E4 Worms, Ger.
91/K5 Worthington, Minn.
85/K3 Wrangell (mts.), Alaska
85/K3 Wrangell-St. Elias Nat'l Pk., Alaska
27/J3 Wrocław, Pol.
59/C5 Wuhan, China
59/D5 Wuhu, China
92/E4 Wupatki Nat'l Mon., Ariz.
29/E6 Wuppertal, Ger.
26/E4 Würzburg, Ger.
55/L2 Wusuli (Ussuri) (riv.), Asia
59/L8 Wuxi, China
94/C3 Wyoming, Mich.
90/F5 Wyoming (state), U.S.

X

94/D4 Xenia, Ohio
61/H3 Xiamen (Amoy), China
61/H3 Xiamen, China
61/G3 Xiangtan, China
54/E4 Xi'an (Sian), China
59/B4 Xi Jiang (riv.), China
107/H4 Xingu (riv.), Braz.
54/E4 Xining, China
59/C3 Xinji, China
46/J5 Xinjiang (reg.), China
59/C4 Xinxiang, China
61/G3 Xinyu, China
59/D4 Xuzhou (Süchow), China

Y

54/E6 Ya'an, China
54/F1 Yablonovyy (range), Russia
90/C3 Yakima, Wash.
47/N3 Yakut Aut. Rep., Russia
47/N3 Yakutsk, Russia
55/J3 Yalu (riv.), Asia
57/G1 Yamagata, Japan
78/D5 Yamoussoukro (cap.), Iv. Coast
62/D2 Yamuna (riv.), India
61/H2 Yangtze (Chang Jiang) (riv.), China
91/J5 Yankton, S. Dak.
59/E3 Yantai, China
57/L10 Yao, Japan
76/H7 Yaoundé (cap.), Cameroon
68/C4 Yap (isl.), Micronesia
42/H4 Yaroslavl', Russia
51/H4 Yazd, Iran
97/F3 Yazoo City, Miss.
43/P4 Yekaterinburg, Russia
55/J4 Yellow (sea), Asia
55/H4 Yellow (Huang He) (riv.), China
86/E2 Yellowknife (cap.), N.W.T.
90/G4 Yellowstone (riv.), U.S.
90/F4 Yellowstone Nat'l Pk., U.S.
52/E5 Yemen
46/J3 Yenisey (riv.), Russia
45/H4 Yerevan (cap.), Armenia
59/B5 Yichang, China
55/K2 Yichun, China
54/F4 Yinchuan, China
59/D5 Yingcheng, China
61/G2 Yingkou, China
66/D5 Yogyakarta, Indon.
56/E3 Yokkaichi, Japan
57/F3 Yokohama, Japan
57/F3 Yokosuka, Japan
98/G5 Yonkers, N.Y.
98/C3 Yorba Linda, Calif.
70/G2 York (cape), Austr.
23/G4 York, Eng.
94/E4 York, Pa.
94/E4 York (riv.), Va.
92/C3 Yosemite Nat'l Pk., Calif.
58/D5 Yŏsu, S. Korea
94/D3 Youngstown, Ohio
99/E7 Ypsilanti, Mich.
101/H5 Yucatán (pen.), Mex.
61/G2 Yueyang, China
40/E3 Yugoslavia
86/B2 Yukon (riv.), N. Amer.
85/L2 Yukon (terr.), Can.
92/D4 Yuma, Ariz.
60/D3 Yunnan (prov.), China
59/E5 Yuyao, China

Z

28/B4 Zaandam, Neth.
27/K3 Zabrze, Pol.
40/C3 Zagreb (cap.), Croatia
51/F2 Zagros (mts.), Iran
74/E5 Zaire
82/F4 Zambezi (riv.), Africa
82/F3 Zambia
67/F2 Zamboanga, Phil.
94/D4 Zanesville, Ohio
82/G2 Zanzibar (isl.), Tanz.
82/G2 Zanzibar, Tanz.
59/D4 Zaozhuang, China
42/E3 Zaporozh'ye, Ukraine
35/E2 Zaragoza (Saragossa), Spain
79/G4 Zaria, Nigeria
59/C2 Zhangjiakou (Kalgan), China
59/D4 Zhanjiang, China
59/C4 Zhengzhou (Chengchow), China
44/D2 Zhitomir, Ukraine
61/G3 Zhuzhou, China
59/D3 Zibo, China
60/E2 Zigong, China
82/E4 Zimbabwe
99/Q15 Zion, Ill.
92/D3 Zion Nat'l Pk., Utah
37/E3 Zug, Switz.
31/E3 Zugspitze (mt.), Europe
37/H3 Zürich, Switz.
26/G3 Zwickau, Ger.
28/D4 Zwolle, Neth.